bringing up
GIRLS

bringing up

GiRLS

DR. JAMES DOBSON

Tyndale House Publishers, Inc.
Carol Stream, Illinois

Visit Tyndale online at www.tyndale.com.

TYNDALE and Tyndale's quill logo are registered trademarks of Tyndale House Publishers, Inc.

Bringing Up Girls: Practical Advice and Encouragement for Those Shaping the Next Generation of Women

Designed by Julie Chen

All Scripture quotations, unless otherwise indicated, are taken from the Holy Bible, *New International Version,*® *NIV.*®
Copyright © 1973, 1978, 1984 by Biblica, Inc.™ Used by permission of Zondervan. All rights reserved worldwide.
www.zondervan.com.

Scripture quotations marked NKJV are taken from the New King James Version.® Copyright © 1982 by Thomas
Nelson, Inc. Used by permission. All rights reserved. *NKJV* is a trademark of Thomas Nelson, Inc.

Scripture quotations marked KJV are taken from the *Holy Bible*, King James Version.

Scripture quotations marked NASB are taken from the New American Standard Bible, *Holy Bible,*® copyright © 1960,
1962, 1963, 1968, 1971, 1972, 1973, 1975, 1977, 1995 by The Lockman Foundation. Used by permission.

Library of Congress Cataloging-in-Publication Data

Dobson, James C., date.
 Bringing up girls : practical advice and encouragement for those shaping the next generation of women /
James Dobson.
  p. cm.
 Includes bibliographical references (p.   ).
 ISBN 978-1-4143-0127-3 (hc)
 1. Parenting—Religious aspects—Christianity. 2. Girls—Religious life. I. Title.
 BV4529.D6315 2010
 248.8′45—dc22   2010001869

ISBN 978-1-4143-3648-0 (International Trade Paper Edition)
ISBN 978-1-4143-3649-7 (softcover)

Printed in the United States of America

18 17 16 15 14 13 12
 7   6   5   4   3   2   1

*This book is dedicated to my only daughter, Danae Ann
Dobson, who has brought incredible joy and love to my life.
As I wrote in the first chapter of the book you are about to
read, "The passion I feel for the subject at hand is related to the
daughter who still calls me Dad.
She is grown now, but I love her like I did when we were first
introduced in the delivery room.
Something electric occurred between us on that
mystical night, and it endures today."*

*I thank God for the privilege of being the
father of this remarkable woman!*

TABLE
OF
CONTENTS

ACKNOWLEDGMENTS

There have been numerous colleagues, friends, and associates who have assisted mightily in the writing of this book. At the top of the list is Paul Batura, who was instrumental in locating and summarizing huge quantities of research relevant to the topics addressed. He was always the first one to read a section, and I came to depend on his feedback. Paul and I worked side by side on this project for three years, often during evenings, weekends, and other inconvenient times. There were numerous occasions when I called him to say, "Paul, you gotta find something for me, and I need it right now." He usually went straight to the source and put precisely what I needed into my hands (or on my computer). I thank him profusely today for standing with me as the book gradually took shape.

My personal assistant, Becky Lane, is highly intelligent and made her own significant contribution. She is, by temperament, a "detail person" who almost never lets anything hit the ground. And as you would expect, there were countless details to be chased in the completion of *Bringing Up Girls*. It would still not be finished without Becky's oversight. Her colleague in our office Corinne Sayler worked alongside her on the project. I appreciate them both.

There were so many others who were so helpful and gracious to me. Pollster Frank Luntz allowed me to quote from his own book, which was not yet in print. It is in the bookstores now and is entitled *What Americans Really Want . . . Really*. You will find his writings at the end of chapter 16 of *Bringing Up Girls*. Thank you, Frank, for your generosity.

Bob West is a remarkably talented man who can solve the most complicated technical problem. I'll never forget calling him early one morning in a panic. I said, "Bob! You won't believe it! My screen has gone blank, and days of work are gone." I was ready to run screaming down the road. Within minutes, he had straightened out the mess, and my text was restored. What a friend!

Bob Waliszewski allowed me to use a portion of his unfinished and untitled book, which comprises chapter 21 of mine ("Protecting Your Daughter from Invasive Technology"). Thank you, Bob. I'm no techie. Thank goodness you are.

Ron Reno is a vice president at Focus on the Family. He is a wordsmith and a thinker. Ron read a large section of my book in its final stages and made many helpful suggestions.

When the book was completely finished, Dave Salkeld was the engineer who recorded my spoken words as I read. It was a chore, and Dave was wonderfully patient as my tired voice cracked and squeaked through 275 pages of content. I recommend Dave to anyone who needs his technical talent.

Columnist Peggy Noonan was kind to allow me to quote her commentary entitled "Embarrassing the Angels." It comprises chapter 6.

At my request, three young women wrote statements for my book dealing with the princess movement. They are Danae Dobson, Kristin Salladin, and Riann Zuetel. The opinions they expressed made a significant contribution to chapter 12, titled "The Obsession with Beauty."

Drs. Joe McIlhaney and Freda McKissic Bush came to Focus on the Family to appear as guests on our broadcast. They are both obstetricians and gynecologists. These physicians were invited to talk about their own book, *Hooked: New Science on How Casual Sex Is Affecting Our Children*. An edited transcript of our interview has been included in chapter 15. Every parent should read this section and, indeed, *Hooked* in its entirety. Appreciation is expressed to these friends and colleagues.

Dr. Roy Stringfellow is also a gynecologist in private practice in Colorado Springs, Colorado. He is also one of my closest friends. Dr. Stringfellow reviewed my writings about female physiology and adolescent endocrinology and made many helpful suggestions.

Randy and Lisa Wilson are the creators of a wonderful program for girls called the Purity Ball. You will want to read about this concept in chapter 11 and then implement their suggestions on behalf of your budding Cinderellas.

John and Stasi Eldredge made a unique contribution to this book with their description of the female soul. What they wrote is wonderful.

Several dozen young women participated in a free-form discussion about their relationships with their fathers. They were attending the Focus on the Family Institute at the time, and they agreed to talk to me at length. Their edited comments appear in chapter 9. This is one of the most insightful sections of the book. To all these students, I want to say thank you for participating in this discussion.

Kim Davis wrote a personal story about her life in "The Obsession with Beauty." Thank you, Kim, for your transparency and insight.

One of my favorite short writings in *Bringing Up Girls* was written by Sarah Kistler. It is entitled "The Charm Bracelet." Don't miss it!

Chapter 10, entitled "Fathers to Daughters," offers one hundred proverbs written or compiled by Harry Harrison. They are excerpted from his book *Father to Daughter: Life Lessons on Raising a Girl*.

Three other people made their own unique contribution to this book through their poetry and songs: Steven Curtis Chapman, Stephanie Bentley, and Edgar Guest.

Randy Negaard is a CPA and a comptroller for my personal corporation, which owns the copyrights for my books. In that capacity, he handled all the contractual negotiations and implementation for *Bringing Up Girls*. Randy and I work together closely, and he is diligent in addressing all business concerns that would otherwise be a distraction for me. I would rather write about marriage and parenting than crunch numbers. Randy makes that possible.

Senator Rick and Karen Santorum were guests on *Focus on the Family* to talk about Karen's book *Everyday Graces: A Child's Book of Good Manners*. An excerpt of that interview appears in chapter 5 of this book, titled "Teaching Girls to Be Ladies." My gratitude is expressed to the Santorums for sharing their helpful advice on child rearing with our radio listeners and for permitting me to include their remarks in *Bringing Up Girls*.

Mark and Becky Waters describe their personal loss at the end of the book. I will never forget Mark's personal letter to me, nor will you.

I am very grateful also to my friends at Tyndale House Publishers who were midwives at the birth of this baby. They are Doug Knox, Lisa Jackson, Becky Brandvik, Sarah Atkinson, Stephanie Voiland, Mafi Novella, and Sarah Rubio, among others. These very gifted people were there for me at every turn.

Finally, my greatest appreciation is reserved for my wife, Shirley, who prayed for me, supported me, and was my sounding board through this process. It may not surprise you that she sees things from a mother's point of view, which influenced my own writings. There's no doubt about it. I love and appreciate this lady enormously.

Enjoy the book.

THE WONDERFUL WORLD
OF GIRLS

A FEW YEARS AGO I wrote a book called *Bringing Up Boys*,[1] which has sold more than 2 million copies. Ever since it was released, people on the street, in restaurants, or in airports have approached me and asked, "When are you going to write *Bringing Up Girls*?" My publisher has posed the same question every time we've been together. Now, even kids have begun to hound me. This scrawled letter came to my office recently:

> *Dear Dr. James Dobson,*
> *I'm 6 years old. I have two older brothers. I would like to know when you are going to write* Bringing Up Girls? *Because my mom really wants to train girls. I appreciate your work on the book.*
> *Julie*

Okay, Julie. You win. I'll do it. And I thank you for the nice note. I'll bet your mom put you up to writing me, because the girl she wants to train . . . is *you*. I hope to meet you someday because you sound like a very special six-year-old.

I have received thousands of other interesting letters from boys and girls, most of whom are older than Julie. Some have been rather angry with me because they blame me for the way their parents disciplined them. A college student sent me a poem to express that sentiment a few years ago. It read:

Roses are red and violets are blue
When I was a kid, I got spanked 'cause of you

One of my favorite letters came from a fourteen-year-old girl named Tiffany, who was steaming when she wrote. She came right to the point:

> *I hate you dr dobson.*
> *i had to watch the dumbest movie today about sex. you made the movie. HA! like you'd know anything about it. also my mom has started not letting me go to movies she has not read reviews about, thanks to your gay little "plugged in" program. now i have no social life since all my friends go to the movies and see good movies. all i can watch is ella enchanted. woo-pa-dee-do!*

Then Tiffany took off the gloves. She must have seen a very old picture of me wearing out-of-date glasses, which prompted this last jab:

> *i hope you get some new glasses. because physiologist or not, your other ones take up your whole face.*
> *Love Always, Tiffany*

What a sweet girl. Only a fourteen-year-old could start a letter declaring that she hates me and end with assurances of eternal love. I'll bet Tiffany is a challenge for her mom and dad, but there are better days coming. The parents I am advising today were testy kids like Tiffany when I wrote my first book on child rearing, but now something rather funny has happened. They have grown up and produced strong-willed children of their own, and they're looking for help. It is rewarding for me to watch a second generation of moms and dads learn to deal with the same issues and problems that they presented to their parents twenty-five years ago. Who knows? Maybe I'll have an opportunity to advise a third generation when Tiffany's first baby comes along. She and other young moms from her generation will see things from an entirely different perspective then. But I am getting ahead of myself.

The title I have chosen for this book, *Bringing Up Girls*, makes a fundamental assertion. It assumes that parents have the responsibility of not simply overseeing the growth and development of their girls (and boys) but of raising them purposely—building into them certain qualities and traits of character. Wise King Solomon addressed that obligation more than 2,900 years ago when he wrote, "Train up a child in the way he should go: and when he is old, he will not depart from it" (Proverbs 22:6, KJV). The apostle Paul added another dimension when he said, "Fathers, do not exasperate your children; instead, bring them up in the training and instruction of the Lord" (Ephesians 6:4).

Think for a moment about the implications of those Scriptures. Do they mean that a child should be taught to revere God and His Son, Jesus Christ, and to understand the spiritual dimension of life? Yes, that is their first and most important meaning. But I believe they instruct us to do more than that.

Children are a gift from God, and we are stewards of their welfare. Training up our daughters in this sense implies helping them to navigate the cultural minefields that lie in their paths—teaching them eternal values, talents, and perspectives. It means instilling within them an appreciation for truthfulness, trustworthiness, self-discipline, self-control, generosity, and sweetness of spirit. It means teaching them modesty, morality, and manners. It means helping them overcome the natural inclination toward selfishness, aggressiveness, violence, and slovenliness. It means teaching them to work and learn and think. That is just the beginning, which is why parenthood is such a daunting responsibility, requiring careful forethought and planning. This is what we will be talking about in the pages that follow.

The passion I feel for the subject at hand is related to the daughter who still calls me Dad. She is grown now, but I love her like I did when we were first introduced in the delivery room. Something electric occurred between us on that mystical night, and it endures today. When Danae was three years old, I was a professor of pediatrics at a medical school and a researcher at a large children's hospital. Five days a week, as I prepared for my long commute through Los Angeles traffic, Danae would cry. She didn't want me to go. I always gave her a big hug and promised to hurry home that afternoon, but she was heartbroken. I can still see this precious kid standing in the doorway crying.

Danae was particularly upset one morning as I explained again why Daddy had to go to work. Her beautiful blue eyes welled up with tears, and she said sorrowfully, "It's all right, Daddy. I forgive you."

I asked my daughter a few weeks ago if she remembered those days. She has a remarkably vivid memory of her childhood, which is almost scary at times. She not only remembered her tears on the morning I was describing, but she recalled something that I had forgotten.

One day when she was three, she and her mother came to the front yard to wave at me as I drove away. I had already backed out of the driveway, however, and didn't see them standing there. Danae recalls that she sobbed in disappointment. But when I was a long block away, I happened to catch a glimpse of my little family in my rearview mirror. They were still frantically waving good-bye. As I was going around the corner, I put my arm out the window and waved in return. Even after all these years, Danae remembers the excitement she felt at that moment when her daddy saw her and returned her wave.

How could I, and indeed, how could *we* allow ourselves to get so busy with the cares of life that we would neglect our vulnerable little boys and girls and leave them unprotected from evil influences? How could we fail to give them the love and attention they crave? And how could we send them into a dangerous world without laying a secure foundation to hold them steady? No other priority comes close to this responsibility to raise our children, as Solomon said, in the way they should go. This is where we will head in the pages that follow.

We will be discussing information, approaches, answers, solutions, and recommendations that have stood the test of time. Our focus will be on the influence of mothers, fathers, teachers, and peers. We'll deal with girls of all ages, from babyhood to adulthood, and will consider the land mines that surely lie ahead. We'll talk about teaching girls to be ladies. We will discuss the search for self-worth, sexual awakening, single parenting, emotional development, and the how-tos of raising girls. And of course, we'll deal with puberty, adolescence, and the obsession with beauty.

Ultimately, we will talk about spiritual training at home and why moral purity must be taught from the preschool years to the empty nest. Therein lies our hope. There is so much to be said here. More than three thousand pages of research and reference material have been accumulated in preparation for this book. It is my thirty-third and has taken me more than three years to complete. What took me so long was trying to decide what to leave out. Everything seemed significant to me.

What I will share with you, moms and dads, has become my obsession. I get a lump in my throat when I think of those precious kids who know so little about life, and I worry about how we can protect their innocence and preserve the joys of childhood.

That is our task. So get a cup of hot coffee or put on a kettle of tea, settle down in a comfortable chair, and let's talk together.

GIRLS IN PERIL

THE RESEARCH SUPPORTING my earlier book, *Bringing Up Boys*, showed unequivocally that boys were in serious trouble on many fronts. From preschool to adulthood, they were doing poorly on almost every measure of emotional, educational, and physical health. Boys were two times more likely than girls to have learning disabilities, three times more likely to be registered drug addicts, and four times more likely to be emotionally disturbed.[1] They were at greater risk for schizophrenia, autism, sexual addiction, alcoholism, and all forms of antisocial and criminal behavior.[2] They were ten times more likely to commit murder,[3] and their rate of death in car accidents was greater by 50 percent.[4] Seventy-seven percent of delinquency-related court cases involved males.[5]

There is every reason to believe that boys generally continue to flounder today. Compared to girls, they have serious liabilities in school. There is hardly a place anywhere in the world where they read better than girls, on average. Here in the United States, boys are outnumbered 124 to 100 in advanced placement courses.[6] According to sociologist Andrew Hacker, three out of four girls who are seniors in high school report spending an hour or more on homework per day, compared with only half of the boys.[7]

As might be expected from these statistics, fewer boys attend and graduate from college today. Fifty-nine percent of all master's degree candidates are women, and the percentage of men in graduate-level professional education is shrinking every year.[8] When eighth-grade students are asked about their future aspirations, girls are twice as likely to say they intend to pursue a career in management, the professions, or business.[9] Boys, by contrast, often don't know what they want. I've found that even in the latter years of high school, they are less inclined to set goals or consider working hard enough to achieve them.

This lack of academic motivation in many boys carries major implications for girls and women. Already, professional women are finding a shortage of men of comparable education available for possible marriage. Someone has said with a smile, "There are so many Cinderellas and so few princes." Males and females have been designed for one another, and they are interdependent in countless ways. Anything that affects one sex is certain to influence the other, both positively and negatively. That's why the war between the sexes, which has continued at a fever pitch for nearly forty years, is so unfortunate and foolish.

Well, that brings us to the subject of girls. How healthy are they emotionally and physically? Although our daughters are doing rather well academically and on some measures of social and personal health, I have to tell you that, in many ways, I am even more concerned about girls than boys. So much has changed for the worse in recent years. Girls are under enormous pressures rarely experienced by their mothers, grandmothers, and other women in previous generations. Today's little girls are being enticed to grow up too fast and are encountering challenges for which they are totally unprepared. That is a generalization with many exceptions, of course, but far too many females are in trouble.

Their turmoil is evident within an array of behaviors that make no sense to family members, friends, and onlookers. For example, a rising incidence of eating disorders, including anorexia and bulimia, is besieging the young. This obsession with extreme thinness has swept through Western nations like a viral epidemic. Although it has numerous and complex psychological causes, it is driven primarily by a fear of being fat, or even chubby, during the childhood and adolescent years.[10] Ninety percent of those affected are girls, beginning as early as five or six years of age.[11] Imagine that! Some of the tiny anorexics are still in kindergarten! According to the American Academy of Child and Adolescent Psychiatry, 40 percent of nine- and ten-year-old girls have attempted to lose weight.[12] Never before have children been so preoccupied with the shapes of their bodies.[13] Eventually one-third of these girls will turn to dangerous methods of losing weight, such as diet pills, laxatives, vomiting, fasting, and extreme exercise.[14] By the time they are fifteen, more than 60 percent will be using these harmful substances and methods.[15] We'll talk in upcoming chapters about how this fear of obesity often leads to anorexia, bulimia, and other maladies.

There are other serious concerns for middle and high school students, some of whom are cutting and mutilating themselves and piercing their tongues, lips, noses, eyebrows, ears, navels, nipples, and private parts with spikes and rings. Some try to symbolize darkness and death in their fashion choices and bodily adornment. Others are involved in sexual aggression, drugs and alcohol, bullying, deceit, and rebellion at home and in school.

Helping to promote some of this dangerous and antisocial behavior is an array of "bad girls" on parade throughout the culture. They are pop icons, starlets, and American idols who are highly influential among teens. Although the in-crowd is constantly changing, today's superstars include Paris Hilton, Nicole Richie, Britney Spears, Lindsay Lohan, and numerous other sexpots who help to warp this generation of young girls. The most brazen among them don't wear undergarments at times and have even allowed themselves to be photographed by the paparazzi from strategic angles.

Another of the "bad girls" is Angelina Jolie, who said in an interview with a German women's magazine, "I doubt that fidelity is absolutely essential for a relationship. It's worse to leave your partner and talk badly about him afterwards. Neither Brad nor I have ever claimed that living together means to be chained together. We make sure that we never restrict each other."[16]

Never restrict each other? I guess that means Angelina and Brad sleep with whomever they please and expect their relationship to be unaffected by it. Time will reveal that they are tragically wrong.

The unfortunate fact is that these brash superstars have become role models for millions of girls. They lead vulnerable wannabes to despise the way they look. How can awkward, newly minted teenagers with braces and acne measure up to the perceived standard of perfection? Obviously, most cannot. So they hate themselves for what they are and what they can never be.

A growing number of today's kids are also binge drinking, according to the Center on Alcohol Marketing and Youth (CAMY) at Georgetown University.[17] In one specific six-month period, 31 percent of girls drank liquor as compared with 19 percent of boys.[18] Though the numbers are smaller, there is a disturbing trend for teen girls to strip off their clothes for money.[19] Prostitution is related to that behavior, of course, and appears to be spreading. Those involved in sex for hire are getting younger, and they tend to be middle class.[20] The majority of them are not runaways or "lost kids." They are ordinary teens looking for attention, adventure, money, and a way to fill the void inside.

Columnist Steve Lopez reflected on the implications of these and other burgeoning concerns about girls in a column published in the *Los Angeles Times* entitled "A Scary Time to Raise a Daughter." He wrote:

> Three months ago, with my wife's contractions getting closer and closer, we flicked on the TV as a distraction before going to the hospital.
> Bad idea.
> No one expects a great deal of enlightenment from the tube these days. But as we switched from one tawdry and vapid reality or dating show to another, I wondered if we should have our heads examined for bringing a child into this world.
> Especially a girl.
> It's not just television that scares me. It's the Internet, pop music, radio, advertising. The most lurid elements of each medium now dominate pop culture, and the incessant, pounding message, directed primarily at young people, is that it's all about sex.
> Sure, some of us boomers had our flower child days of free love, but that was a social revolution, not a corporate-driven campaign.
> Today, if you haven't just had [sex], you're a loser. If you don't expect to have it in the immediate future, try plastic surgery, because sex appeal—the one true standard of human achievement—is the only thing worth aspiring to.
> Yes, I'll admit it: I'm frazzled about all of this because I have a baby girl. Each day, I feel a little more like Dan Quayle, who was once ridiculed for wagging a finger at television's Murphy Brown, an unwed mom.
> Where's Dan Quayle when you need him?[21]

Steve Lopez is right. Like their brothers, many girls are being victimized by cultural influences that are increasingly more violent, hypersexualized, and spiritually impoverished. And this is the key: our society is at war with good parents who are trying desperately to protect their kids from the harmful forces swirling around them.

Let me ask some rhetorical questions to those of you who are raising girls. Do you hope your daughters will be sexually promiscuous even from their early teen years? "Certainly not!" I can almost hear most of you saying. But indulge me for the purposes of illustration. Do you prefer that your girls be brash, loud, and aggressive in their relationships with males?

Do you hope they will be easy marks for boys seeking sexual conquest? Is it your desire that they imitate rogue masculine behavior, such as being quick-tempered, immodest, insensitive, and disrespectful of others? Do you want them to be foulmouthed, crude, rude, profane, and discourteous?

Is it your desire that they dress provocatively in order to attract the attention of guys, revealing more than they conceal? When they become teenagers, do you want them to look like prostitutes, pumping up their lips with collagen and their breasts with silicone? Would you like them to dangle rings from their body parts and dye their hair green, orange, purple, and pink? Do you want them to be so ashamed of their bodies that they feel compelled to diet at nine years of age and are afraid to eat by thirteen? Are you comfortable with professors who will encourage your nearly grown daughters to experiment with lesbian relationships and tell them that bisexuality is an even greater trip? Do you hope that your girls will learn that marriage is an outdated institution that should be redefined or discarded? Do you want them to disdain the cherished spiritual beliefs you have been teaching them since they were babies?

If these are your aspirations for your vulnerable little girls, and I'm sure they are not, then you need do nothing to achieve them. The popular culture will do the job for you. It is designed to turn this generation of kids into politically correct little MTV clones. The influence of the entertainment industry, Madison Avenue, the Internet, hip-hop musicians, some public schools, liberal universities, and other institutions is shaping and warping youngsters and infusing them with harmful ideas that will rob them of the innocence of childhood. As a result, some of our girls will lose their prospects of having a productive and happy life. The stability of their future families is hanging in the balance. This is what lies in the paths of children whose parents are overworked, distracted, exhausted, and uninvolved. Without their care and concern, the culture will take them to hell. I have witnessed it a thousand times. Even with proper parental supervision, many of our kids are on the bubble.

I am most concerned about the children among us who are chronically lonely. Their parents are gone much of the time, leaving them to fend for themselves. Human beings desperately need each other, and those who are isolated do not thrive. Not only do lonely children tend to get into trouble, they also become sitting ducks for abusers who understand their emptiness and use it for their own purposes.

One thing is certain: your children are being targeted by businesses that are willing to exploit them for quick profits. Is there any doubt that the pornography industry wants to sell salacious and perverse images to curious adolescents, regardless of where that exposure leads? The dirty old men (and women) who sell this stuff don't wait for "customers" to come knocking on the door. They go out looking for them. According to former attorney general John Ashcroft, nine out of ten teens have been exposed to pornographic images.[22] Those who stumble across this wretched stuff on the Web or in other media are highly susceptible to what they see. Boys as young as thirteen are easily trapped in addictive and progressive behavior that will plague them for a lifetime. Girls are directly affected because their boyfriends expect them to imitate what is depicted in obscene products.

A myriad of other businesses are also seeking to manipulate girls. Mattel, Inc., for example, released a sexy little doll called "My Scene My Bling Bling Chelsea Doll."[23] Critics called it "Hooker Barbie."

Not only are toys becoming sexier, they are also undergoing something called "age compression." It used to be that girls from six to ten were the prime market for Barbie and other dress-up dolls. Nowadays, Barbie is targeted at three- to five-year-olds. As Stacy Weiner wrote, it's "good-bye to girlhood."[24] Writer Bruce Kluger commented, "You've come a long way, Raggedy Ann."[25]

Child development experts warn that parents could be baiting pedophiles by dressing their daughters as raunchy women. The American Psychological Association (APA) warns that sexualizing children leads to three of the most common mental health problems among girls and women: eating disorders, low self-esteem, and depression.[26] Does the APA really have to convince moms and dads that making their six-year-olds into sexpots is just plain stupid?

The unanswered question at this point is, "Where are the parents?" Five-year-old girls certainly can't buy thongs or jewel-encrusted underwear or dolls that look like little prostitutes. Their parents have to be forking over the cash. Sales receipts from a few years back indicated that parents spent $1.6 million on thong underwear for their seven- to twelve-year-old daughters.[27] I fear that many adults who ought to know better have abdicated their responsibility to guide their precious children.

It should not surprise us that many teen girls who have been raised in the sexual idiocy of the twenty-first century have made adolescent promiscuity a way of life. And most of them are lost—hopelessly lost. Michelle Malkin, one of my favorite columnists and television commentators, is urging us to recognize what is happening to our children. She wrote:

> As a mother of a 4 year old girl and an 8 month old boy, I am increasingly dismayed by the liberal assault on decency, the normalization of promiscuity, and the mainstream media's role as shameless collaborators. . . . You would think that it's

normal to dress up in [Little Miss Hooters] outfits at 5 years old, to wear sex bracelets and discuss oral sex at 10, to flash your breasts for the cameras at 15, to get paid for anal sex at 20, to keep Excel spreadsheets of sexual conquests, and to use abortion as birth control until menopause. When conservative women say, "Have some self-respect," liberals in the media call us self-righteous. When conservative women say promiscuity is degrading and self-destructive, liberals in the media call us prudes. When liberal women raise their voices, they are praised as "passionate." When conservative women raise their voices, we are condemned as "shrill."[28]

Malkin concluded with this advice for parents:

Be "prudes." Be "rude." Be "shrill." And never, ever feel ashamed for asking out loud, "Have you no shame?"[29]

Obviously, the culture has our children in its crosshairs, and either we can go with the flow or we can fight back with all our resources. Heaven help our kids if we remain passive and disconnected.

I hope you understand now why I am so concerned about girls. They are at maximal risk today. They are tender and more easily wounded than their brothers. And politically correct or not, I maintain that their inherent emotional nature makes them more easily manipulated. A longing for love and connectedness lies deep within their feminine souls. This is why they open themselves without commitment to guys who might, given a miracle, give them the affirmation they crave. They don't seem to get much pleasure out of the perverse acts they perform. They are hoping against hope that some adolescent boy out there will fill the void and ease the ache inside. And increasingly, those unmet needs are created by something missing in the girls' relationships with their mothers and/or fathers. Usually it *is* the father! We'll delve into that matter in depth, momentarily.

For now, parents, this is the world in which your kids are growing up. Not all of them have succumbed to the temptations and pressures I have described, of course, and I will soon share with you some very encouraging trends that are beginning to emerge. Nevertheless, the forces that are enticing the younger generation are still having their tragic impact. Our children desperately need us to guide their steps and set reasonable boundaries to protect them.

They remind me of little bunny rabbits running through the meadow, unaware that owls and coyotes and bears and hawks are out there trying to catch them and tear them apart. At times it seems as though every predator in the field is after those same vulnerable little creatures. You, Mom and Dad, are their only defenders. Your public school can't be counted on to do what is clearly your responsibility. Not even your church can save them. The clergy is trying to counter a culture much further gone into moral decline than the world into which we were born. Meeting together with teens on Sunday mornings or Wednesday nights is helpful, but even it is not enough.

You, however, can provide the care and guidance that is needed, and most important, you can fill the void that will otherwise send your bright-eyed kids into the meadow in a desperate search for nurturance and the warm company of other lost bunnies.

Together, perhaps we can protect some of today's children and teens from the dangers I have described. But first I want to talk to you more about these delightful little creatures we call girls.

3

THE FAIR SEX

LET'S EXTEND OUR journey further now into the wonderful and complex world of girls. Every one of them is beautiful, precious, and unique. I wish I had about a dozen granddaughters like the little ladies whose pictures grace the cover design of this book. By the way, wouldn't you like to know what secret is being shared between the giggly little girls shown on the front cover? I'll bet it would make us smile.

I love the way God created girls, romanticized in a classic song written by Alan Jay Lerner and Frederick Loewe for the movie *Gigi*. It contains these lyrics:

> *Thank heaven for little girls*
> *For little girls get bigger every day!*
> *Thank heaven for little girls*
> *They grow up in the most delightful way.*

Indeed they do. Boys are treasures too, of course. I spent three years writing about their uniqueness and what makes them tick. But the female of the species captures our hearts in a different way. It is their sensitivity and tenderness that are so charming. They feel everything intensely and make a habit of hugging those they love.

Let's talk about the soft, feminine nature of girls and explore why (and how) parents should respond in accordance with it. First, I need to acknowledge that girls not only possess a compassionate and gentle spirit, but they can also be catty, rebellious, and downright brutal to their peers. All of us as human beings, both males and females, are capable of exhibiting the best and the worst of characteristics. These polar opposites coexist within people of all ages, and no one is free from the dark side. It would be naive to claim otherwise. It is why we need a Savior, because "all have sinned and fall short of the glory of God" (Romans 3:23).

Nevertheless, the Creator has placed within the fair sex a winsome and caring nature that should be recognized and cultivated. Gratifying and protecting it during the formative years is like pouring cool water at the base of a delicate flower. "Grown-up girls" need careful nurturing too.

A popular love song written in the 1930s by "Irving King" and Harry M. Woods offers valuable counsel to men about dealing with women. It is called "Try a Little Tenderness" and was later recorded by Frank Sinatra and many other vocalists. The lyrics convey this romantic advice:

> *She may be weary, women do get weary*
> *Wearing the same shabby dress*
> *And when she's weary, try a little tenderness*
>
> *She may be waiting, just anticipating*
> *Things she may never possess*
> *While she's without them, try a little tenderness*

These songwriters clearly knew a thing or two about women. But I wonder if he observed similar characteristics in little girls. I certainly have.

When my daughter was young, we took a long car trip and made many pit stops along the way. (You can be sure of that.) While I was pumping fuel at one of the gas stations, a little stray dog came wiggling over to our car and became our "friend." Danae instantly fell in love with this homeless mutt that was begging to go along with us. We had to leave him behind, of course, and I shooed him away so I could shut the door. The little fellow stood looking up at us forlornly, as though he were thinking, *I know. You don't want me. And no one else does either.* Then he followed our car as we drove away, running down the highway after us. It was a sad moment for all of us, but especially for Danae. She was crushed. She sobbed inconsolably and said, "Daddy, you have to go back. He doesn't have anyone to care for him. Turn around. You have to go get him. We can't just leave him back there alone. Who will feed him tonight? Please, Daddy. Go back." Her tears fell like rain.

I wish I could tell you that we returned to pick up the little dog and that he was our pet forevermore. That didn't happen. Though we are all dog lovers in our family, there are times when a mom and dad have to make the hard decisions. We just couldn't take an animal with us on our trip, staying in hotels and parking our car in the hot sun. Besides, we already had a much-loved dog that we had rescued from an animal shelter. For Danae, however, her sorrow overrode all counterarguments. She couldn't stop crying.

Our daughter never forgot that dog. She could tell you about him to this day. And she never completely forgave me for driving away from the lonely pup. In fact, I let her read this just-written story over dinner last night, and a cloud came across her face. She said, "You *really* should have gone back, Dad. You could have made it work." She is still half-ticked over my decision.

Those of you who don't like dogs will not understand the way Danae feels about things, but I do. She has a very tender spirit, and I wouldn't have her be any other way. It is why she has been "Daddy's girl" since she was born. It also explains why she regularly visits lonely elderly people who languish in nursing homes. She genuinely cares for them, which makes me very proud of her.

Danae's compassionate and gentle temperament is not unusual among members of her gender, although it is more pronounced in some girls than others. You will see in the next chapter why girls are typically more sensitive, perceptive, and relational than boys. These are among the characteristics that draw men to women, although guys usually don't understand them very well. It is also why girls and women are easily hurt and given to self-doubt. Beginning in puberty and lasting throughout life, girls and women often struggle with recurring crises of confidence. Some never fully overcome them.

One of my early books was titled *What Wives Wish Their Husbands Knew about Women*. It was based on surveys I administered initially to seventy-five women and then to five thousand more. I shared with them ten common sources of depression that I had heard in my counseling, as follows: problems with the children, menstrual and other physiological difficulties, financial stresses, in-law conflict, sexual problems, absence of romantic love in marriage, low self-esteem, fatigue and time pressure, loneliness/isolation/boredom, and aging. Then I asked the women to rank these items in their own lives. The study was not intended to meet the rigors of the scientific method, because the sample was not randomized and had no control group. Nevertheless, the results were very interesting and revealing.

The most frequent source of depression among these women was low self-esteem, far exceeding any other option. More than 50 percent listed it in first place, and 80 percent marked it in the top five. The seventy-five women who served as the test group were young, attractive, and married. All were mothers with young children and lived in upscale neighborhoods. Most had college degrees and were members of strong Christian churches. Nevertheless, almost all of them reportedly dealt with recurring bouts of depression and flagging confidence.

When I administered the short questionnaire to five thousand more women, my initial findings were confirmed. It is my conclusion, based on these and other more rigorous studies, that the sensitivity of which I have written has a downside: adolescent girls and women are more easily wounded than males, and many of them experience a lifelong sense of inadequacy. The pain that results from being ridiculed, bullied, or left out as a child or teen—as well as from wounds originating within dysfunctional families—is remembered painfully thereafter.

I served as a school psychologist before moving into academia and saw evidence of this vulnerability in most of our female students. They didn't feel pretty enough or accepted by their peers. They just weren't valuable in their own eyes. Here are some examples of that common pattern in highly successful women.

Chris Evert is the former number one tennis player in the world. She was cute and perky and everyone's little sweetheart when she made her stunning debut into the sport at sixteen years of age. There was no prize in tennis that she didn't eventually win, and yet this is what she said of herself:

> I had no idea who I was, or what I could be away from tennis. I was depressed and afraid because so much of my life had been defined by my being a tennis champion. I was completely lost. Winning made me feel like I was somebody. It made me feel pretty. It was like being hooked on a drug. I needed the wins, the applause, in order to have an identity.[1]

Provocative singer and perennial star of the stage and screen Madonna describes herself in similar terms:

> I have an iron will and all of my will has always been devoted to conquering some horrible feeling of inadequacy. . . . I'm always struggling with that fear. I push past one spell of it and discover myself as a special human being of worth and then I get to another stage and I think I'm mediocre and uninteresting and worthless and I have to find a way to get myself out

of that again and again. My drive in life is from this horrible feeling of being inadequate and mediocre and it is always pushing me, and pushing me and pushing me. Because even though I have become somebody, I still have to prove that I am SOMEBODY. My struggle has never ended and it probably never will.[2]

Oprah Winfrey has been the most successful woman in television for more than twenty-five years. Millions of viewers have tuned in to her talk show every day and been influenced by what she has to say. She is also one of the wealthiest women in the world. This, however, is how she sees herself:

> I discovered I didn't feel worth a d--n, and certainly not worthy of love, unless I was accomplishing something. I suddenly realized I have never felt I could be loved just for being.[3]

Melissa Gilbert played the role of "half-pint" Laura for many years on the popular television series *Little House on the Prairie*. But the story of her adult years is sad, because she chose her career over every other aspect of her life. A series of broken relationships attests to the fact that what we see on television is often a facade. An article in *TV Guide* revealed this dark side to her story. Gilbert, who was thirty years old at the time, said she faced the stark realization that the path she had chosen betrayed her. She said, "Didn't I tell you what my greatest fear is? That they'll write on my tombstone: 'She had an incredible career, but no life.'"[4]

Joan Kennedy, first wife of the late Senator Ted Kennedy, was one of the most glamorous women in the world. She was a model who could turn the heads of every guy in the room. I was one of them. I saw her and the senator at close range in 1968 at an American Academy of Pediatrics conference in Chicago. They both sparkled with beauty and charm, but Joan hardly perceived herself in that light.

During the 1980 presidential campaign, she began seeing a psychiatrist regularly. She said, "I had really lost my self-confidence. The only thing I knew that I was sure of was that I was a very attractive young woman and that I had a pretty good figure. . . . The Kennedys are so good at everything and I'm a flop."[5] When hearing reports that Teddy was a womanizer, she said, "[That] went to the core of my self-esteem. . . . I began thinking maybe I'm just not attractive enough or attractive anymore, or whatever, and it was awfully easy to then say . . . if that's the way it is, I might as well have a drink."[6] Joan soon became an alcoholic.

There is no end to the examples I could cite of admired, respected, and gorgeous women—from Ava Gardner to Marilyn Monroe—who were never entirely comfortable in their own skin. Alas, the problem even showed up in my own home. I was shocked to learn shortly after I married Shirley that she had the same feelings of inadequacy. She had been Miss Everything in college—homecoming queen, most outstanding junior girl, senior class president, Who's Who among Students in American Colleges and Universities, and one of the most popular girls in school. She was beautiful and had guys pursuing her from the time she arrived as a freshman. Everybody loved Shirley, and so did I. Yet I discovered during our first year of marriage that she harbored secret doubts about herself that she had concealed from me during our three-year courtship. The fact that Shirley disliked herself made absolutely no sense to me.

I understood that some of her feelings came from being the daughter of an alcoholic and growing up in a poor neighborhood, but those influences lingered long after she had moved away from home. Nevertheless, those feelings of inadequacy were real, and because I loved her, I needed to help her deal with them. I went to work to repair the damage. Shirley has completely recovered now and is, I think, one of the most respected Christian women in the country. I have seen her confidently step to a podium facing an audience of sixteen thousand men and women. But as I discovered in my wife, the phenomenon of low self-worth can be irrational and is not always linked to obvious causes. To some degree, it is "every woman." And it begins in childhood.

John and Stasi Eldredge described this nature in their book entitled *Captivating: Unveiling the Mystery of a Woman's Soul.* They wrote:

> You see, every little girl—and every little boy—is asking one fundamental question. But they are very different questions, depending on whether you are a little boy or a little girl. Little boys want to know, *Do I have what it takes?* All that rough and tumble, all that daring and superhero dress up, all of that is a boy seeking to prove that he does have what it takes. He was made in the image of a warrior God. Nearly all a man does is fueled by his search for validation, that longing he carries for an answer to his Question.
>
> Little girls want to know, *Am I lovely?* The twirling skirts, the dress up, the longing to be pretty and to be seen—that is what that's all about. We are seeking an answer to our Question. When I was a girl of maybe five years old, I remember standing on top of the coffee table in my grandparents'

living room and singing my heart out. I wanted to capture attention—especially my father's attention. I wanted to be captivating. We all did. But for most of us, the answer to our Question when we were young was "No, there is nothing captivating about you." Get off the coffee table. Nearly all a woman does in her adult life is fueled by her longing to be delighted in, her longing to be beautiful, to be irreplaceable, to have her Question answered, "Yes!" . . .

And down in the depths of our hearts, our Question remains. Unanswered. Or rather, it remains answered in the way it was answered so badly in our youth. "Am I lovely? Do you see me? Do you want to see me? Are you captivated by what you find in me?" We live haunted by that Question, yet unaware that it still needs an answer.[7]

Some of my readers are undoubtedly asking, "Well, what can we as parents do about this 'unanswered question' within our daughters? How can we raise them to be confident women? Is there a way to preserve their softness and femininity while strengthening their sense of personhood too?"

I believe there are many approaches to instilling healthy self-worth in girls, but it begins within the security of a loving family. Specifically, it depends on a caring and affirming father. Moms are vital in countless ways too, but self-worth for girls hangs precariously on their relationship with their dads.

That understanding is spelled out in another wonderful book that I hope you'll buy and read (after you have finished reading mine, of course ☺). It was written by pediatrician Meg Meeker and is entitled *Strong Fathers, Strong Daughters*. Here is what Dr. Meeker writes about the way girls are made:

> I have watched daughters talk to fathers. When you come into the room, they change. Everything about them changes: their eyes, their mouths, their gestures, their body language. Daughters are never lukewarm in the presence of their fathers. They might take their mothers for granted, but not you. They light up—or they cry. They watch you intensely. They hang on your words. They hope for your attention, and they wait for it in frustration—or in despair. They need a gesture of approval, a nod of encouragement, or even simple eye contact to let them know you care and are willing to help.
>
> When she's in your company, your daughter tries harder

to excel. When you teach her, she learns more rapidly. When you guide her, she gains confidence. If you fully understood just how profoundly you can influence your daughter's life, you would be terrified, overwhelmed, or both. Boyfriends, brothers, even husbands can't shape her character the way you do. You will influence her entire life because she gives you an authority she gives no other man.

Many fathers (particularly of teen girls) assume they have little influence over their daughters—certainly less influence than their daughters' peers or pop culture—and think their daughters need to figure out life on their own. But your daughter faces a world markedly different from the one you did growing up: it's less friendly, morally unmoored, and even outright dangerous. After age six, "little girl" clothes are hard to find. Many outfits are cut to make her look like a seductive thirteen- or fourteen-year-old girl trying to attract older boys. She will enter puberty earlier than girls did a generation or two ago (and boys will be watching as she grows breasts even as young as age nine). She will see sexual innuendo or scenes of overt sexual behavior in magazines or on television before she is ten years old, whether you approve or not. She will learn about HIV and AIDS in elementary school and will also probably learn why and how it is transmitted. . . .

You need to stop in your tracks, open your eyes wider, and see what your daughter faces today, tomorrow, and in ten years. It's tough and it's frightening, but this is the way it is. While you want the world to be cautious and gentle with her, it is cruel beyond imagination—even before she is a teen. Even though she may not participate in ugly stuff, it's all around her: sexual promiscuity, alcohol abuse, foul language, illegal drugs, and predatory boys and men who want to take something from her.

I don't care whether you're a dentist, a truck driver, a CEO, or a schoolteacher; whether you live in a 10,000-square-foot home in rural Connecticut or a 1,000-square-foot apartment in Pittsburgh—ugliness is everywhere. Once upon a time ugliness was somewhat "contained"—gangs, drug pushers, and "the bad crowd" stayed in defined pockets, in certain neighborhoods and schools. No more. The ugliness is all around. . . .

You will make the difference in your daughter's life.

You have to—because, unfortunately, we have a popular culture that's not healthy for girls and young women, and there is only one thing that stands between it and your daughter. You.

Fathers inevitably change the course of their daughters' lives—and can even save them. From the moment you set eyes on her wet-from-the-womb body until she leaves your home, the clock starts ticking. It's the clock that times your hours with her, your opportunities to influence her, to shape her character, and to help her find herself—and to enjoy living.[8]

Dr. Meeker's perspective is brilliant, including her unsettling reference to the "ugliness" in today's world. Indeed, the culture *is* "cruel beyond imagination" and threatens the emotional and physical health of this generation of girls. It is aimed squarely at female sexuality, beginning in early adolescence (or even earlier) and continuing into adulthood. Without their fathers to protect and defend them, girls are often on their own against formidable forces. In short, the influence that dads wield for good or harm in their daughters' lives touches every dimension of life. Especially, it shapes and stabilizes girls' senses of worth and keeps alive their tender spirits.

I urge all parents, but especially fathers, to work at building your daughter's self-concept throughout her childhood. Tell her she is pretty every chance you get. Hug her. Compliment her admirable traits. Build her confidence by giving her your time and attention. Defend her when she is struggling. And let her know that she has a place in your heart that is reserved only for her. She will never forget it.

Mom, it is your job to bring out the best in your little girl's nature. She needs your affirmation and encouragement too. We'll talk more about your role in chapters 5 and 7. To both mothers and fathers, let me share a suggestion that you may not want to hear: good parenting almost always requires sacrifice. Childhood lasts for only a brief moment, but it should be given priority while it is passing before your eyes. Watch your kids carefully. Think about what they are feeling, and consider the influences they are under. Then do what is best for them.

Let me acknowledge that successful family life is difficult to achieve. It is never perfect and is often problematic. I am sure you have your own set of challenges as you seek to meet the needs of your children. You may be a single parent with very limited financial resources. Perhaps you suffer from illness, disability, or addiction. Or maybe you have strong-willed kids who are tough to handle. The last thing I want to do is add to your pressures or sense of frustration. Nevertheless, if there is any way you can give priority to your children amid those limitations, even if it requires serious sacrifice, you will not regret giving it to them.

This might mean staying married when your impulse is to divorce. It could cause you to make choices that will handicap you professionally. It might mean financial hardship for the family because Mom is staying at home with her children. It might mean giving up your four-hour golf outing every Saturday. What I am saying is that from where I sit today, children are worth everything they cost us.

It was this perspective that led me to walk away from my position as a professor of pediatrics at the University of Southern California School of Medicine. My responsibility in this rewarding position required me to visit fifteen major medical centers across the country twice each year, taking me away from home repeatedly. When my father pointed out to me what my absence was doing to my family, I resigned so I could spend more time with my wife and kids.

I admit that at first, professional accomplishment with all its perks had seemed to be like low-hanging fruit for me, and it was very sweet for a time. Honestly, I thought I was walking away from the good life when I left academia. It was difficult for a type A guy to do, but it was the right decision. As the years unfolded, I realized that I hadn't actually given up much of anything. I just found other ways to use my training and opportunities, and I was more fulfilled than I had been in my "other life." I thank God now that my father urged me to give priority to my family. The wonderful relationship I enjoy with our grown son and daughter today is the payoff.

In summary, I hope you will find a way to give your little girls (and boys) the great benefits of a secure, loving home. That is the surest way to preserve the light that shines in their eyes.

We're going to take a close look in the next chapter at the female brain. It is a marvel of uniqueness and design. It is impossible to understand girls without examining the physiological, neurological, hormonal, and genetic influences that make them who they are. I think you will find this discussion interesting and helpful in dealing with your daughters. About the time you get your youngsters figured out, puberty comes in like a tornado and scrambles all the rules and expectations. That is what makes the parenting task one of life's most challenging experiences. These little creatures called girls are far more complicated than their brothers. Trust me on this one!

I'll close this chapter with the lyrics of a song I love. Its title is "The Hopechest Song" by Stephanie Bentley.

Her mama bought her a hopechest
To keep her dreams inside
All the precious memories
Little things she'd like to hide
A magic wand, an old rag doll
Some plastic pearls 'cause after all

A little girl is only a little girl so long
And tender hearts need their stars to wish upon
'Cause one day you will turn around and she'll be
   gone
A little girl is only a little girl so long

One day when she got home from school
She slipped a little note
Beneath the tattered lining
And here is what he wrote
"Roses are red, violets are blue"
"Put an X in the box if you like me too"
A little girl is only a little girl so long
And tender hearts need their stars to wish upon
'Cause one day you will turn around and she'll be
   gone
A little girl is only a little girl so long

They married in the garden on a perfect July day
In a horse and carriage they waved and rode away
Mama went inside to put away her wedding dress
And spotted a letter lying on the old hopechest

It said . . .

A little girl is only a little girl so long
Your lonely heart might need a star to wish upon
So look inside once in a while to bring the memories
   home
A little girl is only a little girl
And I will always be your little girl
So long . . .[9]

WHY SHE IS WHO SHE IS

AFTER READING *Bringing Up Boys*, a mother shared a humorous story with me about taking her four-year-old daughter, Marla, to meet her three male cousins for the first time. It must have been quite a shock for this little girl to see how aggressive, tough, and unruly they were, compared to her female friends. On the way home that night, Marla shook her head and said, "Mom, those boys are wusser [worser] than I thought."

It hadn't taken Marla very long to figure out that boys are not at all like girls. I wish all adults were as observant, although between 1965 and 1995, many grown-ups failed to notice. During those three decades, some of the most highly educated and sophisticated people drew the conclusion that males and females were different only with regard to reproductive anatomy and physiology. The prevailing view was that every other distinguishing feature between the sexes had resulted from patriarchal upbringing. Boys, it was said, were coerced into being traditionally masculine, which was a serious problem for society.

That belief, promoted with great passion by what was then called the Women's Liberation Movement, served to blind most psychiatrists, psychologists, neurologists, pediatricians, educators, politicians, writers, social activists, television personalities such as Phil Donahue and Barbara Walters, and millions of mothers and fathers throughout the Western world. Or maybe it just seemed that way.

I was a graduate student in child development at that time, and it was perplexing for me to watch this notion called "unisex" gain acceptance among professors and others who should have known better. They seemed to be ignoring the overwhelming evidence to the contrary, including the fact that females, unlike males, have a menstrual cycle, which affects emotions and behavior dramatically. Males and females also carry a different chromosome pattern in every cell of their bodies. How could boys and girls be identical if their DNA is different?

Finally, working with kids as I did every day convinced me that boys and girls are breeds apart. Even Marla could see that. Nevertheless, the unisex idea caught fire under a barrage of disinformation from the media. People began nodding in agreement like little plastic poodles bobbing their heads in the rear windows of cars.

This popular view of masculinity and femininity stood in stark contradiction to what parents had known intuitively for thousands of years. Up to this point, the issue had not even been up for debate. Moms and dads had simply smiled knowingly and said, "Girls are made of sugar and spice and everything nice, but boys are made out of snakes and snails and puppy dog tails."[1] It was a joke, of course, but everyone knew there was some truth to it.

Activists clearly didn't agree. They began a pervasive campaign to change the way boys and girls were raised in an effort to homogenize their behavior. Parents were told that boys were far too aggressive, flamboyant, rowdy, and, well, defective in many ways. They needed to be put through a reorientation program that would teach them to play with dolls and tea sets instead of trucks and balls. They also needed to learn how to cry often and to be more sensitive. In short, these advisers said there was an urgent need for boys to be "fixed" while they were young by making them more feminine.

Girls, conversely, were considered far too passive, frilly, compliant, and "motherly." That had to change too. They needed to be taught to be aggressive, tough, tomboyish, unemotional, and, yes, much more masculine. The net effect was a concerted effort to redesign child rearing from the nursery up. Somehow that was expected to work to the political advantage of women. For a time, parents tried valiantly to comply, but without much success. They were working against irresistible genetic forces.

As we now know, the notion of sexual universality is completely false and never had any basis in scientific fact. It would still be dominant in the culture if it were not for the development of marvelous imaging technologies, including MRIs, CAT scans, and PET scans. These devices permitted neurologists and other professionals to examine the human brain without opening the skull. What they saw on their screens was shocking. Male and female brains were not only different structurally, they also "lit up" in different places when subjected to similar stimulation.[2]

Then a dazzling array of unique hormonal factors began to be better understood. The prevailing beliefs had been dead wrong. The professional community had to acknowledge that behavioral differences between the sexes are not produced by paternalistic biases in child rearing. They are the result of compelling influences that are set in motion at conception.

Well, that takes us back to our theme, which is to offer some insight into the challenging task of bringing up girls. To do that job properly, we need to gain an understanding of what it means to be female—neurologically, hormonally, and emotionally. What is known about the brain and how it affects behavior would fill many libraries, and additional pieces of the puzzle are being learned every day. I can't begin to present the wide scope of those findings in this context, but I can share some useful information that will assist you in interpreting your daughter's behavior and explain why she is who she is. The nuances of a child's personality are undecipherable without knowing some of the basics of her neurobiology. Let's see if we can shed some light on what can be a confusing picture.

Perhaps the best book available to introduce us to this topic is *The Female Brain* by Louann Brizendine. Dr. Brizendine is a Yale-trained psychiatrist who, in the 1970s, observed an absence of research on female neuroanatomy as distinct from that of males. She began seeking answers to such questions as why depression occurs more than twice as often in women as in men and why females perceive the world very uniquely. That led later to her clinical work at the Women's Mood and Hormone Clinic, which she founded at the University of California, San Francisco. It also led to her valuable book, based on more than one thousand scientific studies representing the fields of genetics, molecular neuroscience, fetal and pediatric endocrinology, and neurohormonal development. Brizendine has placed this fascinating medical explanation within easy reach of parents and other laymen.

This is what Brizendine wrote, for example, about the uniqueness of males and females:

> Common sense tells us that boys and girls behave differently. We see it every day at home, on the playground, and in classrooms. But what the culture hasn't told us is that the brain dictates these divergent behaviors. The impulses of children are so innate that they kick in even if we adults try to nudge them in another direction. One of my patients gave her three-and-a-half-year-old daughter many unisex toys, including a

bright red fire truck instead of a doll. She walked into her daughter's room one afternoon to find her cuddling the truck in a baby blanket, rocking it back and forth saying, "Don't worry, little truckie, everything will be all right."

This isn't socialization. This little girl didn't cuddle her "truckie" because her environment molded her unisex brain. There is no unisex brain. She was born with a female brain, which came complete with its own impulses. Girls arrive already wired as girls, and boys arrive already wired as boys. Their brains are different by the time they're born, and their brains are what drive their impulses, values, and their very reality.[3]

Michael Gurian articulated a similar perspective in his book *The Wonder of Girls*, which is loaded with useful information about the fair sex. He quoted Brenda Goff, a middle-school teacher in Kansas City, as she described her own family experience. She said:

> Before I became a parent, I firmly believed that behavior of boys and girls was mostly molded by society and parents. Girls learned to be feminine, boys learned to be masculine. I had a girl first. At fifteen months, this little girl cried about her socks not having flowers on them. She was even born with feminine qualities that I do not have, so how could she have learned them? I was stunned!
>
> Then I had a son. I was still convinced that I could have a boy who wasn't aggressive—no guns, war toys, etc. No violent TV shows—actually very little exposure to TV at all. Then my son "shot" me with his banana around the time he turned two! And my hair dryer became a space gun at around three. It was extremely obvious that he was different from her and yet we felt, as parents, that they've been treated in much the same manner.[4]

Gurian said in response, "Brenda's story has been the story of many parents. And why shouldn't it be? It is human nature."[5]

Indeed! But what aspect of human nature drives behavior associated with masculinity and femininity? It begins at conception, when males and females start their developmental journeys down two very different paths. That juncture will affect the way they think, feel, and act for the rest of their lives. The brains of both sexes appear to be "female" until about the eighth week, when a male brain is washed by a huge surge of testosterone. It is then transformed radically and even takes on a different color.

This male sex hormone kills some of the communication cells, including a portion of the bundle of nerves called the corpus callosum. It is a rope of fibers that connects the right hemisphere, where emotion is processed, with the left, where language is focused. Although the corpus callosum survives the testosterone bath, the male brain will never be able to "cross talk" as effectively thereafter, which has major implications for future masculine behavior. Testosterone also causes an increase in the volume of neurons and circuits located in the boy's sex and aggression centers. Why does that surprise us?

A male has up to twenty times more testosterone than a female,[6] which is why his play often involves running, jumping, roughhousing, grabbing hair, making loud noises, and playing with cars, trucks, airplanes, and tanks. He finds it really funny to pass gas that is SBD (silent but deadly). He likes to throw things and "fire" toy guns (bang-bang!) or shoot cucumbers or carrots or anything that looks vaguely like a gun. Testosterone is the driver for it all. It is the reason his mother, who loves him dearly, has her hands full trying to keep him from killing himself. He is a boy, after all. That's what boys do.

Because the female brain is not subjected to a comparable surge of testosterone in the womb and beyond, its communicative and emotional centers remain intact. In fact, these structures will grow larger and become better networked neurologically. A girl's corpus callosum is up to 25 percent larger in a male's,[7] and becomes an eight-lane superhighway capable of carrying great quantities of emotional information from one side of the brain to the other. (For boys it is a country road.)

As a result, a girl is likely to be more expressive and emotional than most boys almost from birth. She will probably feel things more deeply and respond to subtle cues in her environment that boys are likely to miss. She will be far better at reading character and motives in others, although she probably won't be able to explain how she does it. She will also cry more often, even as an adult. Every man knows that, and he is typically rattled by it. She is a girl, after all. That's what girls do.

To understand the personalities and inclinations of young girls, it is important to understand what is called "infantile puberty."[8] It refers to a period between six and thirty months of age when the ovaries produce huge amounts of estrogen, comparable even to adult levels. As testosterone marinates the male brain in early gestation, estrogen bathes the female brains of babies and toddlers. Estrogen is called the "intimacy hormone" because it stimulates brain circuits that create an urgent desire for bonding, nurturing, and communication. Thereafter, both as a girl and as a woman, she will be a friend, a lover, a feeler, a talker, and even a bit of a conniver. It is what makes her feminine.

It is the nature that I was describing in the previous chapter. The softness and sensitivity that we see in girls are the result of her neurological development. The hormonal forces that shape and influence her behavior are the cause.

Let's turn again to Dr. Brizendine to help us understand female brain structure and how it affects thinking. She describes it like this:

> What if the communication center is bigger in one brain than in the other? What if the emotional memory center is bigger in one than in the other? What if one brain develops a greater ability to read cues in people than does the other? In this case, you would have a person whose reality dictated that communication, connection, emotional sensitivity, and responsiveness were the primary values. This person would prize these qualities above all others and be baffled by a person with a brain that didn't grasp the importance of these qualities. In essence, you would have someone with a female brain.[9]

We can see evidence of this hard wiring and its hormonal underpinnings in the behavior of infant girls. They gaze at faces for signs of emotional expression shortly after birth and draw meaning from a particular look or touch. When they encounter a face without emotion, however, such as a mime or someone who has had too much Botox, the child tends to be confused. A girl will turn her face to others nearby that are more expressive. Mutual facial gazing will increase by over 400 percent in the first three months of life, whereas this response will not increase at all in boys during this time.[10]

Girls have innate skills of observation, including the ability to hear human vocal tones in a broader range of frequencies. A study at Harvard Medical School found that newborn females less than twenty-four hours old are able to distinguish the cries of another baby from various sounds in the room.[11] Girls a little older can also hear even the slightest tightening in Mother's voice, which tells them they should not be touching something forbidden. A little boy, on the other hand, will be less able to recognize mild displeasure in his mother's voice and probably won't care anyway. He will have to be restrained physically to keep him from plunging ahead.[12] A girl of two can tell whether or not an adult is listening to her or if she is being ignored. If disregarded, she will often toddle away in indignation.

Brizendine shares an interesting story that occurred one day when she was mildly depressed. At eighteen months, her daughter noticed immediately that something was wrong. She climbed onto her mother's lap and caressed her hair, glasses, and earrings. Then she looked straight into her mother's eyes, held her face in her hands, and soothed her mom's feelings. Dr. Brizendine said, "That little girl knew exactly what she was doing."[13] We know now that this kind of female nurturing is a precursor to bonding in motherhood. That is what was going on when the three-year-old told her "little truckie" not to worry because everything was going to be all right. She was a future mom in training.

In short, females are finely tuned machines that operate according to fixed timetables. Once again, the behavior we see throughout childhood results from hormones activating preprogrammed receptor sites as they interact with environmental influences. One affects the other, positively or negatively. Maternal stress during pregnancy, for example, can upset the biochemical balance by stimulating a stress hormone called cortisol. It can alter the normal neural wiring, posing lifelong implications for future emotional health. Research also reveals that girls in their first two years tend to absorb the emotional climate in the home.[14] Mothers who are greatly stressed, such as during times of marital conflict or financial worries, can pass along their anxieties to their female offspring. Parents must always remember that perceptive little people, especially their girls, are watching their every move.

Dr. Brizendine elaborates further on the way young females value relationships, as contrasted with males:

> If you're a girl, you've been programmed to make sure you keep social harmony. This is a matter of life and death to the brain, even if it's not so important in the twenty-first century. We could see this in the behavior of three-and-a-half-year-old twin girls. Every morning the sisters climbed on each other's dressers to get to the clothes hanging in their closets. One girl had a pink two-piece outfit, and the other had a green two-piece outfit. Their mother giggled every time she'd see them switch the tops—pink pants with a green top and green pants with a pink top. The twins did it without a fight. "Can I borrow your pink top? I'll give it back later, and you can have my green top" was how the dialogue went. This would not be a likely scenario if one of the twins were a boy. A brother would have grabbed the shirt he wanted, and the sister would have tried to reason with him, though she would have ended

up in tears because his language skills simply wouldn't have been as advanced as hers.

Typical non-testosteronized, estrogen-ruled girls are very invested in preserving harmonious relationships. From their earliest days, they live most comfortably and happily in the realm of peaceful interpersonal connections. They prefer to avoid conflict because discord puts them at odds with their urge to stay connected, to gain approval and nurture. The twenty-four-month estrogen bath of girls' infantile puberty reinforces the impulse to make social bonds based on communication and compromise. It happened with Leila and her new friends on the playground. Within a few minutes of meeting they were suggesting games, working together, and creating a little community. They found a common ground that led to shared play and possible friendship. And remember [their brother's] noisy entrance? That usually wrecked the day and the harmony sought out by the girls' brains.[15]

Michael Gurian referred to these bonding tendencies as "the intimacy imperative," which he defined as "the hidden yearning in every girl's and woman's life to live in a safe web of intimate relationships."[16] He gave as an illustration his own daughters' early experience in soccer, which was more social than competitive. In contrast to the aggressive way boys play the sport, when one of his girls would knock down another player as she ran down the field, more often than not, she would stop to check on the other girl's welfare. Meanwhile, the opposing team would score while parents were yelling from the sideline, "Watch out, watch the goal!"[17]

Winning on the field was less important for these girls than friendship and intimacy. That is usually the case, especially when girls are young. Estrogen, the "queen" of female biochemistry, is at work. It elevates relationship to the highest priority.

But what about girls who are very shy and do not connect easily with others? Are they wired differently from their gregarious sisters? No. Gurian writes that even those who prefer to be alone are often focused mentally on how relationships have been going and how they might be improved. He found this characteristic of female nature remarkable and not at all like the impulses of males. He wrote, "I know I am different from my wife and daughters. There is something about the female experience of intimacy that I will never fully know because I don't live it."[18]

While considering the hormonal influences that make a girl who she is, we must not overlook the actual structure of the brain. There is 15 percent more blood flowing in the female brain than in that of a male, and it is more likely to surge to both hemispheres.[19] When you talk to a girl, she is concentrating on what you say with both sides of her brain, whereas a boy is listening with predominately one side. This is why females typically like to process ideas before deciding or acting on them. It is also why women often agonize over routine decisions. Neuroscientist Ruben Gur observes, "There's more going on in the female brain than the male. The female brain is more revved up."[20] True, brother, true.

Gurian then asks, "Have you ever noticed how hard it is for a girl or woman to 'turn her brain off'?"[21] That is true too. I noticed this characteristic when my wife, Shirley, and I were first married. If we had an argument over something I considered trivial, I would simply put the matter out of my mind until morning. I knew we could work it out after a good night of sleep. Shirley, however, would lie on her side of the bed (her "brink," as I called it) until she couldn't stand the silence any longer, and then she would wake me to say, "You *are* going to talk to me!" I was forced to deal with whatever was bothering her. Unless I was willing to wake up and fly right, neither of us would get any sleep. Therefore, we would talk through our disagreement, and when the matter was settled, she was able to slumber like a baby. Believe me, it is a male-female thing.

It is impossible to overstate the importance of talking in the lives of girls and women. Though estimates vary, it appears that males use about seven thousand words per day; and females, twenty thousand.[22] Women not only talk more, but their enjoyment in conversation is far more intense. Connecting through talking activates the pleasure centers of a girl's brain, providing a huge emotional reward for her. It is why teen girls are obsessed with text messaging and computer chat rooms. It also explains why one of the most common sources of disappointment women express about married life is that the guys won't talk to them. Show me a husband who keeps his thoughts to himself, and I will show you a frustrated wife.

I have sat in restaurants numerous times and watched what appear to be husbands and wives sitting together at nearby tables. They eat their entire meals with nothing to say to each other. Their eyes are glazed and unfocused, or the women are watching other people. It is always a sad spectacle to see these couples whose minds have to be meandering through hundreds of memories and an array of feelings but can't find anything worth sharing. My sympathies are always with the women in those situations because of my awareness of how badly they need to converse. Some of them appear to have given up on the effort.

Little and not-so-little girls need to talk too, especially about what they are feeling. Let me speak directly to the busy mom and dad who are too exhausted at the end of the day to get your kids talking, either at the dinner table or in those intimate few minutes before bedtime: you may be making a serious mistake. You need to know what your children are thinking, and they need the pleasure of telling you about it. Even though some loquacious kids will "talk the horns off a billy goat" and you come home too tired to listen, it is imperative that you tune in—especially to your girls. There will come a time when they will be talking primarily to their peers, and the missed opportunities for understanding and intimacy today will be costly down the road.

This is why we should engage our kids in activities that encourage conversation, including eating together as a family, playing table games, inviting friends with kids to dinner, cooking together, building things, adopting a lovable dog or cat, cultivating mutual interests, or learning a sport such as skiing or tennis as a family. Remember how your daughter is made, and seek invitations into that private world. You won't regret it.

I'll acknowledge again what you already know: girls are not always supersweet and cooperative. They can be just as contentious and sassy as boys when they don't get what they want. In some cases, they are much more so. As they get older, those who are particularly strong willed can argue, scream, slam doors, and make life miserable for the entire family. Still, most preadolescent girls are easier to deal with than most males. However, as the years go by and the menstrual cycle comes into play, girls tend to bring out their claws, which can be tough for parents (especially mothers) who are trying to reason with them.

Let me summarize what we have discussed. Little girls between three and six months of age experience the beginnings of what is known as "juvenile puberty."[23] Their tiny ovaries start producing adult doses of estrogen, up to twenty times as much as is produced within males, along with other hormones. These girls will be transformed physiologically and behaviorally, and will thereafter be "forever female." This estrogenic bath will continue until girls are approximately three years of age, when it abruptly subsides. At the end of this period of juvenile puberty, girls enter a "quiet stage" of childhood.[24] It will continue for five to eight years, during which time their bodies will be preparing for another huge surge of estrogen in puberty.

How this interaction of physiology, neurotransmitters, hormones, receptor sites, and emotions work together in perfect synchrony is a marvel of intelligent design that reveals the handiwork of the Creator Himself. When the first man, Adam, saw the woman God had specifically designed for him, he shouted, "Wow! Now You're talking, Lord." Well, that isn't exactly what he said. He actually responded with awe, "This is now bone of my bones and flesh of my flesh" (Genesis 2:23). Eve was wonderfully unique, and Adam apparently had the good sense to recognize it.

We will set aside this developmental story now and return to it again in chapter 18, where we will deal with the arrival of puberty, adolescence, and the capacity for motherhood. That is another remarkable journey that explains so much of what it means to be a girl, a preteen, and then a young lady. If you understand what is going on inside your daughter, you will be better equipped to guide her through each fascinating (and challenging) phase. Those years will fly by in the blink of an eye.

Teaching Girls
to Be Ladies

HAVING EXPLORED A few of the neurological and physiological intricacies of the human female brain, let's take the next logical step and consider how girls should be raised. That will take us from *nature*, where we began, to *nurture*, which is another infinitely complex subject. To address it, I want to step back a couple of hundred years and get a running start at the principles that matter most. The ideas and perspectives I will share were true two centuries ago, and they are precisely on target today.

We'll begin by revisiting the beliefs and writings of the second president of the United States, John Adams. He was a prolific reader, statesman, and author, and he made an incalculable contribution to our country. He was not a perfect man, but he lived by a standard of righteousness throughout his adult life. In his autobiography, Adams wrote a commentary on the subject of moral behavior, which he called "manners." Though the language is formal and dated, I urge you to read these words carefully and thoughtfully. They carry great meaning for us today.

> From all that I had read of History of Government, of human life, and manners, I [have] drawn this conclusion, that the manners of women [are] the most infallible Barometer, to ascertain the degree of Morality and Virtue in a Nation. All that I have since read and all the observation I have made in different Nations, have confirmed me in this opinion. The

Manners of Women, are the surest Criterion by which to
determine whether a Republican Government is practicable,
in a Nation or not. The Jews, the Greeks, the Romans, the
Swiss, the Dutch, all lost their public Spirit, their Republican
principles and habits, and their Republican Forms of Government when they lost the Modesty and Domestic Virtues of
their women. . . .

The foundations of national Morality must be laid in
private Families. In vain are Schools, Academies and universities instituted if loose Principles and licentious habits are
impressed upon Children in their earliest years. The Mothers
are the earliest and most important Instructors of youth.[1]

How insightful it is that Adams placed the responsibility for the essential moral character of the nation squarely on the shoulders of mothers.
Fathers play a key role too, of course, but moms are absolutely indispensable. It is their primary task to transmit enduring principles of right and
wrong to the next generation. The old proverb "the hand that rocks the
cradle rules the world" is still true. If women grow weary of that responsibility, or if they lose sight of their own moral compass, no other institution
or governmental agency will be able to save the nation. So wrote President
John Adams.

On another occasion he elaborated on the link between national character and the preservation of a democracy. He wrote:

We have no government armed with power capable of con-
tending with human passions unbridled by morality and
religion. Avarice, ambition, revenge, or gallantry, would
break the strongest cords of our Constitution as a whale goes
through a net. Our Constitution was made only for a moral
and religious people. It is wholly inadequate to the government of any other.[2]

To paraphrase, Adams was saying that a representative form of government
such as ours cannot survive without a spiritual foundation, because its citi-
zens are masters of their own destinies. That is the great vulnerability of a
democracy. Our political system, which Abraham Lincoln said is intended
to be "of the people, by the people, for the people,"[3] can be no more stable
than the collective character of its citizenry. It's all up to us. There is no
king, dictator, or tyrant to restrain our behavior. If we choose evil, there
will be no stopping us. In short, our national sovereignty depends on the

transmission of the nation's morals and manners to children, and that task should begin in the nursery.

But what form does this early training take in today's world? It begins with basic civility, because manners and morals are directly connected. As Horace Mann said, "Manners easily and rapidly mature into morals."[4] The first tends to lead to the second. In centuries past, cultured and religious families understood this relationship. They were aware that girls and boys, and all of humanity, are flawed and inherently sinful. Thus, Old English and Early American societies worked diligently at teaching what were called the "social graces." Teaching manners was their highest priority because of the connection to Christian piety.

Alas, American and British cultures in the twenty-first century have swung to the other end of the continuum. Young girls are often allowed, and even encouraged, to be brash, rude, crude, profane, immodest, immoral, loud, and aggressive. Some of this behavior has been consciously taught in recent years under the rubric of "assertiveness training." To the extent that such programs were designed to instill confidence in bashful, frightened young women, I supported them. But some girls have been taught the worst characteristics of "uncivil" males. I know my words must sound horribly old-fashioned and archaic at this point, but there is something important here for us to consider.

Obviously, human nature has not improved much in the past several hundred years, nor will it ever. What *has* changed, as I have described, is that many parents have become far too distracted, overworked, and stressed out to care much about teaching morals and manners to children. Jolene Savage, who runs the Social Graces School of Etiquette in Topeka, Kansas, says society has reached an all-time low when it comes to matters of civility. Exhausted moms and dads seem not to have noticed what has happened to their children. Clearly, instruction in civility is needed now more than ever. Getting that done, however, can be a challenge. As the late dancer Fred Astaire said, "The hardest job kids face today is learning good manners without seeing any."[5] If that is unfair in your case, please forgive him—and me.

Once again, speaking directly to mothers, it is your job to acculturate your daughters and to help them become ladies. Does that sound chauvinistic in our high-tech world? I suppose it does, but even so, it makes sense. As Lisa Fischer, an instructor at the Final Touch Finishing School in Seattle, Washington, says, "Etiquette has to do with knowing the rules."[6] Therefore, girls should be taught how to eat, talk, walk, dress, converse on the telephone, and respond to adults with respect and poise. Parents should demonstrate good posture and table manners for them, such as putting a napkin in the lap, showing them where to place silverware, and not talking with food in their mouths. They should also explain that burping, gobbling food, and picking teeth are rude.

I also firmly believe that you should require your kids to say thank you and please, to demonstrate that ours is not a "gimme-gimme world." Appreciation is an attitude best cultivated at home. Teach techniques of personal grooming, hygiene, and nutrition. Role-play with them about being gracious hosts and how to formally introduce parents or friends to each other. Require them to excuse themselves when leaving the table, and explain how to make friends, how to take turns talking in a group, and how to make eye contact. You might even help them learn how to cook and care for children. Wouldn't that be something novel?

Although I am not an expert in teaching girls some of the social graces I have named (I learned a masculine version of the rules), I know them when I see them. Let me offer a technique that I came across several years ago. It is designed to teach both boys and girls the art of conversation. I have shared it before, but I include it here for the benefit of those who haven't been paying attention.

It begins by facing your daughter about six feet away and telling her that you are going to play a game together. Then call attention to the tennis ball you are holding, which you proceed to bounce in her direction. After she catches the ball, stand there looking at each other for a moment before saying, "It isn't much fun if you hold the ball, is it? Why don't you throw it back?" Your daughter will probably return the ball rather quickly. Stand motionless for few seconds, and then say, "Okay, I'm sending it back to you now." The child will be curious about what is going on. Then sit down together and describe the meaning of the game. Tell her that talking together is a game called conversation, and it only works if the "ball" is thrown back. If a person bounces a question to you and you hold it, the game ends. Neither you nor your partner has any fun. But if you throw it back, you are playing the game properly.

Follow up by saying, "Suppose I ask, 'Did you like the book you have been reading?' I have thrown the ball to you. If you simply reply, 'Yes,' you have caught and held the ball. But if you say, 'The book was very interesting. I like reading about animals,' you have thrown the ball back."

Then tell the child, "I can keep our conversation going by asking, 'What kind of animals interest you most?' If you say, 'Dogs,' you have held the ball again. But if you tell me, 'I like dogs because they are warm and cuddly,' the ball has been bounced back to me. The idea is to keep the game going until the two of us are finished talking."

Kids usually catch on to this game quickly. Afterward, you can build on the concept by commenting on interchanges that occur with friends and adults. For example, you might ask your daughter, "Did you hear Mrs. Smith ask you this afternoon what kind of food you liked? She was starting a conversation with you, but you just said, 'Hamburgers.' Do you think you threw the ball back to her?"

The child may acknowledge that she held it. Then the two of you can discuss what could have been done differently. Suggest, perhaps, that the question could have been tossed back by saying, "I like the hamburgers my mother makes."

Mrs. Smith might then have asked, "What makes them so good?"

"That," you tell the youngster, "is another example of a conversation. Let's practice 'throwing the ball' to each other. Now, start one with me."

While manners tend to facilitate morals, there is another good reason to teach them. They also help develop confidence and poise. A girl who has been trained properly is never completely knocked off balance when she is in an unfamiliar circumstance. She knows what is expected of her and how to deal with it. Her sense of self-worth is reinforced by the way adults react to her charm, poise, and grace. For the mother who wants to give her daughter a head start in life and help her compete socially, this is a great place to begin.

These diverse skills used to be taught to girls in mandatory home-making classes. Alas, most of these programs were canceled after the revolution of the sixties, and America became the worse for it. Road rage, loud cell phone conversations in restaurants, cutting in line, throwing litter from car windows, and general nastiness are now everyday occurrences.

Monica Brandner teaches at an etiquette business for children and youth called Final Touch Finishing School.[7] She says that manners are primarily about how we treat others and ourselves. Sheryl Eberly, who wrote *365 Manners Kids Should Know*, agrees.[8] She says living by the Golden Rule releases the power of a thankful heart to those trained to practice it. She also reminds us—and this is a great point—that when we teach social graces to our children, we are training the next generation in self-government and self-control. John Adams must be smiling from the other side.

In short, teaching manners to girls is about helping them to become young ladies in a not-very-civil world. I assure you that MTV and an increasingly crude culture will do everything possible to carry our daughters (and our sons) downstream toward that which is boorish and uncouth. You can help them paddle upstream.

One technique that my wife used to teach social graces to our daughter was to play feminine games together. For example, they held elaborate tea parties when Danae was four or five years of age. The child loved them!

Their make-believe names were Mrs. Perry (Danae), Mrs. Snail (her mom), and a little boy named Mr. Green who was drafted into service. Other available kids and their moms from the neighborhood were invited on occasion. This fun activity allowed my wife to explain how silverware was supposed to be arranged, how to eat soup without slurping, how to hold and drink from a teacup, how to use a napkin, how to chew with mouths closed, how to hold a conversation, why they should wait to eat until everyone at the table was served, etc. It was amazing how effective these tea parties were in teaching common politeness. I was never invited to join them and definitely felt left out!

But what about moms who haven't been trained in social etiquette themselves? They can hardly pass on what they haven't learned. And what can we suggest for those who are simply too busy to tackle the job? That is where professional etiquette training comes in. Classes are popping up in cities across the country to meet this precise need.[9]

Though these training programs can be expensive, they are worth the cost for parents who can afford them. For those who don't have the resources, some churches and women's clubs are providing assistance. Furthermore, we should never forget what some grandmothers have to offer in teaching these concepts. They are likely to remember a more genteel era, and their granddaughters will enjoy the attention that comes with the training.

Another source of assistance for moms and dads is the array of materials and manuals now available. I've mentioned several of them, which appear in the addendum of this book. Another helpful publication is a four-hundred-page book entitled *Everyday Graces: A Child's Book of Good Manners*, written by Karen Santorum.[10] She is the wife of the former senator from Pennsylvania Rick Santorum and one of the most impressive women I have met. Karen has a law degree from the University of Pittsburgh School of Law and a bachelor of science degree in nursing from Duquesne University in Pittsburgh. Obviously, she could have had a successful career in either medicine or law, but after thoughtful prayer, she and her husband had a different plan. (By the way, it occurs to me that Karen Santorum would make a wonderful first lady for our country.)

Karen is the mother of eight children, one of whom is in heaven, and she homeschools the others. Her youngest was born in 2007, a precious baby girl with a chromosomal anomaly similar to Down syndrome. She is named Isabella, and they call her Bella. Senator and Mrs. Santorum were aware during her pregnancy that their baby might have this condition. They and their physicians were right. Bella will be mentally disabled for what is likely to be a short life. Sadly, over 90 percent of parents today abort babies who have this genetic condition.[11] For the Santorums, however, abortion was never an option. They chose not to even request amniocentesis to confirm the diagnosis. The senator told me, "It wouldn't have made any difference, so why do it?" Bella was welcomed into their home with open arms from a very loving family. Former Alaska governor Sarah Palin made the same choice regarding her baby Trig.[12]

I interviewed Karen and Rick Santorum for our Focus on the Family radio broadcast before Bella was born. Let me share some excerpts from that conversation, edited for clarity:

JCD: You have chosen to be a full-time mother instead of pursuing a career as an attorney or a nurse. Why?

Karen: Oh, I just feel like my role as wife and mother is the most important thing I will ever do. I love raising my children, and I feel very blessed to be able to be at home with them. It's really wonderful.

JCD: Have you ever asked yourself whether you made the right decision to stay at home?

Karen: Yes, when Rick is leaving in a tuxedo for a banquet and I'm on the floor cleaning up milk, I ask myself, *What's wrong with this picture?* [laughter] But then I fast-forward to the end of my life and am standing before God. He will hold me accountable for loving Him, loving my husband, and loving my children.

JCD: Well, you have now written a book that reflects what you are doing at home. It's called *Everyday Graces*. It is different from other books on manners because it focuses primarily on classic literature. Explain that approach.

Karen: Rick and I believe that children learn best through role modeling and by hearing stories. That's why we have read thousands of stories to our kids. Good things happen when a child is sitting on your lap. It lends itself to emotional and physical bonding. He or she identifies with the characters in the stories too, and that allows you to explain the moral lesson being taught.

JCD: Most parents don't have time to read to their children, do they? But I remember fondly the stories my mother read to me when I was a kid. They have stayed with me throughout my adult life.

Karen: Oh, they are remembered. We all need to slow down a bit, turn off the TV and radio, except for your program [laughter], and read to our children.

JCD: Shirley used to take our son, Ryan, to the library, where they would check out an entire stack of books, maybe eight or ten of them. Ryan would have them all read by the next day. Shirley wanted him to get out and play too, so she had to ration the number of books he would bring home. That is a pleasant problem to have.

Karen: Children love good stories such as *Anne of Green Gables*. I've included it and the entire Tolkien series in my book, as well as C. S. Lewis's Narnia series. Now we're reading Brian Jacques's *Redwall*. One of our favorite things is to light a fire and then pray and read together.

Sen. Santorum: Karen becomes the storyteller during those family times, interpreting the readings for our children.

JCD: Explain how you teach good manners through stories.

Karen: We do it through such books as *Aesop's Fables* and similar literature.

JCD: Why don't you give us a taste of something you have read to your kids.

Karen: Okay. Here's a sweet poem called "Mr. Nobody," by an unknown author. Children, of course, never want to admit doing anything wrong, so they say, "I didn't do it." Here's a poem about that situation:

Mr. Nobody

I know a funny little man,
As quiet as a mouse,
Who does the mischief that is done
In everybody's house!
There's no one ever sees his face,
And yet we all agree
That every plate we break was cracked
By Mr. Nobody.
'Tis he who always tears our books,
Who leaves the door ajar,
He pulls the buttons from our shirts,
And scatters pins afar;
That squeaking door will always squeak
For, prithee, don't you see,
We leave the oiling to be done
By Mr. Nobody.

He puts damp wood upon the fire,
That kettles cannot boil;
His are the feet that bring in mud,
And all the carpets soil.
The papers always are mislaid,
Who had them last but he?
There's no one tosses them about
But Mr. Nobody.
The finger marks upon the door
By none of us are made;
We never leave the blinds unclosed,
To let the curtains fade.
The ink we never spill, the boots
That lying 'round you see
Are not our boots; they all belong
To Mr. Nobody.

JCD: And the kids obviously loved it, I'm sure. I notice that you have written a little commentary after each story or poem.

Karen: I have. Would you like me to share an example?

JCD: Please do.

Karen [reading]: Just as your parents do so much for you every day, you can respond by doing loving things for your parents. One of the best ways to express your love for them is through your actions. Even the smallest thoughtful act, like picking flowers for your mother, will demonstrate your love. Remember that Ralph Waldo Emerson said, "Good manners are made up of small sacrifices."

JCD: Karen, didn't you say that before you wrote *Everyday Graces*, you had been looking in bookstores and libraries for good stories and literature, but there were few options? That's why you decided to write your own book.

Karen: That's right. I began writing for my own children. I thought it would be so much fun to have a publication in the tradition of Bill Bennett's *The Book of Virtues*. Instead of giving the kids a list of rules and dos and don'ts, I wanted to teach them through stories. It is so very important for parents to introduce values to their children, and I know of no better way of doing it.

Sen. Santorum: America today is a me-centered culture. It is about doing whatever a person wants to do, regardless of

45

how it affects other people. Manners convey just the opposite. They show respect for others, especially looking out for their interests, whether it's opening the door or waiting in line or just saying a kind word. These social graces reflect an entirely different worldview. But unless parents are consciously working to instill those values and behaviors in their children, the culture will stamp its own perspectives on them. What Karen has done here is to give parents a tool to help them use storytelling to accomplish that purpose.

JCD: Thank you, Karen, for writing this book, *Everyday Graces*. And thank you, Senator, for being my guest. I appreciate the way you both are modeling good family life and parenting techniques for all of us, and for the way you have chosen to live your lives.[13]

The Santorums make a convincing case for teaching manners and morals to children, and I concur with them wholeheartedly. At the same time, I can hear some of my readers objecting vigorously to the goal of teaching girls to become young ladies since that is hardly the direction the popular culture has taken us in recent decades.

Some would question whether it is even desirable for a girl to be feminine in a traditional sense, fearing that it will signal a return to the oppression of a patriarchal era when women had to hide their intelligence and conceal their accomplishments. Hear me out, moms. Not for a moment would I try to take away the hard-won achievements of respect and emancipation enjoyed by today's women. Those cultural advances are here to stay, and may they long endure.

On the contrary, I would point out that femaleness and weakness are not synonymous. Femininity and strength of character are often very close neighbors. I come from a family of strong women who knew who they were and where God was leading them. They took a backseat to no one. My grandmother copastored a thriving church with my grandfather. She could preach up a storm. I can't imagine anyone telling her to sit down, fold her arms, and keep her mouth shut. One of her daughters became my mother, who was also a very confident and accomplished lady. Yet my mother and her sisters were undeniably feminine.

My mom and dad loved each other deeply and had a very healthy relationship based on their identities as a woman and a man. He was very respectful, protective, and supportive of her. I never saw him treat her rudely or harshly. After I was grown, I remember getting upset at my mom for something she said that irritated me. I made the mistake of telling my dad about it. I'll never forget him turning his steely blue eyes on me and saying angrily, "Listen, Bud, your mother is the best friend you have, and I won't stand for you saying anything disrespectful about her." It was the end of our conversation. When Dad called me Bud, I knew it was time to back off.

On the other side of the ledger, my mom honored my dad, not just as her husband, but also as a man. She would not have thought of failing to have a meal waiting for him when he came home. Being from the South, she was not offended when he called from his big chair where he was reading a book. He would say, "Hey, Myrt, bring me a cup of coffee, please." He was her man, and she took care of him. It was a relationship based on mutual respect, and it was highly successful. They both understood manners and morals, and their relationship to spirituality, masculinity, and femininity. My parents modeled them consistently throughout my childhood.

I displayed that training on my first date with a cute coed named Shirley. I took her to a classy restaurant in Hollywood, California, where I told the host where we wanted to sit. Then I helped Shirley with her chair. I asked what she wanted to eat and conveyed her order to the waiter. We engaged each other in conversation for more than an hour, mostly about Shirley. Then I paid the check and took her to my car. I walked on the outside of the sidewalk nearest the street, which was (and still should be) symbolic of a guy's responsibility to protect the woman in his care. I opened the car door for her, and we drove back to our college. I parked, came around to her side of the car, opened the door, and walked Shirley to the front door of her dorm. She thanked me with a smile, and we said good night. I didn't try to kiss her, since that would have put her in a compromising position on a first date—as though she owed me something as a "payback."

I must have done something right on that enchanted evening, because we have now been married for forty-nine years. I think it's going to work. I still try to show her the same courtesies and respect that helped me win her heart in the first place. And she knows all the ways to please me.

By the way, two weeks ago, my wife and I were back in Southern California, and our daughter asked me to take her and her mom to that restaurant where it all began. I was delighted to do that. I pointed out the very table where we sat fifty-two years ago and talked about what we said and did on that significant night where love began.

So much has changed in the culture since then. I will tell you that I am disgusted by the way young men treat their girlfriends today. Some guys will honk from the street, waiting for a girl to come out. They stay behind the steering wheel while she opens her own door, and then they take her to a McDonald's or a Taco Bell. Often, the guy will even expect his date to pay for her food! Do you know why this happens? Because girls tolerate it. I would advise a young lady who is expected to pay for her meal to do so only once. She should then ask to be taken straight home and never agree to see the dude again. Any man who is that disrespectful doesn't deserve a second chance.

Women hold the keys to masculine behavior. Guys are inclined to take what they can get and be no more accommodating than they have to be. To some degree, the lack of culture and refinement we see in many of today's men is the fault of women who ask for, and get, little or nothing. If a girl sees herself as a lady, she will expect her escort to behave like a gentleman. He will respect her if she respects herself. If she wants him to be spiritually sensitive, she should go out with him only if he accompanies her to church. If she objects to his use of profanity, she should simply not accept it. If she wants him to think of her often and call her on the phone, she should wait for him to get the idea himself. Female aggressiveness is a turnoff to most men. I don't care if the rules have changed; it is still a bad idea for a girl to pursue a guy breathlessly. She should let him be the initiator. That is the way he is made.

Parents, teach these concepts to your girls! If your daughter wants her boyfriend to take her to nice places, she should expect him to make the plans for an evening together and to ask her out at least a week ahead of time. If he shows up unannounced on Friday night and says, "Wanna hang out?" she should tell him she has other things to do. If she wants him to be a gentleman, she should require him to act like one, and she should always remember that she is a lady.

If a woman wants a man to marry her, she *must not* make herself available sexually. That wrecks a relationship. Besides, it is morally wrong. Under no circumstances should she live with a guy before marriage. She will probably wind up getting hurt and living to regret it. He will get what he wants, and she will get nothing. The number one reason men give for marrying late or not at all is because they can get everything they want—including love and sex—without commitment.[14] A moral, self-respecting woman simply will not play that game.

If it becomes obvious that a guy is not going to commit, she should send him packing. Period! Don't argue with a jerk about it. Just cut him loose. Don't blame a guy if he is unmannerly and exploitative. Show him what you expect, and if he balks, move on—quickly. If he is a big drinker or uses illegal drugs, run from him. He is trouble on the hoof. Don't give him a beachhead in your heart. There is someone better out there for you if you set your standards high.

It comes down to this: the relationship between a man and a woman throughout their lives together, if indeed they do marry, will reflect the ground rules set by the woman when they are courting. She can change him then, but probably not after. She should not settle for anything less than what she needs emotionally. High on her list of priorities should be a mutual understanding about manners and morals. It is the way men and women have related to each other for thousands of years, and it still provides the basis for healthy families that are equipped to go the distance.

However, teaching girls to be ladies is not enough. We must also give them a strong biblical foundation from which morals and virtues can evolve. Our hope is that our daughters will someday pass along those verities to the next generation. No other priority comes close to this one in significance.

For now, it seems appropriate to return to the words of President John Adams, who gave this solemn charge to the nation's women. You'll recall that he said:

> The foundations of national Morality must be laid in private Families. In vain are Schools, Academies and universities instituted if loose Principles and licentious habits are impressed upon Children in their earliest years. The Mothers are the earliest and most important Instructors of youth.[15]

It was true in 1778, and it is still true today.

❀ ❀ ❀

I gave a speech to students at the Focus on the Family Leadership Institute a few years ago. Then I interacted with them informally about some of the ideas I had just shared. All the while, recorders were rolling. This is an edited transcript of the comments made.

JCD: Let me ask the girls how they feel about guys who expect them to pay for their meals when they are out together.
[A girl's faint voice]: El Cheapo.
JCD: Did I hear someone say, "El Cheapo"?
Girl #1: Yes, it's terrible.
JCD: Explain what you mean.
Girl #1: Well, guys often expect girls to pay their portion. It's kind of like, "I have money and you have money, so we will split the check."

JCD: Do you object when they do that?

Girl #1: I would if I knew better how to handle it. I just go along with them, but I probably wouldn't go out with them again.

JCD: Yeah. How would some of you feel if a guy just showed up at the door without calling?

Girl #2: That would never have happened when I was living at home. My mom told me if a guy sits in the driveway and honks, she would not let me take a step out the door.

JCD: Let's hear it for her mother. [Applause]

Girl #3: My mom would say the same thing. I was taught when I was growing up that boys should call by Monday, or at least Tuesday, if they want to take me out on Friday. It is a precious thing to be taken care of and be appreciated and valued for who you are

JCD: Let me ask you a question. Do you call guys?

Girl #4: No. I might call a friend, but I would never try to start or kindle something on the phone. Never.

JCD: Let me ask the guys who are here. How would you feel about a girl calling you and asking for a date?

Guy #1: Oh, I wouldn't like it very much. If a girl called me and was interested in asking me out, I think it would rob me of my desire to be the one who initiates a relationship.

JCD: Does that happen?

Guy #1: You mean a girl calling and asking me out? Oh yeah! It has happened before. But I'd like also to comment on what someone just said. I don't think all hope is lost. Let me tell you how it is in my family, which is incredible. My brothers and my dad will sometimes just sit around and grunt. You know, uhh, 'cuz that's just being a man.

JCD: Well that's certainly impressive. [Laughter]

Guy #1: But at the same time, my dad is a spiritual leader, and many times I would walk in on my parents and find them on their knees praying by their bed for their kids. And my father wasn't afraid to let us see him cry. He was not only interested in me developing as a male, but he also disciplined me and led me to follow Jesus Christ. I mean, my dad is the most incredible man I've ever met.

JCD: I'd like to meet your dad.

Guy #1: Yeah. You really need to. It has been encouraging for me to watch this man. Not all hope is lost.

JCD: I'm so glad you shared that with us. You're a very fortunate young man. Let me ask you this: were you taught to open doors for a woman?

Guy #1: Yeah! I was taught to walk on the side next to the curb and to pull out chairs for a girl and offer her my arm when we're walking up stairs.

JCD: You know what? There are a lot of women who'd like to know you. [Laughter]

Guy #1: I would get in serious trouble when I was young if I didn't do those things.

JCD: Let me ask the girls if guys open doors and show respect for you.

Girl #3: Yes. We were at a friend's apartment recently, and I was walking back to mine. A guy was walking with me, and we passed his place. I expected him to turn in, but he said, "I live here, but I'm walking you back to your apartment." That really meant a lot to me. We had only known each other for two weeks, and these men in the Institute—I don't even want to call them guys because they are men—have taken an interest in us—not in a guy-girl relationship or anything like that, but as a brother and sister in Christ. They are very protective of us. I have three little brothers, and I am so thankful that my parents are raising them the same way. They already open doors for girls. My question for you is, do you think parents today are teaching their daughters to expect this kind of respect from guys?

JCD: Many of them don't, and that is a problem. This is what I'm trying to address here. The traditional relationship between men and women is wonderful. When it is right, it works for everyone. I think it is unfortunate that many men have no clue about how that's supposed to work. Let me ask the guys: in a formal situation, would you help your date with her chair?

Guy #1: Yeah. I think that would be a good way of showing respect and consideration for a date. I don't know, I probably forget a lot of the time 'cuz maybe we're sitting in a booth or something. . . .

JCD: Well, don't you ever forget it again. [Laughter]

Guy #1: I promise, girls.[16]

Embarrassing the Angels

THE TASK OF teaching your girls to be ladies will be no easy assignment, because our crude and hypersexualized culture will give you no help. Indeed, it will oppose your efforts at every turn. No one seems to understand that assault on femininity better than author, lecturer, and columnist for the *Wall Street Journal* Peggy Noonan. A former speechwriter for President Ronald Reagan, she is one of the most astute culture watchers of our time.

Peggy (I will call her by her first name because she makes readers feel as though they know her personally) wrote a powerful op-ed piece a few years ago on what it means to be a lady. It made me want to stand up and cheer. As you read Peggy's remarks, I invite you to think of your own girls and what you as a parent are up against in the effort to preserve their feminine dignity. More to the point, I hope this article will increase your determination to teach your daughters not only how to be ladies but also why they should think of themselves that way.

These are Peggy Noonan's observations:

Embarrassing the Angels
Or, That's No Way to Treat a Lady

America has become creepy for women who think of themselves as ladies. It has in fact become assaultive.

I start with a dictionary definition, from American Heritage, not that anyone needs it because everyone knows what a lady is. It's a kind of natural knowledge. According to American Heritage, a lady is a well-mannered and considerate woman with high standards of proper behavior. You know one, the dictionary suggests, by how she's treated: "a woman, especially when spoken of or to in a polite way." Under usage, American Heritage says, "*lady* is normally used as a parallel to *gentleman* to emphasize norms expected in polite society or situations."

I would add that a lady need not be stuffy, scolding, stiff. A lady brings regard for others into the room with her; that regard is part of the dignity she carries and seeks to spread. A lady is a woman who projects the stature of life.

These definitions are incomplete but serviceable—I invite better ones—but keep them in mind as I try to draw a fuller picture of what it was like to be taken aside at an airport last week for what is currently known as further screening and was generally understood 50 years ago to be second-degree sexual assault.

I was directed, shoeless, into the little pen with the black plastic swinging door. A stranger approached, a tall woman with burnt-orange hair. She looked in her 40s. She was muscular, her biceps straining against a tight Transportation Security Administration T-shirt. She carried her wand like a billy club. She began her instructions: *Face your baggage. Feet in the footmarks. Arms out. Fully out. Legs apart. Apart. I'm patting you down.*

It was like a 1950s women's prison movie. I got to be the girl from the streets who made a big mistake; she was the guard doing intake. "Name's Veronica, but they call me Ron. Want a smoke?" [She] beeps and bops, her pointer and middle fingers patting for explosives under the back of my brassiere; the wand on and over my body, more beeps, more pats. Then she walked wordlessly away. I looked around, slowly put down my arms, rearranged my body. For a moment I thought I might plaintively call out, "No kiss goodbye?" . . . But they might not have been amused. And actually I wasn't either.

I experienced the search not only as an invasion of privacy, which it was, but as a denial or lowering of that delicate thing, dignity. The dignity of a woman, of a lady, of a person with a right not to be manhandled or to be, or to feel, molested.

Is this quaint, this claiming of such a right? Is it impossibly old-fashioned? I think it's just basic. There aren't many middle-aged women who fly who haven't experienced something very much like what I've described. I've noticed recently that people who fly have taken to looking away when they pass someone being patted down. They do this now at LaGuardia, in line for the shuttle to Washington, where they used to stare. Now they turn away in embarrassment.

They're right to be embarrassed. It is to their credit that they are.

An aside with a point: I almost always talk to the screeners and usually wind up joking with them. They often tell me wonderful things. The most moving was the security woman at LaGuardia who answered my question, "What have you learned about people since taking this job that you didn't know before?" She did an impromptu soliloquy on how Everyone Travels With the Same Things. She meant socks, toothbrush, deodorant, but as she spoke, as she elaborated, we both came to [understand] that she was saying something larger about . . . what's inside us, and what it is to be human, and on a journey. One screener, this past Monday, again at LaGuardia, told me that no, she had never ever found a terrorist or a terror related item in her searches. Two have told me women take the searches worse than men, and become angrier.

But then they would, for they are not only discomforted and delayed, as the men. There is also the edge of violation.

Are the women who do the searches wicked, cruel? No, they're trying to make a living and go with the flow of modernity. They're doing what they've been taught. They've been led to approach things in a certain way, first by our society and then by their bosses. They're doing what they've been trained to do by modern government security experts who don't have to bother themselves with thoughts like, *Is this sort of a bad thing to do to a person who is a lady?* By, that is, slobs with clipboards who have also been raised in the current culture.

I spoke this week at a Catholic college. I have been speaking a lot, for me anyway, which means I have been without that primary protector of American optimism and good cheer, which is staying home. Americans take refuge in their homes. It's how they protect themselves from their culture. It helps us maintain our optimism.

At the Catholic college, a great one, we were to speak of faith and politics. This, to me, is a very big and complicated subject, and a worthy one. But quickly—I mean within 15 seconds—the talk was only of matters related to sexuality. Soon a person on the panel was yelling, "Raise your hands if you think masturbation is a sin!" and the moderator was asking if African men should use condoms, yes or no. At one point I put my head in my hands. I thought, *Have we gone crazy? There are thousands of people in the audience, from children to aged nuns, and this is how we talk, this is the imagery we use, this is our only subject matter?*

But of course it is. It is our society's subject matter.

I was the only woman on the panel, which is no doubt part of why I experienced it as so odd, but in truth the symposium wasn't odd, not in terms of being out of line with the culture. It was odd only because it was utterly in line with it.

Was the symposium the worst thing that happened to me this year? Oh no. It wasn't even the worst thing that has happened to me this week. But I did experience it as to some degree violative of my dignity as a person. An adult. A woman. A lady.

And I have been experiencing a lot of things in this way for a while now.

Have you?

I experience it when I see blaring television ads for birth-control devices, feminine-hygiene products, erectile-dysfunction medicines. I experience it when I'm almost strip-searched at airports. I experience it when I listen to popular music, if that's what we call it. I experience it when political figures are asked the most intimate questions about their families and pressed for personal views on sexual questions that someone somewhere decided have to be Topic A on the national agenda in America right now.

Let me tell you what I say, in my mind, after things like this—the symposium, the commercials, and so forth. I think, *We are embarrassing the angels.*

Imagine for a moment that angels exist, that they are pure spirits of virtue and light, that they care about us and for us and are among us, unseen, in the airport security line, in the room where we watch TV, at the symposium of great minds. "Raise your hands if you think masturbation should be illegal!" "I'm Bob Dole for Viagra." "Put your feet in the foot marks, lady." *We are embarrassing the angels.*

Do I think this way, in these terms, because I am exceptionally virtuous? Oh no. I'm below average in virtue, and even I know it's all gotten low and rough and disturbed.

Lent began yesterday, and I mean to give up a great deal, as you would too if you were me. One of the things I mean to give up is the habit of thinking it and not saying it. A lady has some rights, and this happens to be one I can assert.

"You are embarrassing the angels." This is what I intend to say for the next 40 days whenever I see someone who is hurting the culture, hurting human dignity, denying the stature of a human being. I mean to say it with belief, with an eye to instruction, but also pointedly, uncompromisingly. As a lady would. All invited to join in.[1]

❀ ❀ ❀

Peggy Noonan has graphically illustrated just how commonly our culture assaults the dignity of women and invades the privacy of us all. Unfortunately, those insults are becoming ever more crude and rude every day. Just last week, I saw a disgusting commercial on television featuring three young women who were talking together in a store about the remarkable health of their colons. As though we want to know!

Since Peggy published her commentary several years ago, airport screening procedures have become even more egregious. As you know, it is now possible for images of nude male and female passengers to be created electronically and transmitted to who-knows-who in nearby booths. There we could all be, standing like fools with hands above our heads and as naked as the day we were born. It is small consolation, I suppose, that our private parts and our faces would be fuzzed out. Somebody in one of those little booths may know how to access the naked truth. Can't you imagine this guy and several of his buddies gawking (or laughing hysterically) at the screen?

Everyone recognizes the importance of surveillance and security in this day of terror and mayhem, but surely there are more modest ways to keep us safe in the air. How long will it be before blurred images of a Miss America or a gorgeous movie star appear unwittingly on the Internet? Not only should this prospect be upsetting to the beautiful people of the world, but it ought to irritate those of us who are not so young and sexy. What is more personal and private than our own bodies?

Peggy Noonan was right when she wrote, "America has become creepy for women who think of themselves as ladies. It has in fact become assaultive." It is true. We are embarrassing the angels.

Well, what does this crudity and loss of dignity in the culture mean for girls? It should be clear that parents need to work diligently to teach, shape, and form the character of their daughters. They will certainly not get that training from the wider culture. If MTV, Hollywood, the pop music industry, and peers have their way with your girls, they are likely to curse, dress provocatively, behave like uncultured and uncouth waifs, and have no sense of personal dignity. Remember, Mom, you are the keeper of the keys at home. I hope you will make John Adams proud of you. Teach your girls to be ladies!

GIRLS AND THEIR MOTHERS

EVER SINCE THE WORD got out that I was writing this book about girls, readers have been sending stories and suggestions for my consideration. One of them came from a woman named Marlene who is raising Hannah, a very strong-willed seven-year-old girl.

Recently the two of them were having a bad day. Finally Hannah put her hands on her hips in exasperation and said, "You know, Mom, this just isn't working out. I want a new mother."

Marlene is a very bright woman who knew exactly how to handle the situation. Without flinching, she said, "Well, I think we can arrange that. I know someone who would love to have another child."

She went to the telephone and pretended to call a neighbor. After faking a greeting, she said, "Hannah has decided she doesn't want to live here anymore, and I was wondering if you would like to have her come be your little girl."

Hannah's bluff had backfired. She immediately ran to her mother and said, "No, no, no, Mom! Let's give it another shot." You probably don't need me to tell you that clashes like this one between moms and daughters are standard fare, even when the kids are young. I hear about them often. If you have multiple children, at least one of them is likely to be strong willed. The ratio of testy kids to those who are compliant is about one to one. Raising a tough-as-nails child is no easy task, and at times you need the wisdom of Solomon to keep her on track. And yes, it is more difficult now than in the past because of cultural intrusions.

Despite these stressful times for mothers and daughters, staying in touch with each child emotionally should be a matter of the highest priority. You have to hang in there until the upheaval passes. Your children's successes or failures in many of life's endeavors will depend on the quality of the relationships you share during their childhood years. Indeed, how they navigate the storms of adolescence will be influenced directly by the security of that bond. Let's talk about how it can be enhanced.

Specialists in child development refer to the vital connection between generations as attachment, and the explanation for how it works is called attachment theory. This concept holds the keys to unlocking many of the mysteries of parenting. It was originally formulated in the 1950s by Dr. John Bowlby, an English psychiatrist, and Dr. Mary Ainsworth, an American psychologist.[1] They were responsible for the most exhaustive research into the mother-child relationship ever conducted.

To understand their work, let's pick up where we left off in chapter 4 with findings from brain studies. Imaging technology, which we discussed earlier, has not only revealed brain structure and the hormones responsible for hard wiring, it has also helped us make the connection between environmental experiences and how they influence a child neurologically. I'll try not to get too technical this time, but it is very important for parents to know that the first three years of life are vital to everything that will come later. It is a period of remarkable change in all areas of a child's development. Let me explain: A newborn's brain is about 25 percent of its future adult weight. By the time a child is three years old, her brain will have produced billions of cells and hundreds of trillions of connections, or synapses, between nerve cells. Clearly, something dramatic is taking place neurologically, beginning long before birth. Good nutrition is critically important to brain development between mid-gestation and two years of age.[2]

This breathtaking increase in brain structure and mental capacity helps to explain why *every* experience in childhood is significant. A toddler takes in and tries to make sense of her bewildering world. I have always been fascinated by how this "mantle of humanness" descends on a baby. A newborn who was hanging by her heels in a delivery room just a short time ago will quickly gain fifteen or twenty pounds and develop a sparkle in her eyes, a sense of humor, a unique personality, a curiosity about everything she sees and can get her hands on, and an independent streak that will surprise even her two-hundred-pound father. There is nothing like it in all of nature.

To get a better understanding of attachment theory, it is important to know that there are "critical periods" during a child's early years when certain opportunities for learning must be grabbed or forever lost. For example, babies require normal visual input, or else permanent impairment of the eyes can occur.[3] The rudiments of language skills also occur in a critical period, which is why it is so beneficial to talk, talk, talk to your baby. And when you are not talking, you should be listening. Hearing her imitate your vocal sounds and her coos and laughter makes caring for an infant so rewarding. One of my grandson's first spoken phrases was, "That's cool."

Once again, if these various windows are missed, some of the learning that should have occurred can be lost or distorted for a lifetime. It is one of the reasons children raised amid deprivation and abject poverty are often intellectually and emotionally impaired. Here is the nub of it: in a sense, all of a girl's childhood should be thought of as a "critical period" in the relationship with her mother. If a proper linkage fails to develop between them, the daughter will be affected negatively, some girls more than others, by what was missed.

This brings us back to Bowlby and Ainsworth, who were the first to recognize that infants are highly vulnerable and easily wounded by anxiety, fear, and confusion.[4] Elaborating on a previous point, children who are subjected to prolonged periods of emotional trauma experience surges of stress hormones, principally cortisol, that flood through their immature brains, causing irreversible neurological damage.[5] In extreme cases involving abuse or neglect, an individual may eventually lose his or her ability to "feel" for others, which has implications for violence in days to come.[6] There are tragic cases on record of toddlers who have stood alone in cribs for hours, hungry, sick, and scared. Some of them have even grown up to be cold-blooded killers who murder strangers just for the thrill of watching them die.

It has been demonstrated further that the failure of mothers and babies to attach is linked directly to physical and mental illness of all types. The reason is apparent. If a child is regularly overwhelmed by negative feelings and stressful circumstances, her inability to cope in infancy becomes a life-long pattern. The link between maternal attachment and poor health is not merely theoretical. It is a reality.[7]

By contrast, something wonderful happens when a nurturing mother intercedes lovingly on behalf of her distressed baby. Typically, she talks softly to her frightened infant, cuddles her, changes uncomfortable diapers, sways with her gently, and sings quietly while providing a warm and nurturing breast. The child in her arms is calmed both emotionally and physically, and her fears subside. From that deeply satisfying experience for mother and baby, a bond begins to form between them. It will establish a foundation for all that lies ahead. The relationship the mother and child forge will never be completely abandoned or forgotten, even though it may be severely strained at times. This is why wounded and dying men, hardened by combat on a battlefield, will often utter one last word through their tears: "Mother!"

Infants are like sponges soaking up the affection showered on them. They clearly prefer human stimuli above anything else. As we indicated in chapter 4, girl babies more than boys are attuned to faces, touch, voices, and even smell. They are more sensitive to speech and singing than any other sound. Is this the origin of the lullaby? It must be. A newborn has been listening to her mother's voice from inside the womb for many months, and she is comforted by it.

Brain development is greatly influenced and aided by the care and attention given in a nursery by mothers, grandmothers, or mother substitutes. As the months pass, this attachment provides a secure base that encourages the exploration of the surrounding environment. It also defines a child's style of relating to others, teaches her to trust, helps her interpret her feelings, and acquaints her with intimacy. We cannot overstate the importance of this maternal bonding to the health and well-being of a child of either sex.[8]

To put it succinctly, Mom, you are indispensable. The start your baby gets in life is in your hands—and in your voice and in your heart. What a wonderful privilege and responsibility it is to welcome her with open arms. That little bundle arrives straight from the hand of the Creator as His precious gift. King David wrote about his own formation in one of his most beautiful psalms:

> For you created my inmost being;
> you knit me together in my mother's womb.
> I praise you because I am fearfully and wonderfully
>   made;
> your works are wonderful,
> I know that full well.
>
> My frame was not hidden from you
> when I was made in the secret place.
> When I was woven together in the depths of the
>   earth,
> your eyes saw my unformed body.
> All the days ordained for me
> were written in your book
> before one of them came to be.

How precious to me are your thoughts, O God!
How vast is the sum of them!

Were I to count them,
they would outnumber the grains of sand.
When I awake,
I am still with you.[9]

As indicated, attachment begins prenatally and continues to be vital for years to come. In fact, a two-year-old is still as "clingy" to her mother as she was a year earlier. The encouragement and confidence Mom provides is the primary factor in nudging her toddler out to the edges of her universe. At about five years of age, a child will gradually become more independent and confident, especially if the bond with the mother or mother figure has been firmly established.

Lauren Porter, a psychotherapist and clinical social worker, puts it this way:

> As children continue to age and develop, their needs evolve but their reliance on the attachment system endures. Even adolescence, often viewed as the pinnacle of developmental challenges, has its focus in attachment. Adolescents struggle with the tension between their connection to family and their formation of independence. The foundation built in the early years is the groundwork for this phase of life; if the attachment is secure and established, child and parents can negotiate the events of adolescence with little struggle.[10]

But what about fathers? How do they fit into this attachment phenomenon? As we'll see in the next chapter, when a child is an infant, Mom provides the cornerstone of healthy child development, but Dad is hardly irrelevant. His role is primarily to be supportive of the mother. He should also begin to connect with the baby in the months to follow. His masculine voice, size, demeanor, and gentle discipline provide the security produced by defined limits. In a permissive world where many parents have forgotten or never knew the importance of appropriate authority, it is the responsibility of a father to help guide behavior and teach self-control.

When my grandson, Lincoln, was nineteen months of age, his mother and I were sitting at a table and he was in his high chair. He started to throw a glass on the floor when his mom, who has bonded beautifully with her baby, quietly said, "No." Her manner conveyed, *This is a suggestion.* I could see that the toddler was going to ignore her, so I said with a little more force, "Lincoln! No!" I wasn't gruff with him, but the tone of my voice said, "This is an order." It was the first time I had ever spoken to him in that tone. He instantly turned his head toward me and studied my face. We sat looking at each other for about five seconds without moving, and then we both smiled. He had examined my expression to see if I was angry and realized I was not. But he also recognized that I expected obedience. His smile said, "I get it," and he put the glass down. My smile said, "You're a good boy." This brief two-word interchange and the reading of faces between my grandson and me illustrate how a man typically handles matters of discipline more easily than a gentle mother does.

Here is another example of a father's role as related to gender. Boys are not born with an understanding of what it means to be male. It is a dad's responsibility to introduce that concept over time. Beginning at about eighteen months of age and continuing over the next four years, sexual identity is being formed. During that time, boys need exposure to a loving father or father figure who will serve as a role model for masculinity. They still need their mom's affirmation, to be sure, but not in an overbearing way that prevents them from becoming the males they were made to become. Said another way, the mother is no less significant to her son during that period of identity formation, but something new is being added to the mix. A boy will usually observe as time passes that "Dad is different, and I should be like him." Hopefully, the mother will not be threatened by that realignment and, in fact, should encourage it.

Unfortunately, we live in a culture where family breakup is a common tragedy. Boys, especially those born in the inner city or in poverty-stricken areas, often have little or no exposure to healthy male role models. Too many of them grow up on the streets with older gang members as their only male examples. It is a recipe for violence, drug use, and illicit sex. For more information on boys and their needs, refer to my earlier book *Bringing Up Boys*.

For girls, dads play an entirely different role. Most parents are aware that boys need their fathers and girls are dependent on their mothers. It is equally important to know, however, that the cross-sexual relationship is also of inestimable significance. Girls need their fathers as much as boys do, but for different reasons. We'll address that point and the vital father-daughter connection shortly.

The establishment of attachment between generations is made much more difficult for boys *and* for girls because of dramatic changes in the culture in recent years. Before the Industrial Revolution, fathers and mothers worked side by side on farms or in family-owned businesses. They raised their children together, and except for men in the military or those who sailed the seas, most dads lived and worked close to home. For example, we read in Mark 6:3 that Jesus was a carpenter, a trade obviously learned from his earthly father as a child (see Matthew 13:55). We assume his mother, Mary, was a full-time homemaker living nearby. That family structure is now rarely seen. Only in the last one hundred years have fathers left home all day to make a living. Now, approximately 51 percent of mothers are also employed full-time in the workforce.[11]

This is where establishing attachment encounters a challenge. There are enormous pressures on millions of new mothers to "get back to work" as soon as possible after giving birth. The U.S. Census Bureau indicated several years ago that only 42 percent of new mothers take more than three months at home with their babies.[12] Many return to work within a month or six weeks. Given what we have seen about the importance of early bonding, that can be a big problem. If at all possible, I would recommend that moms take at least a year after birth to heal, bond, and establish a family routine. I recognize that full-time homemaking is not possible for many mothers because of financial pressures and other concerns. Single mothers usually have no choice. It is unfortunate that so many women face that dilemma. Most new mothers know intuitively that the time spent with their babies is precious and fleeting, and they often feel a unique agony when the time comes to hand their babies or preschoolers over to a caregiver and head back to a job outside the home.

Psychologist Daphne de Marneffe, Ph.D., advocates for at-home mothers in her book entitled *Maternal Desire: On Children, Love, and the Inner Life*. After giving birth to her third child, she acknowledged an ache inside to be with her children. She writes, "I felt an invisible tether drawing me home."[13] After talking to many other conflicted mothers in the workplace, she concludes, "Maternal desire is not, for any woman, all there is. But for many of us, it is an important part of who we are."[14] Dr. de Marneffe gave up her practice and became a full-time homemaker.

Freelance writer Ellyn Spragins sought to explain why mothers in the workforce become easily offended when even casual references are made to their employment. She writes:

> What makes a working woman act this way? Having her heart broken each morning by a tearful 2-year-old who has to be restrained from running down the sidewalk after her when she leaves for work? Forcing herself to linger on a phone call about decorations for the fifth-grade Thanksgiving feast when

her client is checking his watch in the reception area? And, of course, needing her paycheck to pay the bills?[15]

Then Spragins turns the coin over and describes the sensitivity of full-time homemakers. She says:

The have-to-work argument isn't believable to many at-home moms, either. Having sacrificed an income and tightened the budget, they see a neighbor's second income as an indulgence, like the new Lincoln Navigator in the driveway.[16]

Spragins continues:

I've straddled these two worlds for most of the last 13 years because I work at home so I can be near my daughter, Keenan, 13, and son, Tucker, 11. Sometimes it makes me feel like a thin-skinned spy. I wince when I hear stay-at-home acquaintances slam an employed mother and become indignant when working friends wonder what stay-at-home moms do all day.[17]

It is a source of powerful internal conflict either way. The system seems rigged against both lifestyles, with mothers at home feeling disrespected for not having a career, and those in the workplace feeling guilty for not being with their children full-time. Combatants in the mommy wars are still in full battle gear.

The trend, it would appear, is moving toward more women staying home. According to a Pew Research Center survey of two thousand women conducted in 2007, only one in five (21 percent) of employed mothers with children under seventeen said full-time work is the ideal situation for them. That is down from 32 percent in 1997. Sixty percent of these moms said part-time work would be their ideal, compared to 48 percent in 1997. One in five (19 percent) said they would rather not be employed outside the home at all. Stated another way, 79 percent of working mothers of minor children would rather not be employed *full-time*.[18]

On the other side of the ledger, only 16 percent of stay-at-home mothers with minor children said their ideal situation would be full-time employment, down from 24 percent in 1997.[19] Forty-eight percent of these stay-at-home moms said not working outside the home would be the ideal situation.[20]

Have I overwhelmed you with these statistics? I must share one more that is significant. In 2007, only 16 percent of mothers with children under five thought it would be ideal to work full-time, down from 31 percent in 1997.[21]

In summary, the majority of stay-at-home mothers are content with their decision not to enter or reenter the workforce, and those who are employed full-time say they would prefer to work less or not at all. These preferences are not widely reported in the mainstream media, but they reveal something significant about mothers. Most of them work outside the home because they feel they must, and the younger their children are, the more they yearn to stay home. What a shame it is that women who desperately want to stay at home with their babies do not have the opportunity to do so. Given the economic downturn since 2008, even more women may be forced by financial need to return to the workforce.

Dare I express my opinion on this volatile subject? It is this: the frantic pace at which "two-career" families run is simply not conducive to what is needed at home when kids are small. I'm sure this statement will be irritating to some of you who are still fighting the mommy wars, but it reflects my firm conviction. Whether or not a woman chooses to be employed full-time when not economically necessary is a complex decision to be made only by her and her husband. No one else should try to make it for her or imply that there is only one way to run a family. I am certainly not trying to do that. All I can say is that parenting is an exhausting experience. Some mothers have the energy and stamina to handle domestic duties and child rearing while also carrying the demands of employment. Others clearly do not. Life for them is one long challenge. The issue at hand, however, is not a matter of the mother's well-being. It is what is best for her children in a critical period of life.

It comes down to this: kids thrive in an environment of order, vigilance, and close supervision, which is very difficult to provide by those who come home every night exhausted, distracted, and frazzled. The question that every family raising small children must answer is one of priorities: where is the best place for a mom to invest her time? All things being equal, I recommend that mothers *who do have an option* consider the welfare of their children first, especially when they are young. Attachment won't wait.

Before closing this discussion about getting your kids off to the most advantageous start in life, I want to make sure I have not been misunderstood regarding the creation of good relationships with children. One could draw the conclusion that because attachment is so important, mothers and fathers have to walk on eggshells to avoid upsetting and driving away independent and self-willed youngsters. That could lead to many problems. You, Mom and Dad, are still in charge, and you must not fear that responsibility.

Loving authority, when properly applied, does not weaken a bond between generations. It strengthens it, because mutual respect is the cornerstone of a relationship. Mothers who are overly cautious around their youngsters deprive them of the guidance, discipline, and boundaries that are necessary for healthy development.

Please don't assume, for example, that you must end every order to your child with a tentative question mark, as in, "Do you want to go to bed now?" "Would you like to eat your vegetables, sweetie?" Or, "I want you to be home by 10 p.m., okay?" If you sound like a wimp, you will be treated like one. You *will not* destroy your mother-child attachment by actively leading that child! Take charge of your youngster from babyhood! God has given you the responsibility of shepherding your precious children through the developmental years, and they need you to fulfill it! At the same time, there are countless ways to show that you love and cherish your child, even in the midst of corrective moments.

I remember my mother punishing me for something (which I undoubtedly deserved) when I was about four years old. After the encounter, she took me onto her lap and told me a story about a little bird. She said the mother bird told her baby to stay snuggled down in the nest, but he didn't obey her. When she flew away to find some worms, the little bird climbed out on the limb and fell to the ground. A big cat saw the little bird fall and quickly caught him.

I'm sure my eyes were as big as saucers as my mother continued, "You see, Jimmy, I am like that mother bird, and you are the little bird. God has told me to protect and care for you, and to keep you from doing anything that could hurt you. That is why you have to obey me at all times. If you don't listen, I will have to punish you like I did today because I love you so much. Now, give me a big hug, and let's go have a snack."

It has been many decades since my mother and I had that conversation, but I remember it vividly today. Did it damage our relationship? Certainly not. It added to the attachment between us, which guided me through childhood. I'm afraid that many parents today have little grasp of the principles involved here. Their confusion will reap painful consequences in years to come.

Carol Platt Liebau is one of my favorite authors. She tells moms in her book *Prude* why they can't afford to be "best friends" with their daughters and sons. She writes:

> Desperate for a good relationship with their children, these adults, mothers in particular, seem to believe that they can win their children's affection only by being "cool." Accordingly,

they behave a lot like their children's peers and unquestioning advocates, offer generous and constant approval whether or not it's merited, toss discipline out the window, and pretend to be little older than their children. . . .

Either unable or unwilling to take charge of their children, they are parents who are committed above all to remaining popular with their own children. . . .

They are able to ignore the most difficult parts of parenting—setting an example, and assuming responsibility for supervising and disciplining their children—and enjoy all the fun of relating to them as friends. But when mothers squander their moral authority, it's the daughters who ultimately suffer, because they are deprived of the wisdom, experience, and guidance of a mature adult. . . .

Many girls with "parent-peers" are allowed to function so autonomously that they alone decide even what morals they will embrace—which, in practice, may mean that peers, the culture, or others who may not have their best interests at heart are shaping girls' principles. . . .

In fact, today's young people are far more open to parental supervision and guidance than their parents often suspect.[22]

What sage advice this is. Dr. Nancy Snyderman addresses the same issue. She suggests that one of the most significant errors mothers make is assuming they'll be their teenage daughter's best friend. She writes, "After your daughter gets through adolescence, you then earn the right to morph into a friendship."[23]

It is my belief that the desire to be liked by one's children reveals a subtle apprehension that they will rebel when they are teens. Perhaps moms think, *If my husband and I don't try to tell them what to do, maybe we can avoid conflict down the road.* But both generations suffer when that happens. Moms and dads who are afraid to say no to a child, which I call "the denial of denial," often produce the very rebellion they dread. Children need firm leadership from the moment of birth onward, and it is cruel to deprive them of it. Trying to avoid conflict by being permissive has a name. It is called appeasement, and it never works in human affairs.

When I was in my early twenties, I taught sixth-, seventh-, and eighth-grade science and math in public schools. Down the corridor from me were several new teachers who were terrified of their students from the first day. They tried desperately to appease them with fun and games and what was then called the "open classroom." The rule was that there were no rules. Kids could do whatever they pleased, simultaneously talking, wrestling, playing, and throwing things. These boys and girls knew intuitively that their teachers were inexperienced and afraid of them. The result was utter contempt.

I remember one teacher who had no idea how to control her classroom. The students became little tyrants who reduced her to tears regularly. When she reached the end of her rope and was completely exasperated, she would climb on her desk and blow a whistle at the kids. They loved it. The ringleaders would plot at lunchtime about how they could get this poor woman to "blow at them." Sometimes she blew all day long. The result was chaos in her classroom.

Children are very perceptive of power games, and they move immediately to fill a perceived vacuum. For them, disrespect and contempt are very closely linked. Adults who are tentative and lacking in confidence often end up being despised by their children. If attachment is the goal of parenting, and it certainly is, that objective is achieved by expressing genuine love, affection, and dedication, combined with reasonable discipline, defined limits, and firm leadership. They work in tandem.

On the cover of my first book, *Dare to Discipline*, was a little scale depicting "love" on one side and "control" on the other. The key to successful parenting is to get those two ingredients into balance. Trouble brews if the scale tips in either direction, whether it is toward permissive and overprotective love or angry and oppressive control. Affection and discipline counterbalance each other, leading to greater bonding.

I'll close with this final thought about attachment. I have been describing ideal family relationships in this chapter, beginning with a loving, nurturing mother and an available, connected dad. In real life, those complex attachments are never perfect. There are countless single mothers and fathers today who are doing the best they can amid difficult circumstances. There are dads who are so committed to their professions that they hardly know the names of their kids. There are immature moms who were still dealing with the emotional upheaval of adolescence when they found themselves pregnant. In these and a myriad of other challenging family settings, parents should try to get as close to the goal of attachment as possible. Nevertheless, children are resilient and usually manage to land on their feet. To all the moms and dads among my readers who recognize their own limitations, take heart. The Creator of families knows your needs and offers His care and concern. Ask and you will receive!

I could devote at least a thousand more pages to this subject, but I will have to move on at this point.

YOUNG WOMEN TALK
ABOUT THEIR FATHERS

WE'VE TALKED ABOUT mothers and why attachment with their children is so enormously important. Now, let me make an appeal directly to fathers of daughters. I urge you to read this chapter and the next one very carefully, for reasons that you will soon understand. Actually, I wish every mom *and* dad would read what I have written, particularly noting the conclusions drawn at the end of this chapter.

What you will find below are insightful—and at times deeply moving—personal comments made recently by some very bright, academically gifted college and university women. They were attending a semester-long Christian educational experience called the Focus Leadership Institute.[1] It is designed for juniors, seniors, and graduate students, and it is one of the finest programs of its kind. The Institute has literally changed the lives of more than three thousand men and women who have graduated since its inception in 1996.

Having these young women (and men) on our campus gave me an opportunity to interact with them at length about *Bringing Up Girls*. The comments of forty female students were recorded and then subsequently transcribed. Though the students were invited to talk about any related subject of their choosing, their conversations typically moved in a straight line to their relationships with their fathers. As you will see, some of them acknowledged that something vital was missing there. Others were grateful for what their dads had done to make them feel valuable and respected.

Almost all of them spoke of the need for greater emotional connection with their dads.

I hope fathers will not be defensive about what was said by these remarkable young women but, instead, will hear within their comments "the language of their hearts." I began by thanking them for participating and asked them to offer suggestions and advice about the content. Then I made this introductory comment:

> I have talked to many college-age women in the process of writing *Bringing Up Girls*, and I can summarize the most frequent comment I have heard like this: "My father is a good man. He has worked hard to earn a living for our family, and he's been faithful to my mother [others said just the opposite]. Still, I never felt that he really admired or wanted to be close to me. He was very, very busy doing what he did, but he didn't have time for me. I felt like I was just there around the house, but he often didn't even seem to notice me."
>
> Was this something that others of you have also experienced?

What followed was a lively and intense discussion:*

> **Girl #1**: What you just said, Dr. Dobson, describes exactly what I feel. And I've heard it from so many of my friends. In fact, our greatest uneasiness about getting married is the fear that our future husbands will not be affirming and caring.
>
> **Girl #2**: It is essential that girls get affirmation from their fathers, because that's something I didn't experience growing up. That is the foundation of all my insecurities—the feeling that I wasn't really loved by my father. It is the root of everything I'm dealing with.
>
> **Girl #3**: That hits home with me, too. My dad was a good father, but he would compare me to girls in the media and complain that I didn't look like them. He told me I didn't work out enough, and he also called attention to what I was eating. He would say, "Do you realize where that's gonna go? That's gonna go right to your hips or to your legs." And so

---

* These comments have been edited to protect the identities of the participants and, in some instances, for linguistic clarity.

. . . I wasn't a full-fledged anorexic, I guess, but I worked out all the time. I was also dieting, and it got to the point where I wouldn't eat anything.

For the longest time I said that I had forgiven my dad, but it affected my relationship with Christ and made me question what it meant to have a heavenly Father who loved me. Fortunately, there are other men in my life who have supported and affirmed me, including my two brothers. But in the past six months, my dad has really worked hard at mending our relationship.

JCD: Did you ever sit down and tell your father how you feel?

Girl #3: Yes, sir. And he actually wrote a letter to me since I came to Focus on the Family about a month ago. He said how sorry he was that he didn't realize what a negative impact his comments had on me. So it's been really good, and I think the only reason I can actually forgive him now is because I have acknowledged Christ as my heavenly Father.

Girl #4: When I was going from a child to a woman—experiencing puberty—my dad just totally stepped back from me. It was as though he no longer knew how to relate to me. But it was a time when I desperately needed him in my life.

JCD: Have you ever asked him why he wasn't there for you at that time?

Girl #4: No. I don't have a good relationship with my father at all. It has led me to get involved in some dangerous behavior.

JCD: Did he spend time with you when you were a child?

Girl #4: No, and even when he did, it was completely on his terms. He was very involved in his profession, so on his day off he had things he wanted to do. He invited me to join him, but his idea of a good time was to shoot firearms. So even at four years old, I was already shooting guns. It wasn't anything that I ever really enjoyed, but it was the only way to get affirmation from my father on any level. He would introduce me to people by saying, "This is my daughter. She just shot eighteen out of twenty on the skeet field an hour ago." He never told them about any of my other abilities.

JCD: He never affirmed your femininity?

Girl #4: No, it was always about guns. I finally just backed away from him.

JCD: Is it too late to connect with your dad?

Girl #4: I don't know. I think God's working on it, but there's a lot of abuse in that relationship too. So . . . I think it's one of those things.

Girl #5: Hearing these heartbreaking stories today makes me thankful that I have a loving and affirming father, but he was not perfect. He was very sarcastic at home, and he joked around a lot. I've never, ever in my life been a skinny child. I'm built like my dad. My sisters and I would wear tank tops and shorts to bed, and in the morning when we came down to breakfast, my dad would pinch my side and make a joke about my weight. He never intended to be mean, but he would talk before he thought and say things that really hurt me.

Girl #6: My father was not like that. He told my sister and me that it was the inner beauty that mattered. He would also tell us how beautiful we were on the outside. And so that's what got me through junior high and high school, because I dealt with self-esteem issues. I'll never forget in sixth grade, having people ask me, "Why don't you look like your sister?" I was a very late bloomer, but she was an early bloomer. So I had four years of extreme insecurity where people would say, "Why are you shorter, and why are you so skinny? What's wrong with you?" My dad got me through that. If it weren't for him, I don't know what I would have done.

Girl #7: You know, I'm just hearing these stories from many of you all [speaking to her classmates], and they make me so sad. I had no idea there were so many broken women in our group. And of course we all have different things that we are going through . . . but wow! I've just had such a different experience, and I realize that much of who I am is because of the affirmation I received growing up. One of the things that I love to hear is when my family says, "Oh, you look cute." That sounds so silly, but my dad told me that all the time, and it has just meant so much coming from my own father. I realize just how blessed I have been.

Girl #8: My father was a good man, but he was very passive, and I just wish he would have set a lot more boundaries and given me more critical input. That is what I missed most from him. Instead of worrying so much about hurting my feelings, I wish he had shown me that he had an opinion of what was right and wrong in my life. He was always trying to make sure that

I was happy with our relationship, but I would rather that he would have been more forthright and said, "You know, I don't think this guy is right for you. This is what I see." I needed him to tell me that I mattered enough for him to guide me.

JCD: I have rarely heard a girl say, "I wish my dad had set more boundaries," but that desire is more common than people think. I believe many teens want their parents, and especially their fathers, to lead them. It is a way dads show they care.

I'm reminded of a single father who works here at Focus who told me something that happened when his daughter was ten or twelve, as I recall. They were watching television together one evening when a program came on that had some bad language and sexual themes in it. He didn't want to be a fuddy-duddy, so he simply went along with it. They watched the program a while longer, and finally he couldn't take it anymore. He turned off the set and said, "Honey, I just don't feel good about our watching this." His daughter said, "I thought you'd never turn it off, Dad." Adolescents need boundaries, even though they often act offended when limits are imposed.

Girl #9: I want to share something neat that my dad did for me. When I was probably seven or eight, we were driving to the beach on a vacation. I was in the back of the car and had my feet on the console between the front seats. My dad was driving, and we were at a stoplight when he reached back and touched my foot. He said, "You have the cutest feet." It meant a lot to me because I was a dancer, and sometimes my feet were not that nice, but to this day I love my feet. I love shoes. Just that simple compliment stayed with me. It was as though my dad selected that one feature to affirm. It still means so much to me. I'll never forget it.

JCD: Some people would consider what your dad did to be an insignificant gesture, and yet you remember it vividly today. It illustrates just how important kindness and compliments are to children, and especially to girls. Conversely, even mild criticism or ridicule, especially about the physical body, can be very hurtful to a sensitive individual.

Girl #10: Just recently I received a Valentine's Day e-mail from my father. It was the first card or e-mail he has sent me since I was seven years old, and it meant the world to me. He was an alcoholic when I was young, but he has been recovering for the past two years. This is the first time in twenty-one years that he's gone more than two days without a drink.

JCD: That is a very touching story.

How many of the rest of you have ever received a Valentine card or e-mail from your father? [counting] That's about half. How many have been taken on a date by your father? [several raised their hands]

Girl #10: When I was seven, my dad would take me to breakfast on Saturday mornings, but there were always about five other men who came along. I was never with him one-on-one. I guess that was why I was always reaching for him. I chose to participate in sports that I thought my dad would be interested in. I love those activities now, but I think I chose them to try to connect with him in some way. I can't explain the love that I have for him, despite the pain that he has caused. I love him in a different way from anybody else on the face of this earth. It is indescribable and unconditional, and I can't explain why.

JCD: Even when a father consistently disappoints and hurts his daughter, he is still her dad and she will always crave his attention. She may be intensely angry at times and blame him for his failures as a dad, but there is usually something inside that longs for reconciliation with him. She is just made that way.

Girl #11: No matter how much your mom affirms you as a child, she can't compensate fully if something is missing in your relationship with your dad. Even if you have a full-time mom when you are growing up, you still need the validation of your dad. When he doesn't provide it, your entire life is affected and even the way you see things is different. That has happened to me.

Girl #12: My dad coached college football, which consumes all of a man's time. It is very difficult for a coach to have a healthy family, especially at the college level. I really didn't know my dad, but he was my hero. And that's what hurt, 'cause he wasn't just my hero; he was the hero of many thousands of kids around the state. He was an amazing man who made mistakes, and he paid for them gravely. In order to get my dad's attention, I would go to practice with him, and

I wondered why he cared more for all those boys than he did about me.

I was the oldest, and he would tell me when he left for a game or for recruiting, "Take care of your mom." I was kind of like the dad of the family, even as a kid. And I felt like I wasn't a pretty enough girl. My mom is a very pretty lady, and men flocked to her. I never felt that way.

When dad was fired, he and my mom drifted even further apart, and they were soon divorced. I only heard them fighting once. They didn't speak much to each other. I just know my mother cried every day until the divorce was over. It really hurt me to watch her struggle. She lost her self-confidence, even though she was, and is, a very godly woman. [crying throughout the room]

My dad did a turnaround when he and my mom were divorced. He went through a time of depression for about four years after he was fired. And he worked his tail off to win back my sister and me, but I kept him at arm's length.

I quit telling either of my parents that I loved them. I decided that since I didn't tell my dad that I loved him, I just shouldn't tell my mom either, 'cause that wouldn't be fair. So I was like the kid who wouldn't let anybody love her. I tried to be tough; I never cried or told anybody that my parents were having problems, and nobody knew. I just tried to carry everybody and fix everything. But my dad worked hard at getting me back. And I put him through some terrible things. We never talked much about the divorce; we only mentioned it about four or five times.

JCD: Have you been able to rebuild your relationship?

Girl #12: Yes, through the Lord. He gave me my dad back.

Girl #13: You are making me cry. I have . . . oh, my goodness. I don't cry, because my dad told me never to cry. And . . .

JCD: Your dad was wrong.

Girl #13: I know. He also knows now. He cries all the time. [laughter]

JCD: These personal experiences that you all are sharing are deeply moving. It is obvious that many of you have walked a similar path. You've done well academically, and yet some of you have experienced the same emptiness inside.

Would anyone else like to share your story?

Girl #9: I remember my childhood only vaguely. I recall going fishing with my dad and taking motorcycle rides, but that's about it. When my parents were divorced, my biological dad quit asking me questions about my life. He still doesn't. I wish he would ask, but he wouldn't care. And so that has scarred me a lot, because I'm hesitant to talk to people about myself. I think what I say really doesn't matter. And I don't know why I'm crying either. I still try to get my dad to do what he ought to do, but I get disappointed every time. [sniffling] I'm just gonna take a breather. [laughter]

My mom and I have been so close, and she will never say anything bad about my dad at all. I admire her a lot for that. [crying] I'm so sorry.

JCD: Please don't apologize. We're dealing with really raw emotions here, and in your case, it is an ache that goes back to when you were very young.

Girl #9: Yeah. I would try to tell my dad some things, but since he wouldn't follow up with it, I'd get disappointed. My mom always warned me about that. She told me not to have expectations for my dad and just let him grow up. And so I've tried. I had lunch with my dad before I came here and told him where I was going. And he just talked about his adopted daughter and what she needs. He totally ignored what I had told him. So I've given up on him. Now I think of him not as a dad but as a "mission field," trying to love him as Christ would, but not as a daughter should.

Girl #15: How often do you see him?

Girl #9: I see him maybe at Christmas and Thanksgiving, times like that. But the good news is that my mom has married a wonderful man who has become a father figure for me. He takes me out on dates often and asks me questions about my life. He never talks about himself. He's made me feel so worthy and tells me how proud he is of me. I've never experienced that before. [weeping] Every time I call my mom, he'll get on the other line too and want to hear. He totally came in and . . . he just cared. He's never missed one of my ball games. My dad never came to any of my games, and that hurt a lot.

So I'm finally getting my confidence back, as though I really do matter.

Girl #16: I don't really have very many memories of

my childhood. I remember having my own golf clubs that my father had inscribed for me. So, obviously, we played golf together. I see him regularly now, but he doesn't ask me questions.

When I told him I was going to college, he asked me which one and what I was doing. But that was basically all he said. He didn't want to know why I was going to college or what I wanted to study. He didn't go to college, or as he said, he only "visited" it for a couple of months and then dropped out. He partied and drank too much and left. I basically have lived my life for myself, made all my decisions, and things like that. He's never wanted to help me make decisions.

I have had an interesting relationship with my father. He was very distant when I was young. He didn't know how to communicate at all, which was hard for my mom. That is something I also struggle with, 'cause I don't know how to communicate with people either. My parents were never intimate. I only saw them kiss once in my entire life. So I had no idea what intimacy was or how to express it.

I know my dad loved us, although he never told us he did. You know, we just kind of knew it. Still, I always loved my dad, and I never wanted him to be alone. Then my mom cheated on my dad and that's why they got a divorce. So that's another behavior I learned—cheating and lying about everything.

My mom never told my dad she cheated; she just filed for divorce. So when my parents got divorced, she married the guy she cheated with. My sister decided to live with my mom, and I went with my dad because no one wanted to live with him and I didn't want him to be alone. And we were kind of all rebelling from God. At the time, my dad was the only godly influence in my life. And it was just amazing how he began to open up. He learned how to love me, you know, and show me that he did. Now he's my best friend.

But it took a long time. I did a lot of things to my dad that my mom had done to him. I lied to him and did the other things I had learned at home. But he stood by me. He was definitely there when I needed him. He told me how much he cared about me and how proud he was of me. And today he'll come to me in tears and tell me how much he loves me and that he's so thankful he has a daughter who follows the Lord and listens to Him.

When my dad started showing me how much he loved me, I realized how much God loves me. I never felt worthy of love by anyone until my dad started showing it to me.

Girl #17: That was true for me. My father came from an abusive home. His dad was an alcoholic, and he was the only Christian out of five brothers. So he purposed in his heart that his family would be different, but at the same time, he's very . . . he's an engineer. He's very mathematical and "equational." For him, A plus B equals C. It is very hard for him to reveal his emotions.

Well, when I was nine years old, I was diagnosed with clinical depression, which was really difficult for my family. There were years of counseling and just battling through it. But during that time, my father stepped outside of himself, and he affirmed me in a very meaningful way. I would apologize for being depressed and say, "Daddy, I don't know what's going on. I can't help it." And he would say, "I love you just the way you are."

You know, that is so huge, and to this day, I know that God has a purpose for my life, because both my dad and my mom affirm me, but my dad did it best. I remember sitting on his lap and hearing him say, "You know, sweetheart, we love you." So I can definitely see how just knowing that has shaped my life. I think it is so important for us as women to hear that we are loved and to be able to feel it. We need to be affirmed—to have a dad say, "You are the apple of my eye" and to let us know it by hugging us.

JCD: Wouldn't it be interesting if the dads you're talking about could have been sitting behind each of you and hearing what you had to say?

Girl #18: I'll bet they'd all be crying too.

JCD: I think you're right. We would need another box of Kleenex.

Girl #19: My parents were both emotionally absent when I was growing up, and that's something I've just come to realize within the last year or two. My mom and dad always provided for my physical needs when I was growing up, and I'm thankful for that, but emotionally there was a void, with my dad especially. I felt like I wasn't worth anything if I wasn't doing everything right.

I never felt like I had my parents' respect until I was in high school and began achieving things. Then they were proud of me. That's when they started giving me attention and showing me that they loved . . .

JCD: You felt like you had to earn it, right? You weren't affirmed for who you were but for what you accomplished.

Girl #19: Yes, but my dad e-mailed me last week to tell me he is proud to have me as his daughter. It is hard for me to accept it now, because of the fact that when I was growing up, he wasn't there. That is something I'm definitely working through right now.

Girl #14: Hearing these comments from the other girls makes me realize how blessed I am to have a father who spent time with me when I was growing up. And I'm blown away by what you all are saying. I had no idea of the hurt that so many of you have been through. I'm the second of ten children, which is pretty much a recipe for having a dad who couldn't give me special attention, and yet he spent a lot of time with us individually. He'd get up at five in the morning to take one of us out to breakfast for a couple of hours. He tried to do that with each child once a month. And then when I turned sixteen, he started taking me out to dinner instead. Those were times when he would ask what was going on in my life, and then he would say, "Do you know how proud I am of you? Do you know how much I love you?" Those were the two questions he always asked as we finished eating.

He had another ritual that, even though it was a small thing, meant so much to me. I depended on it every single night. He went around to each of the kids' beds one at a time, and he sat there and scratched our backs and hugged us. And then he said the same prayer over us. He did that throughout our childhoods. It was such a special part of my growing up. I'll tell you, it was very difficult for me when I was away at college not to have him praying for me at bedtime.

JCD: My goodness, what a blessing! What was the prayer your dad said every night?

Girl #14: He would say, "Heavenly Father, thank You for a daughter like Sherrie. Thank You for blessing her and putting her in this family. Thank You for helping her find You at an early age. Protect her tonight as she sleeps and tomorrow as she goes through her day. Keep her from the enemy and from harm. Help her to find a godly husband in Your time. In Jesus' name, amen."

It was always the same, every night.

JCD: Would you allow me to put that prayer in my book?

Girl #14: Yeah, I would love to have you include it.

JCD: That beautiful prayer will be with you for the rest of your life, won't it?

Girl #14: It will. And I'll pray it over my kids too, and I'll encourage my future husband to do it too.

Girl #20: Wow, I didn't realize this was going to be so emotional. Did anyone else come expecting this? We walked in and saw this beautiful luncheon provided for us. I felt like a princess, and then suddenly, here we are all crying. [laughter]

Girl #21: I, too, have been blessed with a father who wanted to be a part of my life. He is a talented man, very athletic; he just has a sense of authority about him. He knows the Word of God inside and out, and that's where he gains his authority. He could have accomplished anything he wanted, but he became an assistant pastor so that he could be with the family.

Then he started his own church and became the head pastor, but he still had time for me. Every week he would say, "Robin, are we gonna have lunch today?" He would actually be bugging me for a date. He would take me on backpacking trips, something that most girls don't get a chance to do because only boys go backpacking. My sister and I would go backpacking in the Sierras with maybe ten dads and their sons. And he made me feel so special because I was worthy of him wanting to be with me. He wanted to hang out with me.

And one more thing. You asked us for suggestions for dads, and I would like to offer one.

JCD: Please do.

Girl #21: Even though my dad wanted to be with us, sometimes girls have a tendency to be closer to Mom. So when we were little, I mean real little—it started out when maybe I was three or so—we wanted Mom all the time. We wanted Mom to put us to bed; we wanted Mom to wake us up. We wanted Mom to make food. The French toast didn't taste good unless Mom made it. And she began to get worn out, so my dad came up with a little trick. At night my dad made it a priority to put us to bed. Well, at first we didn't want him to do that. So he would say, "Okay, girls, you need to get in bed, close your eyes, and open your mouths. I'm gonna come in there in two minutes, and I have a surprise for you." We never knew what we were going to get. Sometimes it was a little bit of coconut, sometimes it was raisins, but every time my dad would come in and he would put something good in our mouths. We loved it.

JCD: He was bribing you.

Girl #21: Dr. Dobson, it worked. [laughter] We didn't want my mom anymore. [laughter]

But the warmest memory of all for me, and what shaped my life, was waking up very early in the morning and seeing a small light on in another room. It might have been five o'clock or even four. I would get up and find my dad sitting in his chair and holding a cup of coffee. He would be reading the Bible. I would come up beside him and say, "Good morning, Dad." And he would put his arm around me and say, "This is what I just read, Robin. I just prayed this verse for you." And he would put my name beside it in his Bible, and he would pray over me. In fact, right before I came here to the Institute, he prayed for me.

Girl #22: Oh, wow!

JCD: Now you've got to send the Kleenex back down here. [laughter]

Girl #22: That is awesome, Robin.

JCD: Your dad is obviously deeply committed to Christ and to his family, isn't he?

Girl #21: Yeah, he is.

JCD: Well, we are going to have to bring our discussion to a close. This has been a very meaningful and emotional time together, and I deeply appreciate your speaking candidly and from your hearts today. We have used up an entire box of Kleenex, but that is what it was here for.

You are confident and accomplished young women, and yet many of you have revealed a deep "soul hunger" with regard to your fathers. I'm not sure you even knew these things about one another. There has been a common thread here that I didn't anticipate either. I didn't hear great anger or resentment toward your dads—just an ache for affirmation, which many of you never received as a child. You could have talked today about any subject related to *Bringing Up Girls*, but what you have said came from the core of your beings. We have to assume that if you feel the way you do, having come from mostly intact and successful families, millions of other women have dealt with the same unmet need to connect with their dads.

I can't tell you how many women who have read my books or heard my broadcasts have come up to me and said, "You have been the father I never had." I am convinced that few people fully realize just how intense a girl's desire is to connect with the "first man" in her life. If he was absent, or if he is there but not engaged, she will struggle with that vacuum, in some cases for the rest of her life. I will try to convey that message to my readers on your behalf.

Men usually understand that their sons are dependent on them throughout childhood, but I am convinced that girls need their fathers as much as boys do, for this and many other reasons. A girl's sense of self-worth and personal dignity are directly linked to what she believes her father thinks of her. Mothers are important to girls in other ways, but there is something that only a dad can provide to his daughters. That is why the stories you have shared today reflect so much pain. And it is why so many of you cried as you spoke. It is why your identity as women seems to hinge on casual things your fathers did and said. When you read my book, which I hope you will do, this aspect of your femininity will be described.

Let me offer a few concluding words of advice for those of you who are still struggling over what your moms and dads did or didn't do in the past. I'll begin by telling you what you already know—that there are no perfect mothers and fathers, just as there are no perfect human beings. We are all flawed and selfish and shortsighted at times. I remember a father who told me that his grown son was terribly angry with him for being gone so much when the boy was growing up. The father had thought he was doing the right thing at the time but realized too late that he should have given more of himself to his family. That father was dealing with pangs of guilt.

I suggested that he ask his son sincerely for forgiveness but then remind him that parenting is an enormously difficult task. All of us fail at one point or another. And unless I miss my guess, that younger man will probably make some serious mistakes with his own sons and daughters. His errors will probably be different from those made by his dad, but he is likely to have reason someday to ask for forgiveness for his own mistakes as a parent. Life itself is extremely demanding, and we all stumble over challenges that we should have handled better. To the young women here today, I urge you to forgive those who may have misunderstood the little girl you used to be. Someday you will need to ask for that same forgiving spirit from your grown children.

Second, it is healthy to acknowledge painful experiences from the past, as we have done today. It may even be beneficial in that process to talk to a counselor who can help you come to terms with painful memories. But then you need to release them and move on. One of the most costly mistakes you can make is to harbor bitterness that will damage you from deep inside. You must forgive, which is demanded of us in Scripture, and then you need to let it go. It can be done. It must be done.

Third, I hope you won't confuse your earthly fathers with the love of our heavenly Father. Human beings will fail you at times, but God never rejects, ignores, insults, or disdains His children. He is "a friend who sticks closer than a brother,"[2] and we read in Psalms that He is "close to the brokenhearted."[3] We have heard repeatedly today that some of you have felt estranged from God because your dads failed to affirm you. It is a natural mistake to make because our fathers are often a visual image of the Almighty. Nevertheless, the distinction must not be blurred. God is love. Period!

Fourth and last, a mistake commonly made by those who experienced difficult childhoods is to see themselves as victims who are forever doomed to suffer. With God's help and His healing touch, you can overcome even the most painful obstacles from your early years.

I love the chorus written by Bill and Gloria Gaither some years ago with these lyrics: "Something beautiful, something good. All my confusion, He understood. All I had to offer Him was brokenness and strife, but He made something beautiful of my life."[4]

Thanks again for your openness today. What you have shared will be very helpful to parents. God be with you all.

Let's pray. Heavenly Father, I thank You so much for this time together. It has been such a meaningful and candid discussion. I thank You for these young women and for their obvious desire to serve You. We believe each one is here by divine appointment, for purposes that we may not even comprehend. Some have expressed painful memories today that remain unresolved in their hearts. I ask You to heal any damaged emotions that exist and to help them forgive those who may not have fully understood the needs of the little girls they used to be.

There are others who sat at this table, I am sure, who didn't feel comfortable sharing their personal journeys. Be with each of them as the Father, the Encourager, and the Friend we know You to be. Use every tear that has fallen to fulfill Your ultimate plan in their lives.

But also, we want to thank You for the strong families represented here that invested themselves unreservedly in the lives of their children. We all have needed divine guidance along the way. If You should see fit to give families to these young women someday, help them to raise them in the fear and admonition of the Lord. May the experiences revealed today be assets, and not liabilities, in the years to follow.

In the name of our Lord and Savior, Jesus Christ, amen.

WHY DADDIES MATTER

THE SIGNIFICANCE OF our interaction with the Institute students can hardly be overstated. Let me summarize by reminding you that the women who participated in our discussion were young, intelligent, accomplished, and well educated. It might be said that they "had it all." Nevertheless, they hungered for something more—something inexpressible—that could not be provided by money or social and academic success. The majority of the girls spoke of a void inside that was created by the lack of emotional connection with their fathers.

Others were more fortunate, and they expressed appreciation for dads who cared. One girl recalled a single remark made years earlier by her father about her cute feet. That casual comment was probably made spontaneously and quickly forgotten by her dad, yet his daughter never forgot it.

So what was going on there? Was their longing for paternal affirmation and affection unique to the individuals in this group? Certainly not! What the students described is almost universal among girls and women. There is a place in the female soul reserved for Daddy, or a daddy figure, that will always yearn for affirmation. Not every girl or woman is the same, of course, but almost every girl desires a close bond with this most significant man in her life. She will adore him if he loves and protects her and if she finds safety and warmth in his arms. She will feel that way throughout life unless he disappoints her or until one of them dies. She will tend to see all men through the lens of that relationship. If he rejects and ignores her, or worse, if he abuses and abandons her, the yearning within her becomes more intense, though it is often tainted with resentment and anger.

Let me make another thing clear, although some of you will not like what I am about to write: mothers cannot fill this particular empty space. They can and must meet similar needs for love and adoration, and in fact they do occupy their own real estate in a daughter's heart. A girl without a mother's love is a sad spectacle indeed, and I would not minimize the maternal role in any regard. But moms can't be dads, and dads can't be moms. This is why the current advocacy on behalf of same-sex marriage and homosexual adoption contradicts what is best for children.

Some girls will go to great lengths to achieve a close relationship with their fathers. I am reminded of a man who told me about driving a teenage boy to the home of his thirteen-year-old girlfriend. When they arrived, a pretty little teenybopper popped out of the house dressed like a prostitute. She was wearing fishnet stockings and a shocking see-through dress that revealed just about everything, including her panties and bra. Her father was standing in the front yard when she walked past him. He looked up and said, "Have a nice time."

After the girl was in the car, she explained tearfully that she was wearing the sexy dress because she wanted to see if her dad cared enough to stop her. He didn't. It was just a test of his love and concern. He failed it. When they arrived at their destination, she went into the women's restroom and changed her clothes.

Let me elaborate on a fundamental question I discussed in chapter 3: why do girls and women have such intense needs for affirmation from their fathers, and why does the hurt caused by abandonment or rejection often reverberate for a lifetime? As you'll recall, a primary reason for this inner ache is because a daughter's sense of self-worth and confidence is linked directly to her relationship with her dad.[2] What he thinks about her and how he expresses his affection is a central source of her perceived value as a human being. It also affects her femininity and teaches her how to relate to boys and men. Given this vital role in the development of girls, it is a tragedy that 34 percent of these precious babies are born into homes without a father present.[3] They are deprived of fatherly support and influence from the moment of birth!

Counselor and author H. Norman Wright addresses this matter of a woman's sense of identity in his outstanding book *Always Daddy's Girl*. It contains the following cogent observation, written directly for the female reader:

Your relationship with your father was your critical initial interaction with the masculine gender. He was the first man whose attention you wanted to gain. He was the first man you flirted with, the first man to cuddle you and kiss you, the first man to prize you as a very special girl among all other girls. All of these experiences with your father were vital to the nurturing of the element which makes you different from him and all other men: your femininity. The fawning attention of a father for his daughter prepares her for her uniquely feminine role as a girlfriend, fiancée and wife.

If there was something lacking in your relationship with your father when you were a child, the development of your femininity suffered the most. Why? As a little girl, you by nature expressed all the budding traits of the feminine gender. If your father was emotionally or physically absent, or was harsh, rejecting or angry toward you, you automatically and subconsciously attached his disapproval to your femininity. You didn't have the intellectual capacity to understand his rejection, nor did you have the inner defensive structure to insulate yourself against it. You simply and naively reasoned, "I want Daddy to like me; Daddy doesn't like me the way I am; I will change the way I am so Daddy will like me."

When a father does not value or respond to his daughter's femininity, she is stunted in her development. When a daughter has little experience in delighting her father as a child, she is incomplete. She is left to discover her femininity for herself, often with tragic results in her relationships with men.[4]

Wright's insightful analysis explains why the young women I quoted in the previous chapter were so emotional about the rejection they felt from their fathers. It tells us why the most casual negative remark made by a dad years ago still echoes in his daughter's heart. It should also say something profound to today's fathers about their own vulnerable little girls.

Please understand that it is not my purpose to browbeat men or disparage their efforts to meet the needs of their children. Most of them are deeply committed to their families and want to be good fathers. Nevertheless, the pace of living and the pressures of work make it difficult to remember what really matters in the grand scheme of things. Former Beatle John Lennon wrote this lyric in one of his final songs: "Life is what happens to you while you're busy making other plans."[1] How little he knew. Lennon had only a few days to live.

Being a father and a type A personality myself, I look back on my parenting experiences and recall instances where I could have done a better job. I wish I could relive some of those busy days at a slower pace. Unfortunately, none of us is allowed do-overs or mulligans. When our record is finally in the books, not a word or a deed can be altered.

Would it be self-serving to tell you that I also did some things right during my early days as a father, and that the memories of some very special times with my kids rank at the top of my list of accomplishments today? Among my favorites are recollections of my daughter, Danae, when she was five years old. We used to take bike trips together to a nearby park on Saturday mornings. We would play in a sandbox with shovels and buckets. I taught her to build sand castles, explained what a moat and a drawbridge were, and talked about anything else that seemed to interest her. Then we would go to a nearby taco stand and have lunch before riding home. On the way back, we listened every week to a favorite recording of Rodgers and Hammerstein's *Cinderella* on a small Craig recorder, and we sang the songs together. Danae loved those outings, and she can tell you in detail about them today. And guess what? I loved them too.

Our son, Ryan, and I had our fun adventures together too. When he was three years old, I would hide his stuffed bears, lions, deer, and giraffes around the house. Then when it was dark, we'd take my flashlights and his toy guns, and we would creep around on a big game hunt. When he was twelve, we began hunting and fishing together for real. I will never forget those days in the great out-of-doors with my only son. We still hunt together today.

From where I sit today, I can say that nothing, and I mean *nothing*, from that era turned out to be more significant than the hours I spent with my little family. The relationships we enjoy today were nurtured during those years when it would have been very easy for me to chase every professional prize and ignore what mattered most at home.

What I am trying to convey in this chapter is addressed specifically to dads who are still raising kids and want to respond to the desires of their little hearts. My advice is also relevant to fathers whose daughters are grown. The woman who used to be "Dad's little princess" may still long for what she didn't receive when she was young. Even though these fathers can no longer play in the sandbox with their five-year-olds, it is never too late for them to say, "You are precious to me."

I asked our radio listeners to call our organization some years ago and record a message for their dads. More than six hundred people participated. I listened to quite a few of the recordings, and we aired some of them on Father's Day. Not one of these messages focused on what the father did professionally. None of the callers said, "Thanks, Dad, for earning a lot of money" or "Thanks for the big house you provided for us" or "Thanks for the Cadillac [or Mercedes or BMW]." No one mentioned living in an upscale neighborhood. Instead, caller after caller said, "Thanks, Dad, for loving me and for being there for me." Some said with strong emotion, "Thank you for letting me interrupt you, even when you were busy." Nearly all of the calls coming from women mentioned the presence of tenderness in the relationship.

We kept a transcript of those recordings, and there is one that I wish everyone could hear. These are the actual words of a caller. She said quietly:

> Hi, this is Kathy from Georgia, with a letter for my daddy. I don't know where things went wrong, when the pain, prescriptions, and alcohol began. I was just a kid. You tried to never let me down, Daddy, but many times you did. Daddy, in 1978, always and still, I was thinking of you as Father's Day approached. I searched for just the right card for you, my darling daddy, and mailed it late. But Daddy, all day long your phone was busy. You died alone on the floor, beside your upturned phone, on Father's Day. When I got to Portland, my card was still in your mailbox. You never knew, Daddy. I was too late. God, help me always remember that late is better than never, but it's not good enough. Daddy, you died without experiencing my care and my love on Father's Day.

Kathy's words still echo in my mind today: "Daddy . . . ," she said, "always and still, I was thinking of you." Even though decades have passed since the painful experiences of her childhood, this woman continues to grieve for her renegade father. The recording reveals no anger or resentment in her voice—just lingering sorrow because her "darling daddy" was never there for her. I can't tell you how many grown women have told me similar stories about their fathers who disappointed them again and again.

Some years ago, I read a most touching letter to a magazine editor written by a fourteen-year-old girl named Catherine. She described an extremely painful moment of her life and titled it, "That's the Way Life Goes Sometimes." This is what she wrote:

> When I was 10, my parents got a divorce. Naturally, my father told me about it, because he was my favorite. [Notice that Catherine did not say, "I was his favorite."]

"Honey, I know it's been kind of bad for you these past few days, and I don't want to make it worse, but there's something I have to tell you. Honey, your mother and I got a divorce."

"But, Daddy!"

"Well, I know you don't want this, but it has to be done. Now, your mother and I just don't get along like we used to. I'm already packed, and my plane is leaving in half an hour."

"But, Daddy, why do you have to leave?"

"Well, honey, your mother and I can't live together anymore."

"Well, I know that, but I meant, why do you have to leave town?"

"Oh, well, I got [sic] someone waiting for me in Minnesota."

"But, Daddy, will I ever see you again?"

"Oh, sure you will, honey. We'll work something out."

"But what? I mean, you'll be living in Minnesota, and I'll be living here in Pennsylvania."

"Well, maybe your mother will agree to your spending two weeks in the summer with me and two weeks in the winter."

"Why not more often?"

"Well, I don't even think she'll agree to two weeks in the summer and two weeks in the winter, much less more."

"Well, it can't hurt to try."

"I know, honey, but we'll have to work it out later. Now, my plane leaves in 20 minutes, and I've got to get to the airport. Now, I'm gonna go get my luggage, and I want you to go to your room, so you don't have to watch me. And no long good-byes either."

"Okay, Daddy. Good-bye. Don't forget to write me."

"I won't. Now, good-bye. Now, go to your room."

"Okay, Daddy. Daddy, I don't want you to go."

"I know, honey, but I have to."

"Why?"

"Well, you wouldn't understand."

"Yes, I would."

"No, you wouldn't."

"Oh, well. Good-bye."

"Good-bye. Now go to your room, and hurry up."

"Okay. Well, I guess that's the way life goes sometimes."

"Yes, honey, that's the way life goes sometimes."

After my father walked out that door, I never heard from him again.

It is still painful to read Catherine's words, written more than thirty years after her father left home. I wonder if she still thinks about the father who abandoned her for a new flame in Minnesota. I wonder how that devastating experience affected the remainder of Catherine's teen years, her choice of a husband, and her life today. I wonder if her dad has any regrets about breaking his little girl's heart so long ago. We can only wonder, but I think I know. Yes, I'm *sure* I know.

Let's consider how family dynamics tend to play out at home and explain why daughters often come out on the short end of things. First, husbands understand that their wives have certain romantic needs that are different and more urgent than their own. Not all men seek to meet those needs, of course, but they have certainly heard about them.

Likewise, husbands who are fathers usually understand that it is their responsibility to teach their boys to be men. Mothers are not equipped to do that job, and it's up to dads to transmit the meaning of masculinity to their sons. Again, men may or may not be willing to accept that assignment, but they at least know they should.

That brings us to an understanding of the position girls usually hold in the family. Pay attention now, because I am about to tell you something that I consider to be of prime importance: *daughters tend to be third in line for the attention of the man of the family.* I have drawn that conclusion after many years of working with families. I'll say it again for emphasis: fathers know intuitively that their boys require special attention, discipline, and leadership, but they are often unaware of how desperately their daughters also need them. Some dads apparently see this yearning for affirmation among girls as the exclusive responsibility of mothers. The task of bringing up girls is often viewed by dads as "women's work."

It is tough enough for men to understand their wives at times, much less these bubbly little females who are constantly reaching for them. Let me say again that girls need their fathers as much as boys do. This will be a revolutionary thought for some guys, but careful research reveals that it is dead on the money.

We'll conclude our discussion by offering a few how-to ideas for dads about forging meaningful connections with their daughters. It isn't rocket science, but we all need to be reminded of the obvious every now and then. One of the cornerstones of human relationships is embodied in a single word: *conversation*. Girls and women, more than boys and men, connect emotionally through spoken words. When communication breaks down between them and people they love, females are often wounded and frustrated. Girls often feel abandoned by fathers who won't engage them verbally.

You'll remember that two of the Institute women addressed this issue through their tears. One said that her dad was completely disinterested in who she was or what she was doing. Another said her father "didn't know how to communicate at all," and as a result, she has never understood what intimacy is all about. She never witnessed or experienced it.

Every professional counselor has heard similar personal accounts. Females of all ages tend to interpret masculine silence as evidence of rejection. Based on this understanding, the best thing dads can do to connect with their daughters is to talk to them about whatever is of interest. Ask questions and then listen carefully to what is said in return. This interaction helps to produce the affirmation I have been describing. Meaningful and affectionate dialogue with a daughter is evidence that she is worthy, secure, and loved. Those beneficial effects can be achieved so easily through simple, genuine conversation.

Touch is another point of connection that is essential to girls. Just like their mothers, our daughters need to be hugged regularly, perhaps every day. Hugging is easy to do when girls are young and they see their daddies as champions and best buddies. However, with the arrival of puberty and evidences of sexual maturation, fathers often feel uneasy and tend to avoid physical contact. Girls can read that discomfort with the accuracy of a laser.[5]

During our discussion with the students, one girl gave us a textbook example of the way fathers often respond to their daughters during puberty and adolescence. It is worth repeating:

> When I was going from a child to a woman—experiencing puberty—my dad just totally stepped back from me. It was as though he no longer knew how to relate to me. But it was a time when I desperately needed him in my life.

The awkwardness of this girl's father, I would guess, was related to her breast development and womanly appearance. Some fourteen- or fifteen-year-old girls already have the bodies of women, and their dads are not supposed to notice—but they do. A loving father is afraid he will touch her in the wrong place or otherwise offend her. So he tries to keep a discreet distance.

On the other side of the ledger, a girl who has wrestled with her father and hugged and kissed him throughout childhood can't possibly understand why he leans away now when she throws her arms around him. One commentator called that "the leaning tower of Pisa." There is no way a father can explain what is making him nervous. His attraction to her is involuntary and usually quite innocent. What makes the situation worse is that younger children in the family, both boys and girls, still snuggle up to Dad and tell him they love him. The budding teenager sees that affection and wants to cry over what she has lost.

The Institute student observed her father stepping back from her, and it was natural for her to conclude that "Daddy doesn't love me anymore." That scenario has been enacted by millions of fathers and daughters around the world.

I want to say to all these dads emphatically that your pubescent and adolescent girls are going through a time of great insecurity. They desperately need you now. You are their protector and their source of stability. Your love now is critical to their ability to cope with the rejection, hurt, and fears that are coming at them from their peers. Hugs are needed now more than ever.

I urge fathers to continue providing the physical contact that was appropriate during earlier childhood. It should not be sexual in nature, of course, but a loving, fatherly response is still vital. The last thing you want to convey now, even inadvertently, is that your love has melted away. So hide the awkwardness, Dad, and hug your kid like you did when she was six!

I received an early lesson on the importance of touch when my son and daughter were three and seven years of age, respectively. Danae has always been very physical with me from her earliest childhood. When I watched a televised football game on a Saturday afternoon, she often climbed on me with her Barbie doll and played on my lap. Then she would move around to my back and climb on my shoulders. When the USC Trojans scored a touchdown, she would giggle and hang on for dear life as I danced around. She was always Daddy's little girl.

But then Danae and Ryan both came down with the chicken pox. Lucky me! I had never had the disease, and I assure you, I didn't want it! Chicken pox can be a nightmare when contracted as a grown adult. Therefore, I scrupulously avoided both my kids for five days. I tried to disguise what I was doing, but my daughter figured it out. Finally, she went crying to her mom and said, "Daddy won't touch me anymore."

That felt like a knife in my heart. It also told me that my daughter still needed physical contact with me. It was one of the ways I affirmed my love for her. As soon as she began to get well, I wrapped my arms around her again. That object lesson was very useful to me later when Danae began to develop. By the way, I didn't come down with the chicken pox and still haven't had it. I'm saving the experience until I am about eighty so everyone will feel sorry for me.

To dads, let me say, "Just keep doin' watcha been doin'." And keep your tower straight! Your daughter will notice if it is leaning.

Here's a final suggestion, another simple one that is still effective. Dads who want to connect with their little girls, and even those who are not so little, need to spend one-on-one time with them. It is an excellent way to knock down barriers and build bridges. Take your daughter somewhere she will like, such as out to breakfast or dinner. It doesn't have to be a big deal. Just make it a quiet time together when the two of you can sit and talk. Play miniature golf together, or check out a DVD at the library that the two of you can watch at home. If your daughter is younger, go to a kids' movie or a theme park. Put these activities on the calendar, and *do not* let the dates get canceled or postponed. Never leave kids wondering why you didn't show up and didn't even call. That can be more painful to a girl than not promising in the first place.

Once adolescence comes crashing on the scene, your teenager may be embarrassed to be seen with you. That's okay. Play by her rules, whatever they are.

Never forget that girls are made out of the same stuff their mothers are. Put sweet little notes and cards in your daughter's coat pocket or in her shoe. Write a short prayer and put it under her pillow. Girls love flowers. It's in their DNA! They beam when you express pride to others about them. Look for anything that will bring your daughter into your world or you into hers. While you are at it, tell her you love her every time you are together. You will be her hero forever.

I love writing about this subject, because it lies very close to my heart. I'll bet many of you feel the same way. In the next chapter, I'll deal with something you will enjoy as well.

❀ ❀ ❀

When the chemistry is right, fathers make contributions to the welfare of their daughters in almost every dimension of life. Here is a quick overview of some related findings in that regard. After reading it, you'll see again why daddies matter.

Girls whose fathers provide warmth and control achieve greater academic success.[6]

Girls who are close to their fathers exhibit less anxiety and withdrawal behaviors.[7]

Parental connectedness is the number one factor in preventing girls from engaging in premarital sex and indulging in drugs and alcohol.[8]

Daughters who believe that their fathers care about them have significantly fewer suicide attempts and fewer instances of body dissatisfaction, depression, low self-esteem, substance abuse, and unhealthy weight.[9]

Girls with involved fathers are twice as likely to stay in school.[10]

Girls with fathers or father figures feel more protected, are more likely to attempt college, and are less likely to drop out of college.[11]

Girls whose parents divorce or separate before they turn twenty-one tend to have shorter life spans by four years.[12]

Girls with good fathers are less likely to seek male attention by flaunting themselves.[13]

Girls who live with their mothers and fathers (as opposed to mothers only) have significantly fewer growth and developmental delays, and fewer learning disorders, emotional disabilities, and behavioral problems.[14]

Girls who live with their mothers only have significantly less ability to control impulses and delay gratification, and have a weaker sense of conscience about right and wrong.[15]

Both boys and girls do better academically if their fathers establish rules and exhibit affection.[16]

The next study may amuse you. Researchers have observed that women who had good relationships with their fathers during childhood tend to be attracted to men having similar facial features. Some grown daughters have spouses who bear an astonishing physical resemblance to their dads.[17]

Unmarried women may not be thrilled by this information!

Here's a related study that was first published more than thirty years ago but was well documented at the time. It is still valid, in my view. The findings were published in a book titled *Daddy's Girl, Mama's Boy* by James Rue, Ph.D., and Louise Shanahan.[18] Its thesis was that the cross-sexual relationship (girls with fathers and boys with mothers) was found to be a highly significant factor, for better or worse, in all future romantic decisions. Girls with loving, nurturing fathers tended to search for marital partners having a personality and other characteristics similar to those of their dads. Girls with abusive, rejecting, and irresponsible fathers searched for men who were not like them at all. The same was true for boys regarding their mothers. Thus, Mom and Dad continued to shape the romantic interests of their sons and daughters long after childhood.

The bottom line is this: "Choose your parents wisely." You not only carry their genes, but you are also influenced one way or another by their thoughts, behaviors, values, beliefs, strengths, weaknesses, hopes, dreams, biases, intelligence, mistakes, failures, successes, sicknesses, health, joys, and sorrows. It is scary, isn't it? That is why great fathers and mothers are treasures.

FATHERS TO DAUGHTERS

PROVIDED NOW IS a little "serendipity" I am passing along to fathers, and also to mothers. These selected short proverbs were compiled or written by Harry Harrison and published in a delightful little book entitled *Father to Daughter: Life Lessons on Raising a Girl*. As you read these quips and suggestions, you might want to underline those that stand out as particularly insightful. That is exactly what I did.

- ❀ Accept the fact that [your little girl] will melt your heart anytime she chooses.

- ❀ Take part in her life now. Don't wait until she's 15 to try and develop a relationship.

- ❀ Sing to her while you're rocking her. She'll love hearing your voice—and it's a great way to pass the time at 1 a.m.

- ❀ Remember, if you yell at a boy not to play with a wall socket, he'll either stomp off or do it anyway. A girl will cry.

- ❀ Her mom will show her how to bake chocolate chip cookies. You show her how to dunk them in milk.

- ❀ Teach her to count. First her fingers. Then Cheerios, M&Ms, dandelions, and fireflies.

- ❀ Be prepared to watch Walt Disney movies with her some 200 times. Each.

❀ Never lose the wonder of watching her and her mother together.

❀ Relish the moments when she toddles up and for no reason at all throws her arms around your neck. Resist the urge to buy her the world.

❀ Trust her mom to understand the mystery of little girls. You have yet to figure out the mystery of big ones.

❀ Never, ever, make fun of her.

❀ Bear in mind that from the very beginning your personality will shape her.

❀ Never forget that supportive fathers produce daughters with high self-esteem.

❀ Read to her often. Very soon, she'll be reading to you.

❀ Give her a picture of you to put in her first purse. If you're lucky, she'll always carry a photo of you.

❀ Don't tolerate her temper tantrums. Not now. Not when she's 15. Your home will be more peaceful for this.

❀ Restrict her TV viewing, unless you want her to grow up with the values Hollywood teaches.

❀ Little girls are fascinated by escalators. Make sure you hold hands.

❀ Make her a Valentine's Day card—every year.

❀ Lie on your backs in the grass together and look for shapes in the clouds. It's a good way to approach life when you're young.

❀ Be home for dinner on time. Very important.

❀ Ask her about her day, every day. Share her wonder.

❀ Keep her secrets. This way she will begin to trust men.

❀ Take her for a walk in the woods. Show her what poison ivy looks like, how to cross a stream, how to find her way back.

❀ Let her teach you. About what she learned in school today. About the Pilgrims, or multiplication, or manatees. How to sing her favorite song. How to bake a cake. How to braid Barbie's hair.

❀ Praise her often. Let her know you love her the way she is. If you tell her this often enough she might remember it throughout adolescence.

❀ Make up stories to tell each other at night. Stretch her imagination.

❀ Surprise her by showing up at her school for lunch, bearing Happy Meals or pizza.

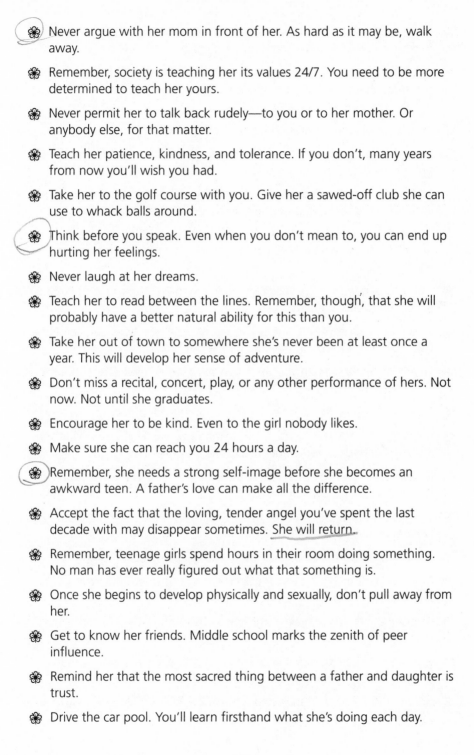

- Never argue with her mom in front of her. As hard as it may be, walk away.

- Remember, society is teaching her its values 24/7. You need to be more determined to teach her yours.

- Never permit her to talk back rudely—to you or to her mother. Or anybody else, for that matter.

- Teach her patience, kindness, and tolerance. If you don't, many years from now you'll wish you had.

- Take her to the golf course with you. Give her a sawed-off club she can use to whack balls around.

- Think before you speak. Even when you don't mean to, you can end up hurting her feelings.

- Never laugh at her dreams.

- Teach her to read between the lines. Remember, though, that she will probably have a better natural ability for this than you.

- Take her out of town to somewhere she's never been at least once a year. This will develop her sense of adventure.

- Don't miss a recital, concert, play, or any other performance of hers. Not now. Not until she graduates.

- Encourage her to be kind. Even to the girl nobody likes.

- Make sure she can reach you 24 hours a day.

- Remember, she needs a strong self-image before she becomes an awkward teen. A father's love can make all the difference.

- Accept the fact that the loving, tender angel you've spent the last decade with may disappear sometimes. She will return.

- Remember, teenage girls spend hours in their room doing something. No man has ever really figured out what that something is.

- Once she begins to develop physically and sexually, don't pull away from her.

- Get to know her friends. Middle school marks the zenith of peer influence.

- Remind her that the most sacred thing between a father and daughter is trust.

- Drive the car pool. You'll learn firsthand what she's doing each day.

❀ Remember, when you're dealing with a 13-year-old girl, for all intents and purposes, you're dealing with a fruitcake.

❀ Talk to her often about decision-making and sex. About her peer pressure, about love, about romance, about God. You never know when it will be just the thing she needs to hear.

❀ Watch your language around her. Insist she watch hers.

❀ Girls this age can be uncomfortable stating what they really need. More often than not, she needs you to be a parent.

❀ Accept the fact that girls squeal when they're happy or confused or excited or scared or because they just saw a certain boy in line.

❀ When she's particularly angry, sit down with her and have her try to describe what's going on. Remember, the longer you listen, the more you'll learn.

❀ Don't subscribe to magazines that exploit women. It makes a statement about how you view all women.

❀ If you don't approve of the way she looks before she goes out, send her back to her room to start over. Be gentle but firm.

❀ There will be days when you think you've raised an alien. Those are the same days she feels she's being raised by one.

❀ Don't let her play you and her mother against each other.

❀ Never call her names. No matter how mad you are. No matter what she did. If you do, she'll remember it for the rest of her life.

❀ Remember—many girls look back on middle school as the worst time in their lives. Stay tuned; stay involved.

❀ Volunteer to drive her and her friends to the movies. Then just listen while they talk.

❀ The day she's born, ask God to guide you in all aspects of raising her.

❀ Drag her to church . . . every week. She may not share your enthusiasm, but after 18 years, the message will have sunk in.

❀ Forgive her when she seeks forgiveness. This is the best way for her to learn to forgive others.

❀ Teach her how to be moral in an age that bombards her with sexual imagery and innuendo.

❀ Ask her every now and then about her spiritual life. If she asks you what you mean, be prepared to have a discussion with her.

❀ Teach her to pray for her enemies. This could possibly include a rotating cast of classmates and ex-boyfriends.

❀ Teach her to treat each day as holy.

❀ Teach her that sometimes God has other plans.

❀ No matter how much you are tempted, don't yell at the refs or insult the umpire. You'll embarrass her and look like an idiot.

❀ You will have to teach her how to drive . . . without making her cry.

❀ Make it very clear that you expect her to wear a seat belt. Even over her prom dress.

❀ Persuade her to buy gas when the fuel tank level is at a quarter tank, not when the needle is buried and the car is riding on fumes.

❀ Odd-looking boys will start showing up at your house. This is to be expected because adolescent boys are odd-looking.

❀ Let her see, by the way you treat your wife, the way a man is supposed to treat a woman.

❀ Teach her how to look a boy in the eye and say "No."

❀ Do not tease her about boyfriends. She may not have one, and you might make her feel like she's supposed to.

❀ Understand that if she suddenly becomes a football fanatic even though she hates the game, you can be sure a boy is involved.

❀ Teach her that if she acts stupid to attract boys, she'll attract stupid boys.

❀ Explain to her that there are dangerous boys as well as honorable ones, and how to tell the difference.

❀ If a boy pulls up and honks for her, go out and have words with him. Explain that your daughter answers to a doorbell.

❀ Wait up for her. Knowing Dad will be greeting her at the door has a very positive effect on her decision-making process.

❀ Remember, every girl's heart gets broken. There's nothing you can do to fix it. Hunting down the boy won't help. On the other hand, she will also break a few hearts herself.

❀ Don't get too emotionally involved in her love life. It will drive you nuts.

❀ Don't let her moods or anger push you away. She needs you now more than ever.

❀ You have no power over how much makeup, shampoo, suntan lotion, skin creams, hair color treatment, mascara, eyeliner, perfume, cologne, body wash, and bath lotion she will buy. Accept this and move on.

❀ Be firm about maintaining family traditions. They will become more important to her than either of you can imagine.

❀ Take long walks with her. If you just listen, she'll eventually tell you everything that's on her mind.

❀ Remember, if her home life is crazy, the rest of her life will be too.

❀ Teach her to respect herself.

❀ Don't let her miss school to get her hair done for a party. Unless all you want is a party girl.

❀ Remember, you're her definition of a man. If you drink and smoke and take drugs, chances are the men in her life will, too.

❀ Understand that when she's 15, and wearing a black dress, with her hair done and face made up, you will be very hesitant to let her leave the house.

❀ Visit college campuses with her in her junior year. (This is not the time to get emotional. There will be plenty of time for that.)

❀ There will be times when you'd rather stick needles in your eyes than have a particular conversation with her. This is when you must act like a father.

❀ Prepare for the day when you're not the most important man in her life.

❀ Tell her the three keys to wisdom: not believing all you hear, not spending all you have, not sleeping all you want. This will be difficult for her until she graduates from college.

❀ Have a look around her room. Take a moment to look at her pictures, her photos, her keepsakes. These are her memories. This was the childhood you gave her.

❀ Remember, she will break your heart when she leaves for college. But you will survive.

❀ Tell her she is the daughter you always dreamed about.

❀ In the end, let her go.[1]

Do you have a lump in your throat now? If not, go back and read these suggestions again.

CINDERELLA
AT THE BALL

RECENTLY, I HAD the pleasure of inviting a very special couple, Randy and Lisa Wilson, to be my guests on the *Focus on the Family* radio program. Randy is the national field director of church ministries for the Family Research Council, an author, and the creator of a concept called the Purity Ball, which has become a national and international phenomenon. Lisa is the mother of seven impressive children whom she has homeschooled.

The Wilsons have been featured on numerous television programs, including the *Glenn Beck* show, NBC's *Today* show, *ABC World News Tonight, Dr. Phil*, ABC's *Good Morning America, The Tonight Show, The View, The Tyra Banks Show*, and evening news programs. Inquiries about the concept are coming in from all over the world.

Articles about the Purity Ball have also been published in *Glamour*; *O, the Oprah Magazine*; *The Economist* magazine; *USA Today*; the *Rocky Mountain News*; the *Denver Post*; and many others. Randy and Lisa have also been interviewed on numerous radio programs in the United States, Canada, Ireland, and Britain.

The Purity Ball Web site, http://www.generationsoflight.com, describes its basic concept and explains the source of all this interest.

> The Father Daughter Purity Ball is a memorable ceremony for fathers to sign commitments to be responsible men of integrity in all areas of purity. The commitment also includes

their vow to protect their daughters in their choices for purity. The daughters silently commit to live pure lives before God through the symbol of laying down a white rose at the cross. Because we cherish our daughters as regal princesses—for 1 Peter 3:4 says they are "precious in the sight of God"—we want to treat them as royalty.

"How can you measure the value of your eleven-year-old looking up into your eyes (as you clumsily learn the fox-trot together) with innocent, uncontainable joy, saying, 'Daddy, I'm so excited!'" wrote Wesley Tullis in a letter describing his grateful participation. "I have been involved with the Father Daughter Ball for two years with my daughters, Sarah and Anna. It is impossible to convey what I have seen in their sweet spirits, their delicate, forming souls, as their daddy takes them out for their first big dance. Their whole being absorbs my loving attention, resulting in a radiant sense of self-worth and identity." Think of it from [a daughter's] perspective. [One girl writes:] "My daddy thinks I'm beautiful in my own unique way. My daddy is treating me with respect and honor. My daddy has taken time to be silly, and even made a fool of himself, learning how to dance. My daddy really loves me!"[1]

The New York Times even featured a full-page article on the Purity Ball written by Neela Banerjee. It was titled "Dancing the Night Away, with a Higher Purpose." In the article, Banerjee describes the ninth annual Father-Daughter Purity Ball, in which seventy young women dressed in floor-length gowns, up-dos, and tiaras were escorted into the Broadmoor Hotel dining room by fathers, stepfathers, and even future fathers-in-law.

"The first two hours of the gala passed like any somewhat awkward night out with parents, the men doing nearly all the talking and the girls struggling to cut their chicken," she writes. "But after dessert, the 63 men stood and read aloud a covenant 'before God to cover my daughter as her authority and protection in the area of purity.'"[2]

Randy and Lisa organized one of this country's first father-daughter purity balls over ten years ago, at a time when their own daughter was nearing adolescence. "The culture says you're free to sleep with as many people as you want to," said Khrystian Wilson, 20, "What does that get you but complete chaos?"

Because we know that premarital sex is especially destructive to girls, fathers play a crucial role in helping them stay pure. "Something I need from Dad is affirmation, being told I'm beautiful," said Jordyn Wilson, 19, another daughter of Randy and Lisa. "If we don't get it from home, we will go out to the culture and get it from them."

In the *New York Times* piece, Banerjee points to several recent studies that have suggested how close relationships between fathers and daughters can reduce the risk of early sexual activity and teenage pregnancy among girls. For this reason, the true focus of purity events is actually on the fathers, who are asked to set an example for their daughters by holding themselves to high moral and spiritual standards.

When the Wilsons and three of their children joined us in the studio for an interview, it turned out to be one of our most popular programs of the year. I began our conversation by asking Randy how the Purity Ball came into existence. He said it was never their purpose to start the movement that has developed. Instead, their initial purpose was to celebrate the "coming of age" of their eldest daughter, Lauren, who was turning thirteen. It was nothing more ambitious than that. Everything since then simply developed from that idea. It soon became obvious that other families wanted to do the same for their daughters.

I then asked Lisa why she has devoted herself entirely and unreservedly to homeschooling her tribe. She immediately got tears in her eyes and said, "Oh, you're going to make me cry." This dialogue followed:

> **Lisa:** The Scripture tells us that fear of God is the beginning of wisdom, and we wanted to teach our children to revere Him. Randy and I knelt before God and asked, "How do we raise them to know and fear You?" The Lord showed us that homeschooling our kids was His calling for us, and we responded to it. This was the best decision we've ever made. The greatest part of it is opening the Word of God every day, which is the foundation for everything that we do. It is such an honor to present God the Father to our children.
>
> **JCD:** Teaching your children at home has also been a sacrifice for you, hasn't it, both financially and personally?
>
> **Lisa:** Absolutely. I've had to say no throughout my adult life—no to many interesting activities and opportunities. But activity doesn't breed intimacy. Instead, I've gathered my children around me and looked into their faces day by day. What a blessing it has been for me. There is no greater calling than to invest in the hearts and souls of these precious kids.
>
> **JCD:** Randy, do you appreciate what Lisa has done for your family?

Randy: Let me tell you, Proverbs 31 says that our brides are a gift from God, and Lisa has certainly been a gift to me.

JCD: My wife, Shirley, has also been a treasure to me. Well, let's talk in depth about the Purity Ball and the ideas behind it. I've been working on a book for several years, which has reflected my growing concern for today's girls. There is no doubt from my research that millions of them are in serious trouble, and it is getting worse by the day. How do you interpret what the culture is doing to our children?

Randy: There is a lost generation of girls out there that has resulted primarily from the absence of committed fathers. Many men are uninvolved and disengaged at home. However, dads are desperately needed to give both girls and boys a strong sense of identity and confidence, and to help them figure out what they believe. I just don't see that happening enough in the culture today. In the absence of such dedicated men, both sexes struggle with the challenges that come their way.

JCD: It is obvious that the popular press is intrigued by what you are doing. As far as I know, you have never hired a publicity agent to get your ideas before the public, but the Purity Ball seems to be popping up everywhere. How accurately has the press portrayed your purpose and intent?

Randy: The reporters don't understand what we are trying to do; they don't seem to want to get it. They come with an agenda and usually put their own spin on what they write. For example, I was talking to the *New York Times* reporter as the girls were practicing before the ball in Colorado Springs. I said, "You know, we've been telling this story now for over a year to many media organizations, and I have said the same things over and over. Purity Ball is about fathers stepping up to the plate. It is about setting a standard of righteousness for their daughters and helping them develop healthy relationships. Our purpose is not about controlling the girls."

Nevertheless, reporters have continued to report just the opposite. They have accused us of being too patriarchal and of sheltering girls too much. It is a distortion. We are trying to support our daughters and help them withstand a confused culture that could cause them harm. How can anyone criticize an effort by fathers who want to show love for their girls and promise to live a godly life before them? That, they say, is "very controversial."

JCD: You are also communicating something to the young men in the lives of your daughters, aren't you?

Randy: Yes, the Purity Ball is designed to provide a model for our sons as well, and to show them how they should treat the women in their lives.

JCD: Tell us more about the ball and what happens on that enchanted night.

Lisa: After eating a wonderful dinner, Randy presents a challenge to the men about their responsibilities as fathers. Then he invites the men to come to the middle of the ballroom. They form a circle around their girls, who are standing all aglow in their lovely ball gowns. The fathers then place their hands on their daughters, and together they pray for purity of mind and body. Then the men read a covenant aloud.

JCD: You have brought a copy of the covenant with you today. Would you read it for us now?

Randy: These are the words I spoke to our oldest daughter, Lauren: "I, Lauren's father, choose before God to cover my daughter as her authority and protection in the area of purity. I will be pure in my own life as a man, husband, and father. I will be a man of integrity and accountability as I lead, guide, and pray over my daughter and my family as the high priest of the home. And this covering will be used by God to influence generations to come."

Lisa: And then all the shutters begin to click throughout the room as pictures are taken of fathers signing this covenant.

JCD: And tears are streaming down faces, I'm sure.

Lisa: Oh, yes! It is a powerful moment. Then the daughters sign as witnesses to the covenant.

Randy: It's a holy moment.

JCD: It's kind of a Cinderella night, isn't it, with everything but the glass slippers and the pumpkin carriage.

[A daughter who was present in the studio said, "Oh, yes, definitely. It is amazing and you feel so loved."]

Another daughter wrote this description of the covenant experience: "As all the dads stood to read the covenant over their daughters, I felt the power of those words sink right into my heart. My father promised to lead a life of integrity and purity for me. He signed his name and I signed as a witness to his words. And as he escorted me to the dance floor, I felt empowered by his promise to war for my heart through his life of purity, and I knew my life would never be the same again."

Lisa: We have invited fathers who've adopted orphans in Africa. We've had foster-care fathers, stepfathers, uncles, and grandfathers come. One woman in her forties called her dad, with whom she had never had a good relationship. He was seventy-nine years old. At first he declined her invitation but later decided to be there. We watched this man dance with his daughter all night with tears streaming down his cheeks. The next morning, he gave his heart to Christ—

JCD: Oh, my goodness.

Lisa: Isn't that exciting?

Randy: The Purity Ball unlocks the heart of a father. This older man then spoke a blessing to his daughter—for the first time in her life. We see it as a means of honoring and treasuring our daughters. It is a call to fathers to take back their area of responsibility. It's a call to restore what has been abdicated in our culture and then to renew and reestablish the father-daughter relationship.

Lisa: You know, the Bible has many examples of fathers blessing their children. To symbolize that blessing, the dads present swords at the cross to show the determination to protect their daughters. Then both fathers and daughters kneel, and the girls lay white roses at the cross to symbolize wholeness and purity before God. It is so beautiful!

We also have microphones set up during the evening so fathers can bless their daughters and daughters can bless their fathers. Through the night, there are individuals waiting to speak. It is very emotional for both the girls and their dads. There is no place in this culture to express honor and blessing between generations, but this event does it, and watching it happen takes your breath away. At the climax of the evening, fathers begin dancing with their daughters, which is something to see.

JCD: You came from a dysfunctional family, didn't you?

Lisa: Yes, my dad left my mom when I was two, and by age twenty-one, she had three babies to care for. My father spent the rest of his life trying unsuccessfully to reconnect with me. Six weeks before he died [choking with emotion], he looked me in the eye and said, "I just want to say I'm sorry and I wish I could do things over."

When I look at my husband, who stands before the children every week and lays his hands on their heads and blesses them, I can't hold back the tears, because we are taking back territory that has been lost. Many dads live with regrets, but God can redeem what has been lost, and that is happening.

JCD: What do you say to the single mother out there who has a daughter and no husband to protect and defend her?

Randy: Well, we often ask, "Is there a grandfather or older brother or an uncle who will become a surrogate father for a girl?" We've even heard repeatedly how a man from another family will take a girl to the Purity Ball and pledge to be the father figure she needs. He will say, "I will fight for you. I will be there to mentor and model for you as you walk this path of life."

JCD: What a great contribution a man can make to a fatherless girl or one whose dad is no longer on the scene.

Randy: Dr. Dobson, I hear often from fathers who tell me their daughters talk about this event all the way home, asking Dad to take them back next year.

Cohost, John Fuller: Randy, going back to something Dr. Dobson said about men before we went on the air, some guys out there must be squirming. They are drawn to what you and Lisa have said, but they're thinking, *I've messed up and I can't straighten it all out now.* But I hear you saying, "It's not too late. Come to a ball, and stand up in front of your peers. Make a covenant, and dance with your daughter. Be the man she needs you to be." How can you give men the courage to move in this direction?

Randy: Well, they can begin by having a conversation with their daughters. Take them to a bagel shop or a restaurant and begin by asking a few questions, such as, "I would like you to tell me what you need from me." "Tell me what your greatest fear is." "Tell me what your greatest joy is." "If you could do anything you wanted in life, what would that be?" Those are windows into your daughter's soul. That conversation can serve to start a whole new relationship. This Purity Ball can also give you an entrée to your daughter's heart.

John: Are some of these guys uncomfortable?

Randy: Absolutely, but it is so easy. They will be in a room full of other fathers. All they have to do is look around and do what they see them doing.

Lisa: There will be other fathers coming for the first time. There will be stepfathers representing blended families. We watch them doing things they never thought they could do. We've had men come to the microphone and ask forgiveness for not being there for their daughters. And it became a new beginning for them. And we weep with them because the heavenly Father, in His Father's heart, is leading the way. Isn't that the story of salvation—asking forgiveness, and then God shows up.

JCD: That is powerful. You know, I was thinking as you spoke. If I were unsure of my relationship with my daughter, I would ask this first question of her: "Do you have any idea [choking with emotion] how much I love you?" What a great place to start—

Lisa: Hmm.

JCD: Well, we have to finish our discussion very quickly. Randy, just tell us where you think the Purity Ball is going.

Randy: Dr. Dobson, we had no idea where the movement was going ten years ago, and I'm still not sure we know. All I can say is that it is growing and spreading. Since the *New York Times* article, I'm getting many e-mails from various places asking if there is a Purity Ball in one state or another. I'm telling them to start an event in their own community. Suggest to fathers that they do it. We can't move around the country ourselves to host events, but people can come to one of ours in Colorado Springs. And . . .

Lisa: We've had inquiries from seventeen countries, some of them calling with interpreters, asking us about the Purity Ball. We've heard from Al Jazeera network, and . . .

JCD: You ain't seen nothin' yet. Focus on the Family is heard in 150 countries. [laughter] Well, Randy, we must not end this interview without giving details about how interested families can get more information about the Purity Ball idea.

Randy: Yes, they can get a Father-Daughter Purity Ball Packet by going to http://www.fatherdaughterpurityball.com. There's also information about our book, *Celebrations of Faith*, and newsy items as well. We will respond to requests and begin a dialogue together.

JCD: Randy, summarize your message for us in closing.

Randy: We are asking families to get on their faces before God and ask Him what He wants done in their lives, in their

homes, and in their communities for this generation. I believe
He will hear the cry of their hearts and begin to bring healing.
And if God is for us, who can be against us?

❀   ❀   ❀

On May 21, 2008, Christian singer Steven Curtis Chapman and his wife,
Mary Beth, lost their beloved five-year-old daughter, Maria Sue, who was
hit and run over by a car. The way this strong family has dealt with Maria
Sue's death has been a model of faith and courage for other families who
have experienced tragedy. Shortly after the accident, Steven rereleased a
heart-wrenching tribute to his precious child and titled it "Cinderella."
Here are the deeply moving lyrics of that song:

> *She spins and she sways to whatever song plays,*
> *Without a care in the world.*
> *And I'm sittin' here wearin' the weight of the world*
>   *on my shoulders.*
> *It's been a long day and there's still work to do,*
> *She's pulling at me saying "Dad I need you!"*
> *There's a ball at the castle and I've been invited and*
>   *I need to practice my dancin'"*
> *"Oh please, Daddy, please!"*
>
> *So I will dance with Cinderella*
> *While she is here in my arms*
> *'Cause I know something the prince never knew*
> *Oh I will dance with Cinderella*
> *I don't wanna miss even one song,*
> *'Cause all too soon the clock will strike midnight*
> *And she'll be gone*
>
> *She says he's a nice guy and I'd be impressed*
> *She wants to know if I approve of the dress*
> *She says "Dad, the prom is just one week away,*
> *And I need to practice my dancin'"*
> *"Oh please, Daddy, please!"*
>
> *So I will dance with Cinderella*
> *While she is here in my arms*
> *'Cause I know something the prince never knew*
> *Ohh-oh ohh-oh, I will dance with Cinderella*
> *I don't wanna miss even one song,*

'Cause all too soon the clock will strike midnight
And she'll be gone
She will be gone.

Well, she came home today
With a ring on her hand
Just glowin' and tellin' us all they had planned
She says "Dad, the wedding's still six months away
but I need to practice my dancin'"
"Oh please, Daddy please!"

So I will dance with Cinderella
While she is here in my arms
'Cause I know something the prince never knew
Ohh-oh ohh-oh, I will dance with Cinderella
I don't wanna miss even one song,
(even one song)
'Cause all too soon the clock will strike midnight
And she'll be gone.[3]

THE OBSESSION WITH BEAUTY

THE IDEA OF Cinderella and other legendary princesses from the land of make-believe has captured the heart of almost every little girl today. Thanks to the creative genius of the late Walt Disney and the company he founded, the princess movement, as it is known, is having an enormous impact on yet another generation of girls. It is also producing more than $3 billion in sales annually for the Disney organization.[1]

Peggy Orenstein made this comment about the phenomenon in the *New York Times*:

> We are in the midst of a royal moment. To call princesses a "trend" among girls is like calling Harry Potter a book. There are now more than 25,000 Disney Princess items. . . . It is on its way to becoming the largest girls' franchise on the planet. . . . Pink, it seems, is the new gold.[2]

This is the way *Huntsville* (Alabama) *Times* columnist and college English instructor Beth Thames describes the movement in her article entitled "Pretty in Pink but Powerful, Too":

> I'm trapped in Princess World.
> In this world, everything is pink, from the sheets on the

bed to the backpack in the corner to the airy costumes made of tulle and gauze.

Princess faces beam down from toy shelves and coat racks, a pantheon of Princess Power.

And the power of marketing. The Disney team put all its female characters together, and, "Bibbi-de-bob-adee-boo," we've got the Princess team. It's made up of such old familiars as Snow White and Cinderella, plus Ariel and Belle, whoever they are.

Each princess has a story line and even a recipe for a favorite food. On the pink Princess stove, a voice announces the ingredients for Cinderella's pumpkin pie (get it?) and Snow White's apple cobbler. The teapot makes a whistling noise and tea is served, along with plastic bananas, hot dogs and cupcakes.

Princesses live on cupcakes. And Disney lives on princess dollars, which are pink, I'm sure.

A stroll at one of Huntsville's malls is a testimony to the power of the princess. Toy stores have princess tea sets and gowns and puzzles. There are princess CDs and princess movies.

All princesses sound alike, so it's hard to tell if you are listening to Snow White or Pocahontas, who has been made an honorary princess in the spirit of cultural diversity. All princess voices are lilting and sweet.

Just because we all read Snow White, and most of us did, that doesn't mean we'll grow up to cook and clean for seven short men, hiding in the dense forest from the evil stepmother who wants to do us in.[3]

The question demanding an answer is, Why are girls so taken with the princess fantasy? Our daughter, Danae, has loved the princess fantasy since she was a tiny girl. I asked her why the story line is so captivating. This is what she wrote in response:

1) *Beauty.* Every girl wants to be considered physically attractive, and princesses take it to the highest level. Snow White was proclaimed "the fairest of them all" by the magic mirror, and all eyes were on Cinderella at the top of the staircase when she walked into the ballroom. (Even the musicians stopped playing momentarily.) One of the gifts given to Sleeping Beauty by the fairies at

the celebration of her birth was the gift of beauty. The description of the blessing, offered in the form of a song, included such phrases as "gold of sunshine in her hair" and "lips that shame the red, red rose . . . she'll walk with springtime wherever she goes."

2) *Song.* Every Disney princess has a beautiful voice, and some of the story lines are based around that talent. Sleeping Beauty was also given the gift of song at birth, and it was her extraordinary voice that attracted Prince Phillip in the forest. The Little Mermaid had such a lovely voice that she was asked by the villain to exchange it for the ability to walk on land. Snow White and Cinderella were always breaking into a cheerful tune while doing chores ("Just whistle while you work"), and every princess sings her dreams instead of talking them out.

3) *Beautiful clothes.* Princesses wear lovely gowns in bright colors, and little girls love to mimic their heroine's attire by donning similar costumes. Just go to Disneyland (or Disney World) and you will see plenty of petite versions of Snow White, Belle, and Cinderella walking around the park in their favorite princess costumes.

4) *Handsome suitor.* A princess is always pursued by an attractive male prospect, and he's usually a prince—someone any girl in the kingdom would love to have. Through all the ups and downs in the story line, a princess always gets her man in the end. Even in the story of Beauty and the Beast, when the curse on the castle is reversed, the Beast turns into a handsome prince, and he and Belle dance across the ballroom floor together.

5) *Rags to riches.* Some of the princesses are already living like royalty (Ariel and Jasmine), others achieve it by marrying a prince (Cinderella and Belle), and still others are princesses by birth (Snow White and Sleeping Beauty) but unable to live in the lap of luxury until the end of the story. One thing is true for all: in the end they all live in a castle with the man of their dreams and with riches galore (enough to buy all the gorgeous gowns they desire).

6) *Happily ever after.* This is true for every Disney princess, but unfortunately not for the rest of us. Nevertheless, the concept of marrying a handsome prince and living happily ever after (no conflicts or problems) is appealing to young dreamers who hope that one day they will have the same privilege. "Happily ever after" sounds so romantic and appealing, doesn't it?

7) *Dreams coming true.* A princess expresses her wishes and dreams early in the story and always sees them come to life in the end. As Cinderella sang so eloquently at the beginning of the film, "No matter how your heart is grieving, if you keep on believing, the dream that you wish will come true." And Snow White sang into the wishing well, "Someday my prince will come. . . ."

To be a princess is to be considered beautiful, to be pursued, and to see all your hopes and dreams come true. Now who wouldn't want to be a princess?

We can all understand why little girls want to join this happy club. But to explore the phenomenon further, I asked a savvy young mom, Kristin Salladin, why her teenage girls have been heavily into the princess fantasy since they were very young. This is what she wrote:

Most girls *love* romance, and princesses fill that need better than anything else. Being a princess also honors girls and "girliness." It separates us from boys. My girls, Jenna and Julia, who are sixteen and seventeen, still like to dress up like the Disney princesses for Halloween. But they also love to read about Esther and Ruth in the Bible. Girls are drawn to stories of successful, beautiful girls who get the "right guy" or the handsome prince, and Disney has cashed in on this desire. Good timing on their part.

You rang the bell, Kristin! Almost every little girl shares her mother's love for romance, and there is always a romantic twist to the princess dream. It gives expression to their inner yearning to love and be loved and to live "happily ever after." That, and many other factors, is driving the Cinderella fantasy.

I asked another young woman, Riann Zuetel, how she feels about the princess idea. Her view was a little different. She saw within this movement a quest for respect and dignity. This is what she wrote:

I think wanting to be a princess is more than just feeling beautiful. Girls and women long to be treated like they are something special and worthwhile. Our culture often treats women like brainless sex objects who are put on this planet to satisfy men's desires, sometimes at the expense of their own sense of self-worth. Young girls grow up bombarded by these messages from the media, such as those seen and heard on the E! channel, MTV, BET, and pop radio stations, and in *Cosmopolitan* and teenybopper magazines. Young kids and especially teen girls are keenly aware of these negative images.

Their mothers, I believe, want their daughters to be treated like intelligent, respected, and equally valuable contributors to society. That is one of the reasons moms buy and dress their daughters in princess attire in hopes of changing their daughters' attitudes toward themselves and other women.

When a girl sees herself as a princess, she feels valued for who she is. Being beautiful is just the icing on the cake, so to speak. She is equal, worthwhile, and special. Most important, she has the confidence to wait for Prince Charming to come and not settle for second best or a loser, no matter how long it takes.

I agree with Riann's perspective too. The princess movement helps to counter some of the degrading stuff thrown at girls. As we have seen, the fashion and entertainment industries continue to market an endless array of highly sexualized products to preteens and even preschool youngsters. These kids are dragged into adolescent behavior long before they are ready to deal with it. Many mothers understand this and are looking for a safe haven for their daughters. Cinderella and her royal sisters help to provide it for them.

Not everyone is thrilled about the reemergence of the princess movement, of course. Some feminists have been clucking nervously about it for years. Indeed, a vigorous debate has been occurring among professors and others in academia who fear the fantasies are undermining politically correct ideology. Writer Jennifer Dowd worries, for example, that princesses convey to children "that women are weaker than men."[4] The last thing these critics want is for girls to read about damsels in distress who are rescued by handsome princes. But the dilemma for them is that their daughters love the princesses.

Peggy Orenstein called the movement "troubling" and admitted she is conflicted with regard to her own child. She says:

> As a feminist mother . . . I have been taken by surprise by the princess craze and the girlie-girl culture that has risen around it. What happened to William wanting a doll and not dressing your cat in an apron? Whither Marlo Thomas? I watch my fellow mothers, women who once swore they'd

never be dependent on a man, smile indulgently at daughters who warble "So This Is Love" or insist on being called Snow White. I wonder if they'd concede so readily to sons who begged for combat fatigues and mock AK-47s.

More to the point, when my own girl makes her daily beeline for the dress-up corner of her preschool classroom— something I'm convinced she does largely to torture me—I worry about what playing Little Mermaid is teaching her. I've spent much of my career writing about experiences that undermine girls' well-being, warning parents that a preoccupation with body and beauty (encouraged by films, TV, magazines and, yes, toys) is perilous to their daughters' mental and physical health. Am I now supposed to shrug and forget all that? If trafficking in stereotypes doesn't matter at three, when does it matter? At six? Eight? Thirteen?[5]

Sharon Lamb, a professor of psychology at Saint Michael's College, came right to the point:

What you're really talking about is sexual purity. And there's a trap at the end of the rainbow.[6]

Lamb is objecting to the fact that purity is making a comeback, at least within the princess movement, and that development is disturbing to her and other liberal commentators. That is strange. I find it difficult to understand how any mother would be disturbed by her daughter's exposure to purity. Modeling virtue is one of the reasons I like the movement. In a subtle way, the Disney stories present a wholesome image of virginity until marriage and then lifelong love thereafter. They also promote femininity, kindness, courtesy, the work ethic, service to others, and "good vibes" about one's personhood. Where else in the popular culture do you find these values represented in such an attractive way?

Rachel Simmons, of Girls Leadership Institute, writes approvingly of princess play. She lauds the way it avoids tough, street-gang behavior that was popular a few years ago. She also likes traditional princess clothing that encourages little girls to be children and is not blatantly sexualized. Cinderella and Snow White do not wear low-rider jeans or thongs, Simmons says. She continues:

So what does the princess phenomenon teach our girls? That it's fun to dress up. That the prince may drop by the castle to give you a kiss or dance with you, but after that, he's out of there. He is peripheral to the whole princess scene.

Princess culture is a matriarchy. See you later, Prince Charming. The shoe may fit, and the carriage may be waiting, but these princesses are very, very busy. The tea water's boiling and the phone is ringing off its hook.

The princesses have a lot to do before the stroke of midnight.[7]

Orenstein and other feminist writers have raised two additional concerns that deserve consideration. The first deals with the eternally optimistic theme of the stories. Everything works out wonderfully in the end, and then "they all live happily ever after." She wants girls, hers and ours, to live in reality, not fantasy. She asks, "Will the girl who is wearing 'Princess' across her chest when she's three be wearing 'Spoiled' across her chest when she is six, and 'Porn Star' when she is 12?"[8]

I've seen no evidence to support the supposition that little girls who think of themselves as princesses are more likely to become brats or strippers when adolescence approaches. That strikes me as ridiculous.

Admittedly, however, life is not always a Cinderella journey, and Orenstein is not the only parent who worries about pretending that it is. But we are talking here about children, after all. There will be plenty of time for them to learn about pain, sorrow, and other intricacies of adult life. Or as one mother put it, they have the rest of their lives to become jaded. Let's let children be children while they are children.

Orenstein raises a final concern about the princess movement, which I think has validity and is worth considering in depth. Not every little girl can be "the fairest in the land" and look like Ariel or Sleeping Beauty. There is, therefore, an aspect to the princess fantasy that parents should recognize and respond to with wisdom and sensitivity. An overemphasis on physical attractiveness throughout childhood can create an expectation that some kids will never achieve. We'll offer some suggestions along that line momentarily, but in the meantime, let me just remind you that there is a downside to just about everything in life. Toys, books, cartoons, video games, and the Internet each have their uses and abuses. We could throw them all out like babies with the bathwater and try to shield our kids from everything that is not perfect.

The better approach, I believe, is to carefully scrutinize and select that which will be allowed into the lives of our children. Our job is to teach and interpret for them what they need to understand. They will learn far more directly from us than from storybook fantasies. The princess movement can be handled in that manner. Ultimately, mothers will have to decide whether or not to introduce their girls to this and other forms of make-believe. It is my belief that the good outweighs the bad in the princess movement, and it is certainly better than Bratz dolls or the adolescent world of Barbie.

Parents do need to be very aware of pressures that children face from the culture. The worship of beauty is so pervasive that it influences every aspect of childhood. It will continue to have an impact throughout life.

I have written about this subject since my early years as a psychologist, and it is still one of my greatest concerns for the well-being of children. I wrote about it in my book *Building Confidence in Your Child*, and I believe my counsel is still valid today.

> Very early in life, a child begins to learn the social importance of physical beauty. The values of society cannot be kept from little ears, and many adults do not even try to conceal their bias. [Every child can figure out] that the unattractive do not become "Miss America," nor do they become cheerleaders or movie stars.
>
> It is surprising just how effectively we teach our small children to accept the beauty cult. Indeed, we seem obsessed by this system of valuing human worth. For example, the approved fourth-grade reader adopted as a California state textbook at one time carried a fairy story about three little girls. Two of the girls were very beautiful, with lovely hair and facial features. Because of their beauty they were loved by the people and given kingdoms in which to rule. The third little girl was very unattractive. No one liked her because she was not pleasant to look at. The people would not let her have a kingdom of her own. She was very unhappy and sad. The story ended on such an encouraging note, however, because this little girl was given a kingdom with the animals. Isn't that a wonderful resolution? Her homeliness got her banished from the world of the elite, as it often does. Her physical deficiencies were described in considerable detail for the fourth graders, so that similar children in the classroom would be pointed out. It is a dull child who fails to notice that nature has created haves and have-nots, and every child in a class can tell who fits where.
>
> What a distorted system of values we propagate! What irreparable damage is done to a struggling child whose parents

do not intervene as allies. She can neither explain nor apologize. She can't even hide. Cruel voices follow her wherever she goes, whispering evil messages in her immature ears: "The other children don't like you." "See, I told you you'd fail." "You're different." "You're foolish." "They hate you." "You're worthless!" As time passes, the voices get louder and more urgent, until they obliterate all other sounds in an adolescent's mind.[9]

As a case in point, I'll share a letter that came to me recently from a teen girl who is struggling with this very issue.

Dear Dr. Dobson,

My name is Renee. I read your article called "True Beauty," and although I have had a very stable childhood and upbringing, I can relate to what you said. I have never been abused or anything, but I found comfort in your words. All people deal with something in their life. I have a very low self-image. I used to find that I could boost my appearance in finding the latest trend and covering my face with makeup. Although I believe that it is wrong to rely on things of this world, I also think that in using this way of hiding my true beauty, I hide my fear. I would never go one day, even if I was sick, without spending hours in front of the mirror perfecting my image. Then everything came crashing down when I had my makeup taken away. [I assume for medical reasons.] I know to most people this sounds pretty stupid, but I really had a hard time accepting this. I would sit at the mirror with red eyes, without makeup, for hours saying that I was an ugly, pathetic, stupid, and unworthy person. I truly believed that I hated myself. My parents and God helped me through that time. I believe the true battle was not about having my makeup taken away, but in realizing that I was, and am, a truly beautiful person in God's eyes. I think that some people need to hear about what I am sharing, because many parents and teens would not believe how many young women struggle with this. I'd love to hear what you all think of this. God bless.

Note that it was Renee's "parents and God" who helped her battle through her self-hatred. I plead with mothers and fathers to be there for your kids when the pressure is on. You hold the keys to their survival, and we must not be too busy to notice what is coming down. My parents were there for me during a similar crisis in my thirteenth year, and they ushered me into a world of broad sunlight. You can do the same for the children who desperately need your love and attention. Teach them skills that will give them a sense of identity; treat them with dignity and respect, even when they fail to earn it at times; choose your words very carefully during periods of greatest sensitivity; and help them make friends by opening your home and your heart to lost kids looking for a safe place. There are no magic answers, but there are *good* answers. Remember that this girl who is driving you crazy will someday be your best friend, if you handle her with care.

Renee and millions of her contemporaries are victims of a false set of values that measures personal worth by that which is temporal, dishonest, and tyrannical. The media and the entertainment industry are largely to blame for this destructive system. They laud images of bodily perfection, including "supermodels," "playmates," "babes," and "hunks." The net effect on children and teens is profound, not only in this country but around the world.

Now I will turn the coin over. Those who are blessed by great beauty often have struggles of their own. Consider the experience of one of the most attractive women in the world, the late Farrah Fawcett. She was drop-dead gorgeous even in high school and became a walking, talking Barbie doll. When she was a freshman in college and went to her first sorority pledge party, the fraternity brothers were invited to choose which particular girls they wanted to meet. Most of the female students were selected by no more than two or three guys. Not so for Farrah. The men wanting to talk to her were lined all the way around the block, including the quarterback of the football team.[10] Wearing a red bathing suit, she later posed for a calendar that sold more than 8 million copies and solidified her image as an international "sex kitten."[11]

Farrah had the qualities that most other girls apparently dreamed about (the guys were dreaming too), and yet we know now that she considered her beauty to be a curse. It made her feel uncomfortable because both men and women stared at her whenever she went out in public. She felt that people didn't take her seriously as a woman or as an actress.

She said during the height of her career, "You're always under pressure to look and feel and be good. How would you like to be photographed every day of your life?"[12]

As you may know, Farrah contracted cancer in 2006 and endured a slow, agonizing decline. She lost her legendary hair, her strength, and much of her beauty. Death came on June 25, 2009, at sixty-two years of age.[13] Millions of us who watched her career from beginning to end felt sadness for her as the ravages of time and a terrible illness took their toll. Alas, so very quickly it seemed, the angel next door was gone.

Is there a message here about our culture, which seems to worship youth and beauty? If so, should it be shared with your daughters? Without a doubt.

Consider another sad example from the life and death of a beauty queen. Her name was Anna Nicole Smith, and she was *Playboy*'s Playmate of the Year in 1993 and a model for Guess jeans. She fantasized about becoming the next Marilyn Monroe and was compared to sultry actress Jean Harlow. Anna Nicole married an eighty-nine-year-old Texas oil tycoon when she was twenty-six.[14] She died on February 8, 2007, after being found unconscious in her hotel room. The cause of death was a drug overdose from nine different types of medications.[15] In that regard, Anna achieved her goal of being like Marilyn. They both died alone after overdosing.

Writer Marc Gellman wrote an insightful and disturbing article about Anna Nicole, published a week after her death. As you will see, he describes graphically the tragedy of beautiful women who are routinely treated like "pieces of meat."

> What men consider beautiful about women changes over time. In 16th-century Antwerp, Peter Paul Rubens taught Dutch men to lust after pudgy brunettes. In 20th-century America, Hugh Hefner taught American men to lust after busty blondes, women just like Anna Nicole Smith. Any reflections on her death must first begin with deep sadness for yet another premature and needless death in our wounded world. Thirty-nine-year-old women should not die. We must also grieve for her infant daughter who, regardless of her possible fortune, is now consigned by fate to grow up without a mother—just as Anna Nicole had been forced by the same cruel fate to grow up without a father. Next we must force ourselves to remember that this front-page story is echoed by a thousand untold stories about unknown women who have died or been killed or driven to fatal addictions just because they were pretty. These women died because they were meat on the banquet table of predatory men. Their deaths must not be seen as merely tragic accidents, but as cautionary tales for us all, and particularly for men who are taught to see women as playthings and not as human beings made, as religious folk like me would say, in the image of God.
>
> Treating women, particularly pretty women, as meat is not a new social pathology or a new sin. It is as old as women

and men. . . . In the Bible the treating of women as meat is called harlotry. In Leviticus 19:29 we read this cautionary law: "Do not profane your daughter by making her a harlot, so that the land will not fall to harlotry and the land become full of lewdness." Read that and tell me you don't believe in prophecy!

Now the PC term for treating women as meat is "objectification." Whatever the label, the essence of this perversion of human dignity is unchanged over time. The idea that half of the human beings on planet earth only matter because of their physical appearance remains an outrageous assault on the human dignity of women.

Anna Nicole was stigmatized as poor white trash. However, it is a cruel illusion to believe that only poor, pretty women must become bimbos, strippers and gold diggers to get out of the trailer park. I see the bimbo-fication of young girls all the time in my affluent suburban synagogue. Sadly, some of the brightest adolescent girls around the age of 12 suddenly try to dumb themselves down so that they can attract a boyfriend who will not be scared off by their intelligence. I also see echoes of Anna Nicole in the successful twentysomethings and thirtysomethings, whose little black cocktail dresses are meant to both reveal their cleavage and conceal their desperation at the thought that pursuing a career means abandoning the pursuit of love and family. The feminist movement has won important victories for egalitarianism, but it has also surrendered women to predatory men who have taken women's newfound freedom as the perfect opportunity to surrender all sexual responsibility, respect and gallantry. One can rejoice at newfound freedoms without distorting their cost.

The problem with treating women as meat is that many of the solutions offered up are far worse than the problem. The Taliban had an easy and perverse solution, and that was to treat women as prisoners. Completely covering up the female form with a burqa and shutting women out of Afghani public and professional life is even worse than being forced to hear about the latest exploits of Paris, Lindsay and Britney. On the other hand, making the case that there is nothing wrong with women freely displaying their bodies and embracing their sexuality in any way they desire is equally perverse because it supports porn, which coarsens our culture, degrades women and led to the death of a woman whose infant daughter needs her now. We need to find a place between prudes and porn. The future of our culture and the dignity of both men and women depend upon us finding such a place now.

An important move in learning not to treat women as meat is to restore the sundered link between love and sex. Porn is not possible if sex is widely seen as a way to express love. If sex is nothing more than scratching an itch, it cannot be the physical consequence of love and trust. Love is never casual, and when sex becomes casual it cannot serve the needs of love. Some say that the best way to reestablish this link between love and sex is to teach that the only satisfying context for this linkage is marriage. I agree, but this need not be the first step in recovering a more modest culture. If men and women just decided to only have sex with people they deeply love and deeply trust, we as a culture would be miles down the right road.

In such a world Anna Nicole might still be alive.[16]

Marc Gellman has illuminated a monumental truth here: our hyper-sexualized culture has made harlots out of beautiful women, and we must protect our daughters from its influence where possible.

For my part, I have not intended to condemn Farrah Fawcett, Anna Nicole Smith, Marilyn Monroe, or any of the other legendary goddesses who have walked a lonely road toward fame and fortune. I feel sadness for them. Rather, I mean to say again that perceptions of human worth should not depend inordinately on physical attractiveness. Furthermore, as we have seen, those who are born with striking beauty might not be better off than those who are more ordinary. To be judged as acceptable or not acceptable based on one's physical attributes is harmful to everyone. Even boys are being hit by the ricochet today.

Before closing, I simply must share another true story about the wife of one of my colleagues. Kim Davis is, by her own admission, not endowed with the beauty she has craved. How she learned to cope with and overcome her self-loathing is both inspiring and instructive. Perhaps her experience will be helpful as you seek to protect your little Cinderella from a culture that is often brutal to both the haves and have-nots. This is her testimony:

Femininity Begins with Self-Respect

I grew up in a solid Christian home. My father was an evangelist who traveled extensively, holding revival meetings. Our entire family traveled with him for four years full time. We lived in a twenty-eight-foot motor home (two adults, four children, and a dog!). I recall my father always seeking a deeper relationship with God. As God shared things with him, he would in turn share them with the family. We were all very close, and each of us knew we were loved without question.

In spite of this godly upbringing, I struggled. From my earliest memory I was thoroughly convinced that I was ugly and unlovable. These feelings shaped many of my choices and behaviors as I was growing up.

My crisis moment came when I entered a conservative Christian college. I recall walking by the boys' dormitory the first day or two after I arrived, and I heard laughter. I immediately felt in my heart, *You see, even here they know who you are. You're laughable, Kim! Who would ever want you?*

The reality is that the guys in that dorm room that day had no idea I was even there. They were laughing about who knows what. But the enemy of our souls is mean and a liar. I was too wounded to recognize him for who he was, and I believed every word.

My mother and sister who had brought me to college were ready to make the four-hour drive back home. In those last moments together I broke down. I had never shown my mother blatant disrespect, but my wounded spirit had reached its breaking point. I yelled at her, "Why did you ever let me be born? I never should have been allowed to live!"

I think God gave my mother an extra abundance of grace that day. She looked at me, and after a moment's pause said, "Kim, I don't know what to do. I have told you your whole life how valued and precious you are. God is going to have to show you now—I can't."

Now that I am a mother of a child in college, I can't imagine the pain [my mother] felt that day as she and my sister pulled away and drove those hours home. She has since told me she spent much time praying.

I went to my dorm room and fell on my face before God. I was broken and wounded. I cried out to God asking Him the same questions I had asked of my mother: "Why, God? Why? Why would You let me be born when You knew what a disappointment I would be? I'm ugly and not worth anything!" The words flowed from my heart; I had been afraid my entire life to be so honest with God. I lay on the floor, facedown, for hours. The room became dark as the sun set. It was then that I heard, *Kim, you are beautifully and wonderfully made.*

"No, I can't be," I responded.

He said without words, *I knit you in your mother's womb. I knew your name. I loved you and you were mine.*

God was so patient with me. He quietly, gently spoke my name, brought to mind Scripture as if He had written it just for me. My spirit began to quiet, and His spirit fell on that room in a beautiful way. God began healing me.

I truly believed I was unlovely, unlovable, and unworthy. Now I know what a lie that was. This is why I am such an advocate for girls to recognize their worth. If respect for ourselves doesn't take root in the heart, we can never realize the full potential of who God created us to be, and we can never really respect others. The more I see myself as God sees me, the more I can see others as God sees them. I've taught in schools off and on since 1984. Through the years I have seen a decline in the behavior of young ladies. My heart has been heavy for them as I see such wounds and pain. Seeing in them the same struggles I had experienced, I began to seek ways to address some of them.

While at a teachers' conference, I saw a rhinestone pin shaped like a crown. I immediately thought of my middle school students who didn't value themselves, who didn't know how to be ladies or respect themselves. I purchased the pin, knowing that the girls would be drawn to the "glitz."

The next day at school I wore it, and sure enough, the girls asked me about it. It was the invitation I was looking for. I began by stating in an offhanded way that it reminds me that if I want to be a princess, I need to act like one and expect to be treated like one. I was amazed by the response. The concept of being so highly valued was foreign. It became the focus of our girls' class (I taught in a single-gender classroom).

These girls had no idea that they could expect to be treated like ladies, let alone act like one.

I have found that many of the girls I teach:

- are being raised by working or single mothers
- are being raised by parents who were themselves raised without a moral compass necessary for healthy behavior
- have no positive male influence in their lives

While many young ladies who come out of homes like these are strong and healthy individuals, I saw more pain and damage than anything else. The girls who didn't have the moral guidance of an involved parent habitually made poor choices. By God's grace, I found that engaging these young ladies helped many of them to realize they were worth more than they knew, and they began expecting others to treat them with healthy respect. And it goes way beyond expecting boys to be gentlemen. With these girls it was about respecting themselves, accepting who they were, and coming to the point of celebrating who they were created to be.

What started with a crown-shaped pin became a yearlong focus on femininity. I had many conversations with the girls as they brought up struggles they experienced that destroyed their self-respect. I've seen lives changed and have even prayed with students (in a public school, no less) as a result of this focus. Girls want to know who they are! They want to be accepted and loved. That's why so many of them make the poor choices that they do. I believe we women have been remiss in giving that guidance, thus the havoc that has been wreaked in our girls. These girls are too precious to lose.

Thank you, Kim, for this beautiful and candid message and for offering advice that parents can use. I appreciate your allowing me to share it with my readers.

I am reminded of a Scripture that places our society's attitudes toward women into proper perspective. It reads, "Charm is deceptive, and beauty is fleeting; but a woman who fears the LORD is to be praised" (Proverbs 31:30). Selling that concept to a girl who hates herself might be a tough assignment, but the case can and should be made nonetheless.

I am not the only writer to decry this false system of values, of course. I am pleased to report that since 2004, there has been an initiative called

"The Real Truth about Beauty: A Global Report."[17] Its purpose is to change the way women and children are perceived. It is sponsored by Unilever's Dove beauty brand, which reported that more than two-thirds of women around the world believe "the media and advertising set an unrealistic standard of beauty that most women can't ever achieve."[18] Their research revealed that only 13 percent of women were very satisfied with their body weight and shape. Only 2 percent considered themselves to be beautiful, and more than half said their bodies disgusted them.[19] This is the world in which your daughters are growing up!

Dr. Nancy Etcoff, a professor at Harvard University and director of the Program in Aesthetics and Well Being at the Massachusetts General Hospital Department of Psychiatry, said this about women and beauty: "When only a minority of women is satisfied with their body weight and shape in a society captivated by diet and makeover programs, it is time for a change."[20]

Yes, it is! That led Dove to launch the Campaign for Real Beauty in 2005, which included a national advertising program. The senior vice president, Silvia Lagnado, said:

> By questioning the accepted definition of beauty, we hope to help women change the way they perceive their bodies and encourage them to feel beautiful every day.[21]

Let's get that message across to our own daughters.

RELATED QUESTIONS AND ANSWERS

Question: You said that girls and women have a lot of influence on men and that they hold the keys to masculine behavior. Sometimes I find that difficult to believe. Can you elaborate on why it works and how I can make use of it as I try to raise my own daughter to be a lady?

Answer: That statement is not always true, of course, but women do have considerable influence on men when the fit is right and the attraction is strong. Typically, a man needs a woman more than she needs him. In fact, she can make or break him. This is why marriage is so important in a culture, because it serves to harness masculine aggressiveness for the benefit of the family. Though there are many exceptions in individual cases, single men are more inclined to move from job to job, drink too much, drive too fast, spend money unwisely, and be sexually irresponsible. Commitment to a woman not only channels a man's energy and passions, it also helps to produce a more healthy society. This male-female connectedness is, I think, part of a divine plan.

God has given women this powerful influence, and they should use it, not to manipulate or control men, but to nudge them in the direction of responsibility, commitment, and morality. A man does not want to be nagged, intimidated, or belittled, and he will dig in his heels if anyone tries it. To the contrary, what he wants and needs is respect, admiration, and appreciation. When a woman genuinely feels that way about him and is proud to stand beside him, he gains confidence and is empowered to succeed in a highly competitive world. That is exactly what my wife did for me early in our marriage when I was still in graduate school. She believed in me and told me she couldn't wait to see what God would do with the talent He had given to me. She also instilled that respect for me in our two children.

It is a wise woman who understands how a man is constructed emotionally and encourages him to perform the four critical roles for which he was designed. These roles are to provide for, to protect, to lead, and to give spiritual direction for his family. When he is comfortable in those responsibilities, it affects how he responds to his wife. It makes him want to give her what she needs from him, notably security, kindness, sensitivity, and romantic love. She also wants him to remember their first date, their anniversary, her birthday, and the things that please her most. It is a smart man who does.

Here's a silly little story from my childhood that will illustrate the influence that a woman (in this case, a girl) holds. Because I was endowed with an abundance of testosterone as a boy, I had a habit of taking risks and doing dumb things. I once fell out of a tree trying to swing down from a limb like Tarzan. Unfortunately, I didn't learn much from the experience. When I was fourteen years old, my mother told me to pick all the cherries off the tree in our backyard. Every limb was brimming with fruit, so I set to work stripping it. When I had picked the low-hanging cherries, I set up a six-foot ladder and began working my way upward. Finally, I stood on the very top rung and leaned out to harvest the center of the tree. Anybody with an ounce of sense would have recognized what was about to happen, but it never occurred to me.

At that moment of destiny, the prettiest girl in my school happened to be walking by. Her name was Laurie, and she lived in my neighborhood. I saw her coming, of course, and was delighted when she stopped to watch. Then she said very sweetly, "You had better be careful, or you will fall." Just to have that gorgeous creature standing there worrying about my safety made my heart skip a beat.

I said, "I'll be fine." I then wiggled the lower half of my body to show her that I was fearless and in control. High-octane testosterone was obviously talking to me. That is when my legs suddenly went to the left and the rest of me went to the right. For the second time in my life, all the air was knocked out of the state of Oklahoma. (The first was at the climax of the Tarzan episode.) Laurie ran to get my mother, and the two of them leaned over me. I was gasping and groaning and wanting to die. It was horrible.

Don't try to tell me that girls can't affect a guy's behavior for better or worse. Of *course* they can. Laurie knocked me off my ladder just by showing a bit of concern for me. I hope mothers will teach this principle to their daughters and urge them not to squander their powerful influence. Someday it will be put to better use.

Question: You mentioned that girls and boys often approach organized sports from entirely different directions. Here's our experience: last year, we signed up our eight-year-old daughter, Marilyn, for a soccer team. Our intent was for her to get some good exercise and fresh air, meet other kids, and just have fun!

She didn't know anything about the sport, but the league was a beginner level and she was on the team with both boys and girls her age. However, many of the boys had already had about three years of experience playing soccer! Putting them together turned out not to be a great idea.

In the first game, Marilyn scored. Unfortunately, she kicked the ball into her own team's goal! The boys gave her a terrible time for doing that. In fact, one of the boys ended up going to Marilyn's school the next year, and the first thing he said to her was, "You kicked the ball in the wrong goal last year!" How embarrassing.

Marilyn had another difficult moment during that first game. She saw a little boy get cleated in the face. It scared her badly. She did everything possible to stay away from the ball for the rest of the season!

I am wondering if things would have been different if they had leagues just for girls and leagues just for boys. After Marilyn participated in the theatrical performance of *Annie* this year, she said, "Mommy, soccer wasn't my thing, but I really like being onstage." We encouraged her to try different things and then figure out what she likes and doesn't like.

She still talks about kicking the ball into the wrong goal. Do you think girls and boys should play on the same teams?

Answer: Generally speaking, I don't think coed sports are a good idea, and certainly not after puberty. Admittedly, my view on that subject is controversial, and many of my readers will disagree. I have been influenced greatly on this matter by sociologist George Gilder, in his classic book *Men and Marriage*. His opposition to coed sports is based on what he believes is best for girls, but especially what the presence of girls does to slow-maturing boys. He says:

> Sports are possibly the single most important male rite in modern society.
>
> Whatever their detractors may say, sports embody for men a moral universe. On the team, the group learns to cooperate, learns the importance of loyalty, struggle, toughness, and self-sacrifice in pursuing a noble ideal. At

a period in their lives when hormones of aggression are pouring through their bodies in unprecedented streams, boys learn that aggressiveness must be disciplined and regulated before it can be used in society. They learn the indispensable sensation of competition in solidarity.

The entrance of a large number of teenage girls, at a time in high school and junior high when they tend to be larger than boys, would be disastrous for all the slow developers. Leaders in Outward Bound physical programs for [inner-city] children, for example, find that the best athletes perform as well—if in a different spirit—with females present. The smaller, shyer, and less developed boys, however, are completely daunted by the girls and refuse to make a resolute effort. In addition, the lessons of group morality are lost. The successful boys, those who work with and encourage the others in all-male groups, simply show off for the females in mixed assemblages. Nor do the girls benefit. Some of them do quite well, but their performances seem directed more toward the boys than to the real values of the undertaking.

In joint athletics, girls subvert the masculinity of the weaker or slow-developing boys without gaining significant athletic reward themselves. The girls who could actually play on an integrated high-school team would be exceedingly rare. But the girls, nonetheless, would disrupt and deform the most precious rituals of young boys.[1]

I agree with Gilder at this point, especially as it relates to boys and girls in puberty and beyond. As for enrolling children in coed sports, that is something parents will have to decide for a particular individual. I would be inclined not to do it even in childhood because of the dramatic differences between the sexes. Marilyn's unsuccessful experience is common.

Question: I have a three-year-old boy and an infant girl, and they are both precious to me. I want the very best for them, which is the highest priority at this stage of my life. My husband feels the same way. However, I also have an exciting job, and I've always intended to return to it as soon as possible after the birth of my second baby. Now, after learning of your comments about mother-child attachment, I'm uncertain about what to do. Everyone is telling me that there are some very good child care centers in my area and that it

would actually be advantageous to my kids to be placed there while I am at work. How do you feel about that?

Answer: Many couples have struggled with that issue since the arrival of their children. As I acknowledged in chapter 7, some families feel they don't have a choice, given their compelling financial pressures. I understand their dilemma. But for those who *do* have options, there is little doubt about what is in the best interest of their children, as I see it. I can say categorically that kids do better physically, emotionally, and intellectually when their parents care for them at home. That is the conclusion drawn from numerous scientific studies, including the most extensive investigation to date. It was a multimillion-dollar long-term study conducted by the U.S. government through the National Institute of Child Health and Human Development (NICHD). It stands today as a landmark study.

Researchers at NICHD demonstrated conclusively that children placed in day care facilities for an average of thirty hours per week, compared with those spending ten hours per week or less, were much more likely to display aggressive behavior, including arguing, cruelty, fighting, bullying, temper tantrums, emotional outbursts, demands for attention, classroom disruptions, and related misbehavior. These kids were still affected by the day care experience at six years of age.[2]

Jay Belsky was one of the collaborating investigators in the NICHD study beginning in 1991. He is also director of the Institute for the Study of Children, Families and Social Issues, and is highly regarded in his field. Belsky said this about the findings:

> Contrary to the expectations (and desires) of many in the field, the NICHD study shows that the more time children spend in day care arrangements before they are 4 1/2 years old the more aggression, disobedience and conflict with adults they manifest at 54 months of age and in kindergarten. These patterns remain even after taking into account multiple features of children's families, as well as the quality and type of day care that children experienced. . . .
>
> Not that you'd know any of this from reading the NICHD's press release or listening to many of the commentators. The results, after all, are not politically popular: many have made their careers representing good child care as a sort of social cure-all. Because child care is here to stay, the argument goes, only the improvement of its quality is

important. Anyone highlighting disconcerting evidence is simply against child care. And a weatherman reporting rain is against sunshine.

One must wonder why, after the government invested tens of millions of dollars, so many are bending over backward to minimize the results. This is particularly astonishing in light of the fact that we are talking about early experience had by tens of thousands of children. It's practically the norm these days for American children to start nonmaternal care in the first year of life, often for more than 20-30 hours per week. They continue at similar levels until they enter school.

The recent results, however disconcerting, are consistent with others that have been reported over the years in the study. Published evidence has shown that more time in care, irrespective of its quality, predicts more problem behavior among two-year-olds, less sensitive maternal behavior when children are 6, 15, 24, and 36 months of age; and lower rates of secure attachment to mother when children are 15 and 36 months of age if their mothers' parenting is relatively insensitive.[3]

Dr. Burton White is another expert on child development whose opinion I respect. He is the former director of the Harvard Preschool Project and a leading authority on the first three years of life. He also commented on the child care issue, as follows:

After more than thirty years of research on how children develop well, I would not think of putting an infant or toddler of my own into any substitute care program on a full-time basis, especially a center-based program. . . .

Unless you have a very good reason . . . I urge you not to delegate the primary child-rearing task to anyone else during your child's first three years of life. . . . Babies form their first human attachment only once. Babies begin to learn language only once. . . . The outcomes of these processes play a major role in shaping the future of each new child.[4]

Why should we be surprised to learn of the serious problems associated with institutionalized child care? It is common sense to recognize that governments can't pay child care workers enough to do what mothers do for free. A mom and dad are likely to be passionately committed to their own children, and no one else will care for them as well. It is also obvious that the individual attention and verbal interaction between parents and children is clearly superior to that provided by paid employees handling large numbers of children. This is a critical issue, because intellectual competence is most influenced by what is called live language between a mother and her child. There is simply no comparison between the quality of mother care and the custodial care available in group situations.

I am convinced that Dr. White, Dr. Belsky, and other authorities in the field of child development are correct in their views, and I share their conclusions emphatically.

So to answer your question, I recommend that you care for your children at home if possible, at least while they are in the preschool years. Nevertheless, this is a decision you and your husband will have to make. If you do return to full-time employment, I suggest that you do your best to find a close family member, perhaps a grandmother, a sister, a trusted friend, another mother, or a small private consortium to provide for your children during the day. Ideally, that key person should be someone the kids know and love. That caregiver should also be a constant in their lives. Children are creatures of habit, and they do not cope well with dramatic change. The more consistency there is in their daily routine, the less stress there will be for the youngsters—and for you.

Question: You referred to various problems associated with child care facilities. Are there any others we should be aware of?

Answer: Yes, there are additional concerns that are deeply troubling. The most serious among them is the spread of infectious diseases. Brian Robertson, in a book titled *Day Care Deception*, addressed that issue head-on. His data are older now, but the findings are still highly relevant:

> The drastically elevated incidence of infectious diseases among day care children is hardly a secret among pediatricians and epidemiologists. The problem surfaced in dramatic form a decade ago when *Pediatric Annals* devoted a special issue to day care–related diseases, headlining their lead editorial, "Day Care, Day Care: Mayday! Mayday!" The statistics are truly shocking. According to one estimate published by the American Academy of Family Physicians, children in day care are eighteen times more likely

to become ill than other children; at any one time, 16 percent of those attending day care are likely to be sick. (Of those sick children, 82 percent continue to attend day care in spite of their illness.) Day care children are anywhere between three and four-and-a-half times more likely to be hospitalized than those raised at home. One study estimated that "children in day care are at a 50 to 100 percent increased risk for contracting [certain] fatal and maiming diseases for each year in day care."[5]

The newer findings regarding the detrimental effects of day care on behavior and the mother-child bond are merely the latest confirmation of warnings from numerous child development experts over the last forty years—warnings that have been largely suppressed by the reigning day care establishment of researchers, journalists, and lobbyists. The truth is, these experts—particularly those who specialize in the field of "infant attachment"—found the evidence against day care for young children conclusive long ago.

I could say more, but it all comes down to the vulnerability and sensitivity of very young children. They need the very best care we can give them as they get their start in life. Though research has not been as definitive about child care during the remainder of childhood, I personally believe they should be cared for at home for as long as possible. Even teens benefit from having a mom there when they get home from school. But that is another question.

Question: I wonder if you understand how difficult it is for me to hear you say that. I am a single mother, and I have to work outside the home to feed my little family. I'm doing the best I can to raise my three kids by myself.

Answer: I *do* understand because I have dealt with many single parents such as yourself who struggle day by day. That is why I have said the task of raising children alone is "the toughest job in the universe." My evaluation of group-oriented child care does not represent insensitivity toward those who must utilize formalized programs. For many years, I have been an advocate for single parents who are in desperate need of compassionate assistance from intact families and others who can lend a helping hand. It is a wonderful thing, for example, when fathers are willing to invite fatherless kids to accompany their sons on fishing trips and sporting events. Too often, we leave single moms to flounder during those early child-rearing years.

I extend my best regards and prayers to you. As you said, you are doing the best you can to cope with circumstances as they are. I applaud you for that. The last thing I want to do is add to your burden, and if I sounded insensitive in my criticism of child care programs, please forgive me. I was addressing my concerns to those who have a choice about caring for their kids and want to know the truth.

Question: My daughter has a friend who has a single dad. They want to have a sleepover at her house. My daughter is eleven years old. I would like to know if it would be appropriate to let her go to the sleepover. I am more than willing to let them have a sleepover at my house anytime.

Answer: Except on occasions when you are sure that your child will be safe, I would not suggest that you allow your daughter—or your son—to spend the night in a home where there is not a mother you trust. The father in that situation may be a fine man, but he is not the only reason for caution. Remember that kids sometimes molest younger kids, as do older brothers and their friends. This is why I believe that the day for sleepovers has passed. There is just too much at stake to put children at risk in this way.

Sadly, the world has changed in the last few decades, and it is no longer a safe place for children. Pedophiles and child molesters are more pervasive than ever. That is why parents must be diligent to protect their kids every hour of the day and night. Some little tykes have actually been abducted from their bedrooms while their parents were in the house. The name of Polly Klaas comes to mind, the twelve-year-old girl who was assaulted and murdered after being taken from her home during a slumber party in 1993.[6]

Until you have dealt with little victims as I have and seen the pain in their eyes, you might not fully appreciate the devastation inflicted by molestation. It casts a long shadow on everything that follows, including future marital relationships. Therefore, parents have to think the unthinkable in every situation. The threat can come from anywhere—including neighbors, uncles, stepfathers, grandfathers, Sunday school teachers, coaches, music instructors, Scout leaders, and babysitters. Even public bathrooms can be dangerous today.

The state of Colorado, in a misguided effort to end what the legislators called discrimination, made it legal for cross-dressing men and homosexuals to use women's restrooms.[7] Is that ridiculous or what? A little girl or a single woman can be using the facilities when, without warning, a man comes in unannounced. Can you imagine the terror and embarrassment a child could experience in that situation? Sadly, few people in Colorado have objected to the ridiculous law.

Now, here is the ultimate challenge. You as a parent have to figure out how to shield your kids from danger without overprotecting them or making them fearful. That is called being between a rock and a hard place. You can begin by teaching your kids the difference between a "good touch" and a "bad touch," urging them to never talk to strangers, and telling them to scream when approached, etc. At the same time, however, you must be careful not to make them feel that *you* are fearful or that their loved ones and teachers are trying to hurt them. Shepherding them between these two harmful alternatives requires great skill and wisdom.

You should know that pedophiles are usually adept at drawing children into their clutches. They tend to gravitate toward malls, pizza restaurants, amusement parks, and even chat rooms where unsupervised boys and girls hang out. They can spot a kid who is lonely in a matter of minutes, and they offer them the "love" and attention they crave. Once these creeps have established a relationship with them, the abuse is easy and lasts an average of seven years. Amazingly, the children usually don't tell anyone about the abuse out of fear and intimidation. Some pedophiles become so masterful at this technique that they abuse, on average, 280 children in a lifetime.[8]

Don't let your boy or girl be one of them! Protect them, and meet the needs that make them vulnerable!

Question: What about leaving your kids with babysitters? Is that wise?

Answer: I think it is relatively safe to leave children with mature adolescent girls, although they should be told they cannot invite their boyfriends to come over. I would not recommend leaving kids of either sex with teenage boys since there is so much going on sexually within males at that age. Although there might be no problem most of the time, you must do all that you can to make sure that the devastation of child abuse does not occur even once in your daughter's entire childhood.

Question: My husband works in law enforcement and has several days off work in a row. I work full time Monday through Friday. Therefore, it is my husband who volunteers in our kids' classrooms. A little girl wants to come to our house for a sleepover with my daughter during a time when only my daughter and my husband will be home. The mom of the other girl does not have an issue with it. However, I do not think this is appropriate. What do you think?

Answer: The motives of your husband are probably entirely honorable. But once again, I think it would not be wise to allow the little girl to sleep over. The potential for disaster, though unlikely, is just too great. I would always err on the side of caution, not only protecting the child, but also preventing any damage to your husband's reputation. Perhaps I am being overprotective here, but it is much better to be safe than sorry.

Question: Why has pedophilia become such a serious problem? Are there really more cases of child sexual abuse now than in the past, or is the reporting mechanism just better?

Answer: Reporting systems are better, I'm sure, but the incidence of molestation has increased exponentially. It has resulted primarily from the proliferation of obscenity on the Internet, including illegal child pornography. Pedophiles try to obtain DVDs or photographs of nude children, taken while they are being assaulted if possible. Those images can then be sold or traded to other child molesters.

I am well acquainted with this tragedy because of my service on the Attorney General's Commission on Pornography from 1985 to 1986. During that time, I witnessed materials from the FBI that I will never be able to forget, including photographs of an eight-year-old boy taken while he was being murdered. I can't get those images out of my mind. During that same meeting, a representative from the American Civil Liberties Union (ACLU), Barry Lynn, who is now executive director of Americans United for Separation of Church and State, told the commission it was the position of the ACLU that child pornography should not be produced, but once it exists, there should be no restriction on its sale or distribution.[9]

If the ACLU had had its wretched way, a child who was being horribly molested under the watchful eye of a camera could do nothing to stop those images from being sold on the open market for the rest of his or her life. The most terrible experience of a child's lifetime would become a pornographer's gold mine. The commissioners were aghast at this testimony.

You must understand this: obscenity is highly addictive and progressive in nature. What begins as an attraction to soft-core porn gradually changes the individual who lusts over it, leading to ever harder and more perverse obsessions. Thus, porn addicts are transformed from having what might be called "normal" sexuality to a passion for increasingly perverse material, such as heterosexual and homosexual violence, the abuse of women, bestiality, necrophilia (sex with the dead), and very commonly today, child pornography. This is where the perversions often originate. It is what led serial killer Ted Bundy, whom I interviewed seventeen hours before his execution in the Florida State Penitentiary, to murder more than thirty women and girls. The last victim before his arrest and conviction was a twelve-year-old girl whom he killed and left in a pigsty.[10]

Though the media rarely reveals the connection, pornography is almost always involved in cases of abduction and murder of boys and girls. This is why these horrendous crimes are occurring more commonly today. When the facts are known, obscene materials are typically found in the houses or garages of the perpetrators. What this means is that moms and dads must be eternally vigilant in protecting their kids. Let me say it one more time. I recommend that you take *no* unnecessary chances, whether during sleepovers, in the mall, in public restrooms, in neighbors' houses, or on the way home from school.

Question: My daughter is very much a "people pleaser." What should I do about it?

Answer: My goodness! What a delightful problem to have. I see no need to "do anything" about it. Your daughter obviously came equipped from birth with a compliant temperament. Usually, people pleasers reflect a sensitivity to and a need for approval from others. Throughout childhood, these kids will be called "sweet" by adults, who are drawn to their pleasant personalities. I remember a song from the movie *Funny Girl*, which features Barbra Streisand singing, "People who need people are the luckiest people in the world."[11] I think the lyricist was rather accurate.

I would, however, offer two cautions. The first is that people who need people can be more easily hurt. Whereas the tough-minded youngster is ready to defend herself against insult or attack, the people pleaser is looking hopefully for affirmation. You as a parent should be aware of that vulnerability as you shepherd that child toward adulthood.

The second "downside" to the emotional apparatus of people pleasers is that they sometimes go through a period of mild rebellion during their late teens or early twenties. Whereas a strong-willed child frequently gets in the face of her parent, a compliant child's late stubbornness shows up in less aggressive ways. For example, eating disorders sometimes occur among mild-mannered "good little girls" who wouldn't have thought of challenging their authoritative fathers. Instead, they express their individuality in the food they consume or don't consume, and they can resist every effort by others to make them eat. Another common reaction of people pleasers is seen in a rejection of the family's faith. Typically, but not always, they come back to it.

For now, I would recommend that you accept the individual personality of your little girl just the way God made her, and enjoy every minute of her childhood.

❀ ❀ ❀

We'll turn our attention now to the children whose temperaments are at the other end of the continuum. I am referring to the kids who challenge and test their parents many times a day. They are just as precious in their own way and may even turn out to be more successful in adult life. They are, however, tougher to handle almost from the beginning. To give you the flavor of life with a strong-willed child, I will share a series of questions that have been submitted to me by frustrated parents. Though their inquiries take various forms, they all focus on the discipline of "testy" children, as follows:

Question: My daughter is six, and lately she has been a little terror. We can be watching a movie and she will turn off the television and start pitching a fit out of nowhere. She will spit on the floor and curse like a sailor. She will be well behaved and then randomly do something she knows is wrong. She recently threw a ball and broke some valuable things just because she wanted to. I really don't know what has gotten into her. She gets a lot of attention—maybe too much—but she has no reason to act this way. I try not to lose my temper, but what can I do when I have a six-year-old screaming in my face? The hand spankings don't faze her anymore. Please help.

Question: My daughter will be four in June and is a very strong-willed child. I am currently in the fifth month of pregnancy with my second child. Call it a coincidence, but ever since I started showing, my three-year-old has been having major behavior issues at home and in preschool. Everything is a challenge, from getting dressed in the morning to listening to authority figures. She does not want to participate in group activities at school and seems to be distancing herself from showing signs of affection to family members. Do you think this type of behavior is directly related to the new baby or could this be a stage?

Question: My twenty-month-old daughter will not go to sleep without a fight. My wife is pregnant with our second child, and I am wondering what to do.

Question: My son and daughter-in-law are having a lot of problems with their four-year-old daughter, who screams a lot and hits them. They are at their wit's end and don't know what to do. What advice do you have for them?

Question: I have a five-year-old daughter who is defiant to her mother but obedient to me, her father. How can we teach her to respect both of us?

I could provide individual answers to each of these questions, and probably should do so, because the circumstances described involve children of varying ages. A twenty-month-old toddler not wanting to go to sleep should be handled very differently from a six-year-old girl who is pitching fits and spitting on the floor. Nevertheless, I will not take the time to provide specific suggestions because that work has already been done. A couple of my earlier books deal with the management of children and address these kinds of issues. They are *The New Dare to Discipline* and *The New Strong-Willed Child*. Instead of reinventing the wheel, I will quote a section from that second book, in which I discuss the nature of tough-as-nails children and then offer some advice for parents. Perhaps I can at least take a moment to point harassed moms and dads in the right direction.

> It is obvious that children are aware of the contest of wills between generations, which can become something of a game. Lisa Whelchel, former child actress on the television sitcom *The Facts of Life*, described a funny encounter with her four-year-old boy, Tucker. She related the story in her excellent book, *Creative Correction*. Lisa and her husband were going out to dinner and left the children with a babysitter. As they were standing at the door, she said to her son, "I really want you to do your best to obey the babysitter tonight."
>
> Tucker immediately replied, "Well, Mom, I just don't know if I can do that."
>
> "Why not?" she asked.
>
> With a straight face, he answered, "There's so much foolishness built up in my heart, I don't think there is any room for goodness and wisdom."
>
> "Well," Lisa said, "maybe we need to step into the bathroom and drive that foolishness out."
>
> With that, Tucker replied, "W-wait a minute. I feel the foolishness going away all by itself—the goodness is coming in right now!"
>
> Lisa's encounter with her son did not represent a serious challenge to her authority and should have been (and, in fact, was) responded to with a smile. But when a real donnybrook occurs between generations, it is extremely important for the parents to "win." Why? A child who behaves in ways that are disrespectful or harmful to himself or others often has a hidden motive. Whether he recognizes it or not, he is usually seeking to verify the existence and stability of the boundaries.
>
> This testing has much the same function as a police

officer in years past who turned doorknobs at places of business after dark. Though he tried to open the doors, he hoped they were locked and secure. Likewise, a child who defies the leadership of his parents is reassured when they remain confident and firm under fire. It creates a sense of security for a kid who lives in a structured environment in which the rights of other people (and his own) are protected by well-defined limits.

With that said, let's hurry along now to the how-tos of shaping a child's will. I've boiled this complex topic down to six straightforward guidelines that I hope will be helpful, the first of which is most important. . . .

First: Begin Teaching Respect for Authority While Children Are Very Young

The most urgent advice I can give to the parents of an assertive, independent child is to establish their positions as strong but loving leaders when Junior and Missy are in the preschool years. This is the first step toward helping them learn to control their powerful impulses. Alas, there is no time to lose. As we have seen, a naturally defiant youngster is in a high-risk category for antisocial behavior later in life. She is more likely to challenge her teachers in school and question the values she has been taught. Her temperament leads her to oppose anyone who tries to tell her what to do. Fortunately, this outcome is not inevitable, because the complexities of the human personality make it impossible to predict behavior with complete accuracy. But the probabilities lie in that direction. Thus, I will repeat my most urgent advice to parents: that they begin shaping the will of the particularly aggressive child very early in life. (Notice that I did not say to crush his will or to destroy it or to snuff it out, but to rein it in for his own good.) But how is that accomplished?

Well, first let me tell you how *not* to approach that objective. Harshness, gruffness, and sternness are not effective in shaping a child's will. Likewise, constant whacking and threatening and criticizing are destructive and counterproductive. A parent who is mean and angry most of the time is creating resentment that will be stored and come roaring into the relationship during adolescence or beyond. Therefore, every opportunity should be taken to keep the tenor of the home pleasant, fun, and accepting. At the same time, however, parents should display confident firmness in their demeanor. You, Mom and Dad, are the boss. You are in charge. If you believe it, the tougher child will accept it also. Unfortunately, many mothers today are tentative and insecure in approaching their young children. If you watch them with their little boys and girls in supermarkets or airports, you will see these frustrated and angry moms who are totally confused about how to handle a given misbehavior. Temper tantrums throw them for a loop, as though they never expected them. Actually, they have been coming on for some time.

Second: Define the Boundaries before They Are Enforced

Preceding any disciplinary event is the necessity of establishing reasonable expectations and boundaries for the child. She should know what is and is not acceptable behavior before she is held responsible for it. This precondition will eliminate the sense of injustice that a youngster feels when she is punished or scolded for violating a vague or unidentified rule.

Third: Distinguish between Willful Defiance and Childish Irresponsibility

[There is a] distinction between what I would call childish irresponsibility and "willful defiance." There is a world of difference between the two. Understanding the distinction will be useful in knowing how to interpret the meaning of a behavior and how to respond to it appropriately. Let me explain.

Suppose little David is acting silly in the living room and falls into a table, breaking several expensive china cups and other trinkets. Or suppose Ashley loses her bicycle or leaves her mother's coffeepot out in the rain. Perhaps four-year-old Brooke reaches for something on her brother's plate and catches his glass of milk with her elbow, baptizing the baby and making a frightful mess on the floor. As frustrating as these occurrences are, they represent acts of childish irresponsibility that have little meaning in the long-term scheme of things. As we all know, children will regularly spill things, lose things, break things, forget things, and mess up things. That's the way kids are made. These behaviors represent the mechanism by which children are protected from adult-level cares and burdens. When accidents happen, patience and tolerance are the order of the day. If the foolishness was particularly pronounced for the age and maturity of the individual, Mom or Dad might want to have the youngster help with the cleanup or even work to pay for the loss. Otherwise, I think the event should be ignored. It goes with the territory, as they say.

There is another category of behavior, however, that is strikingly different. It occurs when a child defies the authority of the parent in a blatant manner. She may shout "I will not!" or "You shut up!" or "You can't make me." It may happen when Junior grabs a handful of candy bars at the checkout and refuses to give them back, or when he throws a violent temper tantrum in order to get his way. These behaviors represent a willful, haughty spirit and a determination to disobey. Something very different is going on in those moments. You have drawn a line in the dirt, and the child has deliberately flopped his bony little toe across it. You're both asking, *Who is going to win? Who has the most courage? Who is in charge here?* If you do not conclusively answer these questions for your strong-willed children, your child will precipitate other battles designed to ask them again and again. That's why you must be prepared to respond immediately to this kind of stiff-necked rebellion. It is what Susanna Wesley meant when she wrote, "Some [misbehavior] should be overlooked and taken no notice of [referring to childish irresponsibility], and others mildly reproved. But no willful transgressions ought ever to be forgiven children without chastisement, more or less, as the nature and circumstances of the offense shall require." Susanna arrived at this understanding 250 years before I came along. She learned it from the nineteen kids who called her Mama. . . .

Fourth: Reassure and Teach After the Confrontation Is Over

After a time of conflict during which the parent has demonstrated his right to lead (particularly if it resulted in tears for the child), the youngster between two and seven (or older) will probably want to be loved and reassured. By all means, open your arms and let him come! Hold him close and tell him of your love. Rock him gently and let him know again why he was punished and how he can avoid the trouble next time. This is a teachable moment, when the objective of your discipline can be explained. Such a conversation is difficult or impossible to achieve when a rebellious, stiff-necked little child is clenching her fist and taking you on. But after a confrontation has occurred— especially if it involved tears—the child usually wants to hug you and get reassurance that you really care for her. By all means, open your arms and let her snuggle to your breast. And for the Christian family, it is extremely important to pray with the child at that time, admitting to God that we have all sinned and no one is perfect. Divine forgiveness is a marvelous experience, even for a very young child.

Fifth: Avoid Impossible Demands
Be absolutely sure that your child is capable of delivering what you require. Never punish him for wetting the bed involuntarily or for not becoming potty trained by one year of age or for doing poorly in school when he is incapable of academic success. These impossible demands put the child in an irresolvable conflict: there is no way out. That condition brings unnecessary risks to the human emotional apparatus. Besides that, it is simply unjust.

Sixth: Let Love Be Your Guide!
A relationship that is characterized by genuine love and affection is likely to be a healthy one, even though some parental mistakes and errors are inevitable.

These six steps should . . . form the foundation for healthy parent-child relationships.[12]

Once again, this brief synopsis provides only a broad outline of a much more detailed discussion of discipline found in my earlier books. Those who need more information can find additional suggestions there.

THE RIVER OF CULTURE

WHETHER YOU HAVE cuddly little preschool girls who are toddling around your house or budding young adults about to leave the nest, it is very important to understand how the culture is influencing their developing hearts and minds. We should never underestimate its force, which is like a powerful river that carries everything downstream with it. You can and must help your youngsters avoid being swept by the current into unknown waters. Protecting them from its ravages is far easier when they are young, of course—it becomes increasingly more difficult with the passage of time. That is why a primary goal of parenting should be to introduce your children to moral and spiritual values during the early years. These underpinnings will help keep them afloat when the floodwaters come in the spring.

Let's talk about that challenge. In years gone by, the River of Culture was a gentle stream that carried children along toward adulthood. Most of my friends and I made the journey with hardly a ripple. Today, parents are aware that the quiet waters have become like the raging Colorado River crashing through the Grand Canyon. There are numerous places where the rapids threaten to drown those whose rafts are not piloted by an experienced oarsman.

Many of today's teens are experiencing a river that flooded its banks in the sixties and seventies, long before this generation was born. That's when a sexual and social revolution inundated the Western world. Overnight, a leftist ideology swept over the landscape and convinced the younger generation that if it felt good, they should certainly do it and that there were no unpleasant consequences for defying time-honored standards of right and wrong. God supposedly died in 1966,[1] and a questionable psychologist named Timothy Leary (some comedians called him "Really Leery") told young people to "turn on, tune in, and drop out."[2] I was there on a university campus, and I saw the impact of Leary's terrible advice firsthand. Though I was young, it alarmed and offended me.

Now, decades later, we're witnessing the effects of that revolution. Marriage as an institution has been devastated, more than 50 million babies have been aborted,[3] violence has shot skyward, sexually transmitted diseases are rampant, and drug abuse still abounds. Yet few contemporary journalists have been willing to admit that something went terribly wrong in those days when caution, convention, and morality were thrown overboard. Do you think?

Those revolutionaries who set out to "change the world" so long ago were highly influential in their time, and in fact, they have had an enduring impact on the River. Most of their names have been forgotten, and some of their antics are laughable today. (Ask someone who lived in that era about the "bra burners" of the late 1960s.) But the passionate beliefs and convictions from the revolution have not only survived, they actually remain ensconced today within politically correct thought. Here's a version of these ideas that the River has carried down to today's adolescent society.

- Early sexual experience is healthy, and for girls, leads to empowerment.
- Virginity results from oppression and should be gotten rid of as soon as possible. It is an embarrassment to be an uninitiated girl. Some parents also feel the same way.
- The white male power structure is a major source of injustice in the world and must be resisted whether it appears in a family or in the culture at large.
- There are no innate differences between males and females, except for the ability to bear children. To be truly equal, men and women should act and think alike.
- Women and girls should imitate the predatory behavior of men. Casual, "no-strings" sexual experience is as satisfying to females as males. It no longer implies or confirms a relationship. Therefore, girls today are much less likely to wonder, *Will he call me in the morning?* For a girl to actually

ask that question of a sexual partner would be a breach of etiquette.

- Modesty is old-fashioned and reflects the oppression of the past. Behavior that would have shocked previous generations doesn't raise an eyebrow today.

- The source of true power for young girls depends on maximizing their sex appeal and then marketing it in the competition for boys.

- For a girl to become what was once considered "easy" or "loose" is now deemed socially acceptable by peers. Therefore, dressing and acting tough or looking like a prostitute is evidence of confidence and strength. Janet Jackson allowed her bra to be torn off in front of 90 million television viewers during the 2004 Super Bowl halftime extravaganza.[4] It was just a "wardrobe malfunction," said Justin Timberlake, who exposed Jackson's breast. Most of the other female performers in that spectacle resembled streetwalkers. Who can estimate how many girls saw the performance that night and decided to change their persona from wholesome to "bad"? The "raunch culture" was on parade.

- Girls are more likely than ever before to be the aggressors in male-female relationships. The traditional understanding that males are the initiators and leaders has been turned upside down. Now girls do much of the calling. They pursue. They often pay. And they regularly take their male friends to bed.

- Homosexuality, bisexuality, and heterosexuality are considered morally equivalent. They simply represent different lifestyles from which to choose.

- Romance has faded in popularity. There is no reason for a man to court a woman if she will offer him sexual favors before the two of them have even developed a friendship. Fewer couples say, "I love you" with deep meaning. Dating has also largely gone out of style. The new relationship is called "the hookup," referring to repeated one-night stands.

- What used to be called "shacking up" or "living in sin" in most Western countries was considered shockingly wicked for centuries. It is now referred to in morally neutral terms, such as "living together" or "cohabitation." It is a noncontroversial housing arrangement without moral implications. Parents may object until they get used to the idea, but peers will not blink an eye.

These are just a few of the concepts that engulfed the baby boomer generation more than four decades ago. Now, the grandchildren of these revolutionaries are growing up to accept and live by ideas that were once celebrated as "the new morality." Behavior that was shockingly racy then has become the pop culture of today. Teenagers are taught its philosophy with an evangelistic zeal. The radicals who set out long ago to "liberate" women and shape the values of their children have been amazingly successful. Most members of the younger generation have no other frame of reference. It is all they have known. I'm reminded of what Adolf Hitler said on November 6, 1933: "Your child belongs to us already . . . what are you? You will pass on. Your descendents, however, now stand in the new camp. In a short time they will know nothing but this new community."[5] Nearly four years later he added, "This new Reich will give its youth to no one."[6] Alas, the new revolutionaries now have our kids.

What does this mean for the mental and physical health of today's children and young people? The answers are striking and can be found in the writings of two brilliant young authors, Wendy Shalit and Carol Platt Liebau. Their books, written separately, are must-reads for every parent who wants to understand the culture and protect his or her girls from those who would subvert their moral character. Shalit wrote *A Return to Modesty* and *Girls Gone Mild*. Liebau is the author of *Prude*. These three books expose the toxic nature of the hookup (or raunch) culture and warn of its devastating impact on both boys and girls. I recommend them highly.

Wendy Shalit's concern about this issue had an interesting origin, which is relevant to our discussion. She was a sophomore at Williams College when she published her first article in *Commentary* magazine. It was a devastatingly effective piece entitled "A Ladies' Room of One's Own." It expressed her irritation about coed bathrooms in college dormitories, including those at Williams. She described the embarrassment of showering and using the toilet in front of male students in a very small and unlocked bathroom. She and the other students had been told that truly liberated women were "comfortable with their bodies" and therefore should not be embarrassed by nudity in front of boys.

Wendy wrote, "Don't get me wrong. I was quite comfortable with my body—had been, all along. It was the intricacies of the opposite sex's body which I wasn't necessarily so eager to study so early in the morning."

Resident advisers at Williams didn't share Wendy's prudish notions. They had said at freshman orientation the previous year that anyone who had a problem with coed bathrooms might want to make an appointment to see a counselor at the campus "Psych Services." In other words, modesty is evidence of mental illness.

To avoid dealing with men in her bathroom, which Wendy called "this lovely garden of togetherness," she carried her toothbrush, toothpaste, and a washcloth to a nearby administration building for the rest of the year. There the bathrooms were still designated "in dear sweet black lettering, with what to me seemed the most reassuring words in the English language: 'Women' and 'Men.'"

The following year, Wendy chose a housing arrangement that was made up of all-girl suites. There she could bathe in privacy. But things didn't turn out quite like she anticipated.

She continued:

> One day, early in the fall, once again I stepped out of the shower to find a strange man in the bathroom with me—or, rather, the rear of him.
>
> "What are you doing here?" I asked.
>
> "Ugh . . . just trying to take a leak."
>
> "Well, I'm sorry if there's been some misunderstanding," said I, clutching my white towel in what I flattered myself was a most emphatic manner, "but this is not a coed bathroom."
>
> For the first time the young man glanced backward to peer at me. He must have been amused at the sight of this small, soaking-wet frame trying to appear intimidating, because he still refused to leave, laughing and protesting weakly instead.
>
> The male student said, "Well . . . there was no sign."
>
> "But see . . . that's what I am here for," I announced. "I am the sign. THIS IS NOT A COED BATHROOM! Do you think you can read the sign now?"
>
> "OK, OK," he mollified, quickly zipping up and scuttling out the door. As he darted down the hall I could hear him muttering, "But you don't have to raise your voice. Gosh— she sounds like my mother."

That led Wendy to put a sign on the door that read, "This is not a coed bathroom—ladies only, please. Thank you for your cooperation, gentlemen." The next day a knock came on her door, and she was asked to join her suite mates for a meeting. Four girls were sitting cross-legged on the floor and wearing very grave expressions. One of them spoke for the others:

"Wendy, we have been talking and we were thinking, well . . . that sign of yours is really very exclusionary of one gender."[7]

Exclusionary of one gender? Give me a break! Bathrooms all over the world are marked *Men* and *Women* in native languages. Now some university men are insulted if they are not admitted into this highly personal and intimate women's sanctuary.

Shalit's article created a sensation, both at Williams and elsewhere. *Reader's Digest* reprinted it the next year, which established Wendy's career as a social commentator. She then elaborated on society's libertine sexual attitudes in each of her two books and warned of the consequences of unrestrained lust. Feminists hated the books, of course, and tried to intimidate Wendy. But her cogent arguments were not easily dismissed. Even the students at Williams later applauded her courageous stance.

The theme of Shalit's books is that modesty, which has represented the essence of womanhood for millennia, has undergone a radical transformation. Virginity is now seen as evidence of weakness and timidity. A modern woman should be brash, profane, aggressive, loud, angry, tough, and independent—anything but feminine and demure. Above all, she must be sexually liberated, which holds the key to her sense of empowerment. Engaging in casual hookups and immodest behavior, and even nudity in coed bathrooms, is thought to build confidence and display strength. This convoluted view of feminine nature turns reality on its head. Nevertheless, the majority of today's teens and young adults, especially those attending secular universities, have been indoctrinated with moral relativism from which libertine behavior emanates. Alas, the River has swept them downstream.

Carol Platt Liebau illustrates the depth of this moral degeneracy:

> Sexual activity has infected middle school with a vengeance.[8] . . . Increasingly, girls define sexual activity as part of what it means to be a typical teen.[9] Previously unacceptable sexual behavior, like same-sex relationships, is increasingly common, and at younger ages.[10]

Liebau is correct. According to researchers at San Diego State University, a review of 530 studies over a period of five decades and involving 250,000 young people between the ages of twelve and twenty-seven revealed that only 12 percent of women approved of premarital sex in 1943. By 1979, it was 73 percent.[11]

The Gallup organization found similar trends. In 2006, 79 percent of young adults said premarital sex was morally acceptable, and 52 percent considered living together no problemo.[12] The sexual revolution that began with a flourish in the late 1960s has survived into the twenty-first century and now encompasses the majority of young Americans.

Another study of Americans corroborated these dramatic findings. Over one thousand adults were asked if they believed in the notion of sin, defined as "something that is almost always considered wrong, particularly from a religious or moral perspective." Eighty-seven percent acknowledged that they did. The responders were then asked to compare thirty behaviors traditionally thought to be sinful. Adultery headed the list with 81 percent; followed by racism, 74 percent; drug abuse, 65 percent; abortion, 56 percent; homosexual sex, 52 percent; gossip, 47 percent; swearing, 46 percent; and alas, premarital sex, 45 percent. For more than half of American adults of all ages, sex outside of marriage is considered to be "no big deal."[13]

The Family Research Council, which reported these findings, writes, "It's encouraging to know that in this day of moral relativism that the majority of Americans still recognize and believe that there is such a thing as sin, even if there are devils in the details."[14]

Previous generations would not have believed this disintegration of traditional morality occurring in our day. Columnist Florence King summarizes it starkly:

> We went from a nation that believed a virtuous woman's price is far above rubies [Proverbs 31] to one that believes a virtuous woman is as sounding brass [1 Corinthians 13]. Meanwhile, the New Woman went from prize to prey. Without the social conventions of modesty, her prerogative to say no was overridden by men's prerogative to expect sex.[15]

It was this dramatic change in cultural attitudes that motivated Wendy Shalit and Carol Platt Liebau to write about their implications for the welfare of girls. We don't know whether they compared notes before writing, but they obviously came to the same conclusions.

Liebau writes:

> In an earlier era, social success was defined by how much a particular girl could inspire a boy to pursue, woo, and do for her. Now girls compete for boys' attention on the basis of how much they, the girls, are willing to do for the boys, sexually and otherwise. What this dynamic means, as girls themselves have pointed out, is that the boys call the shots more than ever. . . .

By offering their bodies so quickly and so easily, girls have essentially surrendered their most effective means for securing the kind of male companionship that they most desire.[16]

Shalit emphasizes that it is foolish to believe a woman can easily detach herself emotionally from the men with whom she sleeps. To the contrary, girls in the hookup culture typically feel rejected, used, and abused when they offer their most intimate gifts and are then cast aside. When that happens, guys get what they want and girls just get angry and depressed. We will see the profound consequences of the hookup lifestyle in the next chapter.

Shalit quotes eighteenth-century philosopher Jean-Jacques Rousseau warning women not to try to be like men. He wrote, "The more women want to resemble [men], the less women will govern them, and then men will truly be the masters."[17] That is exactly what happens to women who engage in casual sex.

Sleazy behavior also affects men, both emotionally and spiritually, but in a different way. This is how the apostle Paul described it: "Do you not know that he who unites himself with a prostitute is one with her in body? For it is said, 'The two will become one flesh'" (1 Corinthians 6:16). That is the way we are designed. An old proverb describes how ancient people viewed virginity. It goes like this: "Chastity is like an icicle; if it once melts, that's the last of it." In other words, virginity can easily be destroyed, but it can never be restored.

References to chastity, and especially nudity, can be found in classical literature from earliest recorded history. The book of Genesis indicates, for example, that before Adam and Eve sinned in the Garden of Eden, they were "both naked, and they felt no shame" (Genesis 2:25). After eating the forbidden fruit, however, the biblical text says that "the eyes of both of them were opened, and they realized they were naked; so they sewed fig leaves together and made coverings for themselves" (Genesis 3:7).

Later, Adam tried to hide from God because he was ashamed of his nakedness. The Creator asked him a telling question: "Who told you that you were naked?" (Genesis 3:11). From that time to this, modesty about the body has been deeply ingrained in human nature, especially among women. It can be overridden and subverted, but at a heavy price.

As we have seen, the popular culture refers to public nudity as "becoming comfortable with your body." Huge numbers of girls have accepted that interpretation and brazenly disrobed for *Playboy*, for movie producers, for soft-core and hard-core pornographers, and for anyone else who offers to pay them. It is another form of prostitution, of course. Some teenage girls seeking attention receive no compensation in return. In a transmission called "sexting," they send nude or sexually explicit photographs through their cell phones or the Internet to boyfriends, who download the images. The guys can then distribute the pictures widely for decades to come. More than 20 percent of teens have engaged in this activity.[18] Whatever happened to the voice of conscience that told generations of young women that disrobing before strangers was wrong and cheap? It has been perverted by a popular culture that instead condemns modesty and morality, urging girls to get comfortable with nudity.

Everywhere teens turn, they hear versions of the same party line. I am reminded of the enormously successful movie *Grease*, which subtly helped to weaken what was left of traditional morality. It was released in 1978 but set in the 1950s as a fluffy, glitzy, relatively tame musical about teenage love. The film starred John Travolta as Danny Zuko, a big man on campus who made the girls swoon. Olivia Newton-John played a cute little blonde named Sandy who was a newcomer from Australia. Clearly, she didn't know the ropes. She was a "good girl" who usually dressed in white or pale yellow. Every other girl at Rydell High seemed to be having more fun than she was, and in fact, her new friends were concerned about Sandy's embarrassing innocence. They invited her to a sleepover to toughen her up.

Sandy's virginity was the focal point of the party. When one of the girls, Frenchy, offered to pierce Sandy's ears, another girl handed her a "virginity pin" to penetrate the lobe. Get it? The blood was symbolic of the loss of virtue. The girls introduced Sandy to wine and smoking, which sent her scurrying into the bathroom to throw up. While she was inside, the brashest member of the clique, Rizzo, said, "Little goody two shoes makes me wanna barf." Then she put on a blonde wig and began to sing, mockingly:

> Look at me, I'm Sandra Dee, lousy with virginity.
> Won't go to bed till I'm legally wed,
> I can't, I'm Sandra Dee.

The lyrics went on to lampoon Sandy's good-girl image. The relationship between Sandy and Danny continued to go sour in the days that followed. He took her to a drive-in movie and gave her his school ring. "That means so much to me," she said. "It means you respect me." Then Zuko made his move. He tried to touch Sandy's breast and then pinned her down on the front seat of his car. Sandy screamed and struggled free, then stumbled from the car. The incident frustrated Zuko and caused a rift between them, after which they drifted apart. Sandy was very confused by what was happening.

Then a drag race was staged at the Los Angeles River, pitting Zuko against his rival. Sandy is seen sitting in the distance and thinking about what had gone wrong in their relationship. Suddenly, it hit her. She realized she was altogether "too good." That led her to sing Rizzo's sleepover song sadly,

> *Wholesome and pure, oh so scared and unsure,*
> *A poor man's Sandra Dee.*

The last words of the song are, "Good-bye to Sandra Dee."[19] Remember that Sandy was said to be "lousy with virginity." That was the big problem.

Sandy knew exactly what she had to do. She asked Frenchy to oversee a makeover, and in the next scene a vampish-looking Sandy emerged wearing a leather jacket, skintight leather pants, and spike heels. She saw Zuko and said, "Tell me about it, Stud." They pranced through a dance number at an all-school carnival, at times moving their hips toward each other symbolically to the beat of the music. Then they got into a futuristic car and soared into the clouds while the students at Rydell High danced with glee.[20]

I have described this entertaining movie in detail, not because it is the worst movie that has ever been produced. It is actually rather tame and quite funny. I have singled out *Grease* because it subtly and convincingly destroys virginity as a virtue. It illustrates precisely the point Shalit and Liebau make in their books. Being "wholesome and pure, oh so scared and unsure" is how girls are told they will feel if they are too virtuous. To get over it, they need to act like men and be tough, brash, and sexually aggressive.

The movie is still having an impact on younger generations more than thirty years after its release. In fact, it played on cable television twice in my area last night. Girls today, like their predecessors, look to Sandy's character as a role model who teaches them why they also need to get rid of their lousy virginity. Today's girls are warned that they'll never get the attention of guys if they continue to look and act like Sandra Dee. Most of them are too young to have seen the perky actress in movies.

The choices for those kids are stark. They can either join the hookup culture or sit at home waiting for Prince Charming to ride in on his white horse. He will probably never come, anyway. That is the underlying message of *Grease*, and any dunderhead can understand it.

Frankly, I resent what the entertainment industry has done to the morals of vast numbers of kids. Just consider how many innocent and vulnerable girls are enticed by movies to rush into sexual experiences for which they are totally unprepared. Some conceive babies they can't care for. Some have abortions they will never forget. Some contract incurable sexually transmitted diseases that will plague them for the rest of their lives. Some are irreparably scarred by rejection and heartache. Some will experience troubled marriages that are destined to fail before they even begin. And all of them will face the spiritual consequences of violating God's moral law. Despite what some people believe, His standard of right and wrong has not been repealed.

The film industry has done tremendous damage to the morals and health of generations of young people, with productions that are infinitely worse than *Grease*. So have many other influences and institutions. They come at kids from every dimension of the culture. Few physicians, for example, tell teen girls that abstinence makes more sense than birth control pills. How I wish they would take the time to tell their patients that contraception *will not* prevent diseases, and condoms often don't either. They should explain why they have so much to lose emotionally and physically by giving themselves intimately to guys who want nothing more than a quick roll in the hay.

Sadly, adults in positions of authority are often unwilling to tell young people the unvarnished truth. Rather, they encourage them to engage in irresponsible and immoral behavior. A case in point: In 2007, a panel discussion was held at Boulder High School in Boulder, Colorado, presented by the University of Colorado. It was a mandatory assembly for the entire student body, during which the subject "STDs: Sex, Teens, and Drugs" was addressed. The various panel members offered outrageous advice to the students on that day. The event was recorded, leaving no doubt about what was said by the participants. What follows is an excerpt from the actual words of Dr. Joel Becker, one of the presenters. He is a psychologist from UCLA, who said:

> I'm going to encourage you to have sex, and I'm going to encourage you to use drugs appropriately. [There was applause and cheering from the students.] And why I'm going to take that position is because you're going to do it anyway. . . . I want to encourage you to all have healthy sexual behavior. Now, what is healthy sexual behavior? Well, I don't care if it's with men and men, women and women, men and women, however, whatever combination you would like to put together.[21]

Becker continued to offer radical fare to impressionable teens straight from the hookup culture. His strongest advice was that they should have lots of "healthy sexual behavior," although he never defined it. He offered no word of caution about devastating diseases, pregnancy, or exploitation of those most vulnerable. Remember that AIDS and thirty other sexually transmitted illnesses plague those who regularly, or even occasionally, have casual intercourse outside of marriage. There was certainly no mention to the students at Boulder High of moral considerations or the beliefs that some of them had been taught at home or at church. That was dismissed with a sneer.

Then Dr. Becker and his colleagues had the temerity to stand there, shrouded in professional authority, endorsing the use of illegal drugs. To repeat, he said, "I'm going to encourage you to use drugs appropriately." What in the name of common sense is an *appropriate* use of drugs? Becker was seemingly encouraging minors to commit crimes. But did school administrators or law enforcement officers in Boulder object to the comments? Dr. George Garcia, superintendent of Boulder Valley School District, said "Overall, the panel was appropriate."[22]

In the spring of 2009, I met Daphne White, who had been a sophomore at Boulder High School in 2007. She was in the audience on that day, listening as her Christian beliefs were belittled and contradicted. After four speakers had prattled on about drugs and sex, the students in attendance were given an opportunity to ask questions but were warned not to express their own opinions or make a statement. Daphne alone stood to confront Dr. Becker respectfully. She said,

> Hello. It's actually really hard for me to get up and say this, but I feel like I have to. So, I'm extremely offended, just by some of the things you say, and I think it's important to understand even though this is Boulder High School, there are people who . . . have different views, and I think that this discussion has been fairly one-sided. Sorry. But some of the things that offended me were just that I think it's inappropriate to discredit religious views on some of these issues. And I know that, Mr. Becker, you discredited abstinence, and this is something that a lot of people feel very strongly about, and I just want everyone to know that there are two sides to the argument. . . . And also, I noticed that you were taking some of these serious issues to be humorous, and I think that, if anything, kind of encouraging teens to kind of [do] the opposite of what I thought this panel was supposed to be about, encouraging teens to be abstinent. So I would just state that

I think that the panelists need to think about what messages they came to send.[23]

I am very proud of this courageous young lady. Daphne defended modesty, abstinence, and her religious faith with conviction in front of eight hundred of her peers, teachers, and the school administration. She also spoke out against the use of illegal drugs. I have worked with teens for many years, including those in public schools, but I have rarely seen such courage as Daphne demonstrated on that afternoon. Unfortunately, she paid a dear price for standing up for what she believed. She was vilified and humiliated in the days that followed. Students made fun of her, and teachers made her feel foolish. Virtually no one came to her defense except Daphne's mother, Priscilla White, who called the school principal, Bud Jenkins. He reportedly defended the program and gave her no support.

Fox News commentator Bill O'Reilly heard about the incident and chastised the school board and administration for the one-sided, liberal agenda of the presentation. I also discussed the situation on *Focus on the Family* and let my listeners hear a portion of the recordings. Then many in the community became outraged in defense of their school. Amazingly, most parents came down on the side of the school. Some were openly rude to Daphne. At a subsequent board meeting, the room was packed with townspeople, and only four or five parents were there to stand in opposition to the program. When Mrs. White tried to speak, her microphone was cut off so she could not be heard. This is what young people and their parents are often up against when they dare to defend their beliefs, especially in liberal communities such as Boulder. At a time when moral clarity is desperately needed, those who ought to be helping to hold the line are adding to the confusion and the enticements of youth. What chance do immature kids have to make right choices when even adults are urging them to do things that are foolish and dangerous? It is hard enough for them to remain chaste in this hypersexualized culture. It is almost impossible if pastors, teachers, coaches, counselors, nurses, grandparents, aunts, and uncles remain silent. Without them, there will be no stopping evil influences. Alas, "Ol' man river . . . he just keeps rollin' along."

As unconscionable as it seems, many moms and dads actually urge their teens to be promiscuous. It is difficult to understand why, given what is at stake. Returning to Wendy Shalit, she addresses that conundrum repeatedly in *Girls Gone Mild*. These are some of her quotes:

If parents knew [their kids were having sex], many would not mind and might even be relieved that the child was "getting [his or her] groove on." Our expectation that young people will be sexually active, and cavalierly so, is clearly making it difficult to call child abuse by its proper name.[24]

The reality is that parents also face a lot of peer pressure to enforce our new low expectations. There is an unmistakable misogyny in our attitude toward the virgin, which becomes all the more obvious when this philosophy is carried to its logical conclusion.[25]

About 70 percent of these e-mails and letters [coming from girls who had contacted Shalit] felt that wanting marriage and children was an aspiration she needed to "hide." . . . I was shocked that according to nearly half of the letters, a girl's own parent thought that something was wrong with her for not being sufficiently casual about sex.[26]

When one mother found out that her daughter hadn't slept with the new boyfriend after a whole weekend away, the mother warned her ominously, "You're gonna lose him!" (She didn't; they eventually got married.)[27]

How sad are the children and teens whose parents accept and endorse the distortions of the hookup culture in this way. Rather than offering wisdom, they add to the confusion and temptations of youth. The ultimate responsibility for guidance and moral training of children lies with mothers and fathers. I will repeat the stern warning to all of us as written in Leviticus 19:29 (NASB). Its meaning is unmistakable:

> Do not profane your daughter by making her a harlot, so that the land will not fall to harlotry and the land become full of lewdness.

Christian parents who take that Scripture seriously and literally (as I do) will appreciate the following statement. It offers the most cogent defense of virginity I have read.

> Virginity actually represents an expression of respect for the awesome power of sexual passion—and a manifestation of fidelity to something higher than momentary desires. It is, as essayist Sarah E. Hinlicky has written, "a sexuality dedicated to

hope, to the future, to marital love, to children, and to God."
It's also an expression of self-respect. Girls who refuse to play
the hookup game are asserting that they deserve something
better than sexual fumbling either with boys who want them
for nothing but their bodies, or with those who may claim to
care about them—but not necessarily enough to commit to a
formal relationship such as marriage (or to promise marriage
should an unexpected pregnancy result).

Being a virgin means being truly in control of oneself:
body, heart, and soul. It's a way of determining which boys
care about a girl for herself, rather than simply for her body.
And although it's no guarantee against heartbreak, virginity
does ensure that a girl will never know the bitter regret of
having given part of herself to someone who was unworthy
of the gift.[28]

Are you listening, parents? This is Truth with a capital T! It must be
taught to your daughters especially, but also to your sons. I can almost hear
some critics saying, "You are espousing the old double standard that told
men they could have their fun while women had to be the gatekeepers for
morality." That is emphatically *not* what I am communicating. The fact is that
while sexual purity is wholesome and morally significant for both sexes, and
the Scriptures make no distinction between them, it remains true that women
clearly pay a higher price for sexual misbehavior, emotionally and physically.
It has always been that way. It will be true for your daughters too.

Begin steering your boys and girls away from the hookup culture when
they are young. Initially, that is accomplished by teaching reasonable standards of modesty and virtue. Tell them that some things are right and
others wrong, and spell out the differences between the two. Explain that
moral principles are eternal and are established by our Creator, to whom
we are accountable. Those standards are a reflection of His very character.
His Word is the basis for behavioral boundaries, which are given for our
benefit. Teach the meaning of marriage, and explain why virginity is a precious gift to a future husband or wife. Tell your sons and daughters they
have no right to give it to anyone else, and assure them that they will never
regret preserving it.

Above all, pray daily for your children by name. Help them avoid jag-
ged rocks and obstacles on the River of Culture. Doing that job properly
may protect them from a lifetime of grief.

CONSEQUENCES

I'M SURE THE previous chapter was disturbing to some of my readers because the world in which children live has become so toxic. I will soon move on to more uplifting and encouraging subjects because raising girls is a wonderful blessing to be celebrated. Speaking personally, however, I must not leave the subject of the hookup culture before providing some extremely important information about the consequences of promiscuity and other irresponsible behavior. I believe even parents of young children will find this discussion helpful. After all, adolescence is just around the corner.

Recently I was talking to a married couple with four children—three girls and a boy. All of them are in their teens. The mother turned to me and said, "I need your help with something. I am very concerned about the culture and what it is doing to kids, especially our own. My husband and I are doing everything we can to protect them from harmful influences, but it is a struggle just to hold them steady. The most distressing thing is that other parents in our social group are not standing with us, including those in the church. They have essentially given up and apparently have decided to let their kids go with the flow."

This mother continued to describe her difficulties in trying to keep her teenagers from being exposed to unwholesome movies, television shows, and Internet sites. Their children's friends are also part of the problem, because it seems that they are free to do whatever they want without rules, discipline, or supervision. She and her husband feel virtually alone in this battle, despite the fact that their children attend Christian schools and are members of a conservative church.

This is precisely the point I have been making. These parents are among millions of others whose children are being carried downstream by the River of Culture. To use another analogy, many concerned moms and dads are in a tug-of-war for the hearts and minds of their kids, and they dare not lose it.

It is a very familiar story, which is why I have described in some detail the forces that are assailing the family today. I doubt if there has been another time in modern history when it has been more challenging to get youngsters through adolescence and into the relative safety of early adulthood. The sexual revolution of the sixties has now become the pop culture of today, although it is no longer as shocking to adults.

Let me return to the comments I made earlier in the book about the turmoil smoldering inside many adolescent girls. Therein lies the key to deciphering some of the behaviors that are otherwise incomprehensible. Specifically, this turbulence is the reason so many teen girls seek to harm themselves in disturbing ways. You've no doubt seen examples of this self-destructive behavior in the teen environment, perhaps by members of your own family. An alarming number of girls harbor deep-seated anger that has turned inward, leading them to starve themselves even to the point of death; secretly binge and purge; take prescription medications and illegal drugs; dull their senses with alcohol; cut and pierce their bodies; permanently ink themselves; engage in things like prostitution, pornography, stripping, violence, bullying, sexual aggression, lewdness, and crudeness; and even attempt suicide, which has spiked in recent years.[1] They all have a common thread.

Why would intelligent teens and young adults, mostly girls, behave in ways that are so self-destructive? The answer, in a phrase, is self-hatred. Such individuals are at war with themselves in the dog-eat-dog world of adolescence. It is a vicious environment, creating winners and losers, haves and have-nots, stars and scars, and paralyzing fear. Those who perceive themselves to be worthless often sink into a despair from which they cannot escape without professional help.

The girls who despise themselves usually harbor painful memories of past humiliations inflicted by boys who rejected and taunted them, and by jealous and gossipy girls who ridiculed and harassed them. They are commonly called names that describe embarrassing body characteristics and are made to feel like fools. Some are referred to as "throwaway girls." Consequently, they perceive themselves to be ugly, stupid, unloved, and unlovable. They seethe with hostility toward parents, teachers, and peers, but mostly toward themselves. They look in the mirror with utter disdain, wishing they could die.

We are beginning to understand how this self-hatred originates. First, I must emphasize that it has many causes in individual circumstances, from early physical or emotional abuse to tragic rejection by one or both parents. I can't catalog the various factors in this limited setting, but there is one concern that is increasingly common today. It is early sexual promiscuity, as we have been discussing. It becomes a superhighway to depression.

Anger, as we know, is a by-product of depression. A naive little girl who loses her virginity when she is oh-so-young and then moves on into the hookup culture is vulnerable to numerous hurtful experiences. In a search for love and affirmation, this girl may have initially trusted and tried to please an immature guy whose motives were entirely different from her own. She engaged in the most intimate of relationships in the hope of being cherished forever. It was a false promise. The boy walked away callously when the wham-bam affair was over. If the girl's desire was for love, his was for conquest and a quick thrill. What she called romantic, he called "getting lucky." She was left feeling used and abused, while he bragged about what he took from her. This is why I have said that sexual liberation, as it was originally called, is the biggest joke men have ever played on women. But it isn't funny.

The sad thing is that most schoolgirls don't learn much from their early unpleasant encounters. Perhaps the next guy will be her Prince Charming. Maybe he will return her love. Instead, she moves from bed to bed and soon finds herself pregnant, alone, and facing an angry parent. She may be whisked off to an abortion clinic by a school nurse or by her mother, where she will undergo a procedure that will be remembered, perhaps with regret, for the rest of her life. Or she may consider having a baby for whom she is woefully unprepared. Hopefully the idea of adoption will be suggested to her, but regardless of the decision, what she has been through will have changed her emotionally and physically. Life will be different thereafter. Why wouldn't she be depressed and angry?

I am not talking here about all adolescent females, of course, or even the majority of them. But even if there is only one girl out there who is on this journey, her situation is tragic. I grieve for her and her family.

Let's look at the evidence linking casual sex, depression, self-hatred, and finally, self-destructive behavior. That is what we have observed. But what does the research show?

According to a study of 19,000 teens by the National Institutes of Health, promiscuous girls were four times more likely to experience depression than those who were virgins.[2] Their symptoms included sadness, loss of appetite, and a sense of despair about the future, among others. Suicide was also found to be more likely among girls who were involved in sexual activity. On the other hand, boys and girls who remained virgins were found to have a lower rate of depression.[3] When girls began to experiment sexually, they suffered emotionally.[4] Boys were less affected. Who said life is fair?

The *American Journal of Preventive Medicine* offers further evidence of the connection between certain behaviors and depression. Their study is titled "Which Comes First in Adolescence—Sex and Drugs or Depression?"[5] The answer, according to the research, is sex and drugs. Depression comes next, followed by self-loathing and attempts to harm oneself.

The American Psychological Association also confirmed this sequence. Their findings indicated that today's hookup culture causes serious psychological and even physical harm, as we have seen. Casual sex interferes with the development of personal identity, resulting in what is called "objectivization." That means girls begin to think of themselves merely as "sex objects" whose sense of worth is determined by how they function in a highly eroticized society. They give themselves to boys indiscriminately to prove they are valuable in the only currency they recognize. Afterward, especially if the relationship ends, they feel abused and discarded.

There is more. The Heritage Foundation reviewed relevant literature and issued a related report entitled "Sexually Active Teenagers Are More Likely to Be Depressed and to Attempt Suicide."[6] These are some of their findings:

> When compared to teens who are not sexually active, teenage boys and girls who are sexually active are significantly less likely to be happy and more likely to feel depressed. When compared to teens who are not sexually active, teenage boys and girls who are sexually active are significantly more likely to attempt suicide. Thus, in addition to its role in promoting teen pregnancy and the current epidemic of STDs, early sexual activity is a substantial factor in undermining the emotional well-being of American teenagers.[7]
>
> A full quarter (25.3 percent) of teenage girls who are sexually active report that they are depressed all, most, or a lot of the time. By contrast, only 7.7 percent of teenage girls who are not sexually active report that they are depressed all, most, or a lot of the time. Thus, sexually active girls are more

than three times more likely to be depressed than are girls who are not sexually active.[8]

Some 8.3 percent of teenage boys who are sexually active report that they are depressed all, most, or a lot of the time. By contrast, only 3.4 percent of teenage boys who are not sexually active are depressed all, most, or a lot of the time. Thus, boys who are sexually active are more than twice as likely to be depressed as those who are not sexually active.[9]

The Heritage Foundation then reported the issue of sexual activity as related to suicide. The findings are startling and should be of concern to every parent of teen girls.

A full 14.3 percent of girls who are sexually active report having attempted suicide. By contrast, only 5.1 percent of sexually inactive girls have attempted suicide. Thus, sexually active girls are nearly three times more likely to attempt suicide than are girls who are not sexually active.[10]

Among boys, 6.0 percent of those who are sexually active have attempted suicide. By contrast, only 0.7 percent of boys who are not sexually active have attempted suicide. Thus, sexually active teenage boys are eight times more likely to attempt suicide than are boys who are not sexually active.[11]

It is unusual for social scientists to be in virtual unanimity regarding the issues they are studying, but most are in agreement about the consequences of early sexual behavior. It is often the first step toward devastating emotional and physical harm, especially among those for whom intercourse has become habitual.

Let's turn now to some specific forms of self-destructive behavior, beginning with the disturbing practice of cutting and piercing. Have you ever driven your car up to the window of a fast-food restaurant and been shocked to see your order being taken by a teenager who has imbedded rings, small diamonds, and other trinkets in his or her nose, ears, and lips? It is a common sight in the culture of the young. Some have even pierced their tongues with small spikes, causing them to slur their speech. Others have slashed or stabbed their arms and legs with knives, leaving ugly wounds and telltale scars.

Why would so many teens assault their bodies in these and other unfortunate ways? The answer, again, is self-hatred. It is an inward cry for help. A surprising number of those who deliberately harm themselves have been raped or otherwise sexually abused. The devastation of that experience often leads to promiscuity, the use of alcohol and drugs, involvement in petty crime, and other delinquent behavior. It is now evident that the use of alcohol and drugs can become a precursor to eating disorders. These expressions of emotional distress do not occur in isolation. They are usually linked together in a familiar pattern, and many of them have sexual overtones.[12]

If you have a youngster who is exhibiting these behaviors, he or she must be given professional help as soon as possible. I will offer specific advice to parents of these kids in chapter 19.

Another devastating consequence of early promiscuity is the contraction of one or more sexually transmitted diseases. It is almost impossible to overstate the scope of this problem. About 19 million new cases of STDs occur each year among all age groups in the United States.[13] Those who "sleep around," even occasionally, will inevitably, and I do mean *inevitably*, be infected with a sexually transmitted illness or an array of them. Condoms may reduce the risk, but they are problematic too. They slip, they break, they leak, and they become brittle with age. Furthermore, kids at the peak of passion often fail to use them properly, if at all. In some instances, all it takes to contract a fine case of syphilis or gonorrhea or chlamydia or herpes or another of the thirty common STDs is to make a single mistake with a carrier. The chances of becoming infected by an infected partner are as high as 40 percent per encounter.[14] Thousands of kids roll the dice every day and come up snake eyes.

According to officials from the Centers for Disease Control and Prevention, nearly half of African Americans and 20 percent of whites aged fourteen to nineteen are infected each year by at least one of four common sexually transmitted diseases.[15] This finding extrapolates to 3.2 million teenage females per year. The viruses, bacteria, and parasites that they carry often have lifelong implications for fertility, marriage, and general health. Yet many of the victims do not even know they are infected.[16]

One of the four dreaded diseases mentioned above is the human papillomavirus, or HPV, which deserves special attention. The Centers for Disease Control and Prevention estimate that 19 million people are infected annually with this disease.[17] At least 50 percent of sexually active individuals will acquire HPV during their lives.[18] By fifty years of age, 80 percent of women will acquire a genital HPV infection.[19] There are more than one hundred strains of this infection, forty strains of which affect the genital area. Some of them cause cancer of the cervix.[20] Most people do not realize they are infected or that they are passing the virus to a sex partner. Girls who contract one of these diseases will need medical evaluation regularly and may require special testing and treatment procedures.

As distressing as that is, studies continue to show that young children are experimenting sexually. An investigation conducted by researchers at the University of Texas and published in April of 2009 carried this headline: "Middle School Youth as Young as 12 Engaging in Risky Sexual Activity." The focus of the study was seventh graders. Here are the primary findings:

> By age twelve, 12 percent of students had already engaged in vaginal sex, 7.9 percent in oral sex, 6.5 percent in anal sex and 4 percent in all three types of intercourse. Markham said, "These findings are alarming because youth who start having sex before age 14 are much more likely to have multiple lifetime sexual partners, use alcohol or drugs before sex and have unprotected sex, all of which puts them at greater risk for getting a sexually transmitted disease (STD) or becoming pregnant."[21]

Other studies indicate that oral sex among teens between ages fifteen and nineteen is more common than sexual intercourse.[22] Seventy percent of those between seventeen and nineteen say they have had oral sex.[23] Unbelievably, most teens view that activity as casual and non-intimate.[24] Some of them apparently choose oral sex instead of intercourse to retain their "virginal status" and to prevent disease.[25] What they don't know is that many of the sexually transmitted organisms they bring home, such as herpes and other viruses, are incurable even though they are treatable. Strains of the human papillomavirus can cause mouth and throat cancer and are spread by oral sexual activity. Those are the cold, hard facts. And discriminatory or not, girls usually suffer more from them than do boys.

It has also been confirmed more recently that men are contracting HPV by performing oral sex on girls or women who have the disease. This was the conclusion of Dr. Joel Ernster, who published his findings in *The Laryngoscope*, a prestigious medical journal for ear, nose, and throat specialists. The incidence of cancer in the pharynx and throat among males living in Colorado increased by 36.6 percent from the eighties to the nineties. That higher incidence corresponds with a similar increase in diagnosis of HPV.[26]

Dr. Ernster says, "Oral sex has implications that are way beyond what we first thought."[27] He said that married men with families who engaged in this sexual activity decades ago can still be carrying the infection.

In study after study we are seeing confirmation of what many of us have known for twenty years but still seems to be a secret among most teens and young adults. That hush-hush fact is that there is no such thing as so-called safe sex. U.S. health officials estimated in 2007 that one-quarter of all women in this country between fourteen and fifty-nine are infected with a virus that causes warts and most cases of cervical cancer.[28] Does that shock you as it does me? Twenty-five percent of the female teens, wives, sisters, aunts, and some grandmothers that you see walking around carry this disease. Some will die from cancers resulting from HPV.

Allow me to be redundant here. These epidemics of sexually transmitted diseases are swirling all around us, but kids still think they can play with fire and not get burned. Yes, and those who invest their precious money in the lottery still think they can win the jackpot against the odds of 200 million to one. When told of the infinitesimally small chance of winning, one not-very-bright man disagreed with the gambling commission on which I served. He said, "You're wrong. The odds are not 200 million to one, they are one to one." We asked how he came to that conclusion, and he said, "If I play the lottery, I have a chance. If I don't play, I have no chance. The odds are one to one." This man probably flunked third grade math. In his case, he only lost a few hundred dollars on the lottery. When the kids play the "safe-sex game," they gamble with their bodies and perhaps their lives.

That brings us to one of the most important questions I will deal with in this book. This is it: given the fact that casual intercourse and other forms of sexual intimacy are wreaking physical and emotional havoc among teens and young adults, why are they not being warned of the consequences of promiscuity? Many so-called safe-sex programs in public schools invest time and energy teaching very young children the mechanics and anatomy of intercourse, while almost endorsing the act for those who think they are "ready." Tell me, what hot and bothered teen *doesn't* think he or she is ready, especially when everyone seems to believe it is the thing to do?

Some teachers and guest speakers in schools go even further, as Dr. Joel Becker did when he addressed the entire student body at Boulder High School. Remember, he said, "I'm going to encourage you to have sex, and I'm going to encourage you to use drugs appropriately."[29] The man should have been driven out of town by outraged parents and teachers! Instead, the teachers, the principal, members of the school board, and many parents defended the racy doctor. I would like to know why.

Why do psychiatrists, psychologists, university professors, sex education teachers, and bureaucrats in the health business, all of whom must be familiar with the studies I have cited, continue to pretend that the hookup culture carries no significant risk? They have to know better. Why do they withhold this vital information from students who desperately need it? Why did the U.S. Congress eliminate the pittance allocated for abstinence education in 2008, in favor of tens or even hundreds of millions of dollars in support of same-sex ideology?[30] It is difficult not to conclude that there is a conspiracy of silence by those in the professional community to shield young people from the truth.

I am not the only one puzzled and angered by what we are doing to kids. Dr. Miriam Grossman, a psychiatrist at UCLA's Student Psychological Services division, was also intrigued by the taboo preventing the discussion of sex and health. She posed a question similar to those I asked: "Why are students inundated with information about contraception, a healthy diet, . . . coping with stress and pressure—but not a word about the havoc that casual sex plays on young women's emotions?"[31]

After years of clinical practice, Dr. Grossman addressed this silence by her colleagues in a book titled *Unprotected: A Campus Psychiatrist Reveals How Political Correctness in Her Profession Endangers Every Student*. Because of the taboo against discussions of sexual behavior, she was fearful of professional and employment reprisals. Thus, she called herself simply "Anonymous, M.D." for several years. Only much later did she reveal her identity.

Grossman added:

> We ask [our patients] about child abuse, but not last week's hookups. We want to know how many cigarettes and coffees she's had each day, but not how many abortions in her past. We consider the stress caused by parental expectations and rising tuition, but neglect the anguish of herpes, the hazards of promiscuity, and the looming fertility issues for women who always put career first. [32]

The psychiatrist concluded, "The message must get out: Casual sex is a health hazard for young women."[33] I would add, it's a bad bet for young men too!

It is my guess that the message is not getting out because it is politically incorrect. Anything that smacks of morality or Christian ethics is offensive to the liberal community. Meanwhile, young people are falling into the same snare that entrapped their parents when they were young. Some taboos are not just foolish—this one is downright ridiculous!

In conclusion, I want to share the edited transcript of a radio interview I conducted for *Focus on the Family*. It featured two board-certified obstetricians and gynecologists, Drs. Joe McIlhaney and Freda McKissic Bush. Dr. McIlhaney was in private practice for more than twenty-five years before resigning to found the Medical Institute for Sexual Health. This organization, now called the Medical Institute, is designed to inform physicians, educators, parents, and teens about sexually transmitted diseases and related topics. Dr. Bush is still in private practice and serves on the clinical faculty at the University of Mississippi Medical Center.

These physicians have written an outstanding book that is a must-read for parents and teens. It is titled *Hooked: New Science on How Casual Sex Is Affecting Our Children.*[34]

> **JCD**: I have used the term "hookup culture" in my writings. Tell us what you mean by it.
>
> **Dr. Bush**: The kids use that terminology to mean everything from casual kissing to sexual intercourse. They don't know it, but when they have sex they are also "hooking up" emotionally.
>
> **JCD**: And what are the effects of doing that with multiple partners?
>
> **Dr. McIlhaney**: It has very dangerous implications. We now know this because of our ability to examine the human brain directly, using MRIs, PET scans, and other imaging technology. These devices have revealed recently that repeated sexual experience with multiple partners over time permanently changes the wiring of the brain and damages the way it was designed to function.
>
> **Dr. Bush**: To understand why this occurs, we also have to consider how three neurotransmitters work in the brain. They are dopamine, oxytocin, and vasopressin. These chemicals operate to give great pleasure to a man and woman during sex and then bond them together emotionally. They also explain why sex partners often have "flashbacks" or recurring memories of that first experience that make them want to continue having sex.
>
> **Dr. McIlhaney**: But here's the catch. When a person has sex with multiple partners outside of marriage, this bonding mechanism is interfered with, and he or she loses the ability to connect in the same way. A man and woman who "sleep around" when they are single will often have a weaker bond with the person they marry.
>
> **Dr. Bush**: The illustration we gave in the book is that of a Band-Aid. The first time you put it on your arm or knee, it sticks firmly. But each time you pull it off and put it back on, the stickiness gets weaker, until it will no longer stay in

place. This is what happens in the hookup culture. Those who have had sex with numerous people actually have a seriously weakened ability to bond permanently in marriage.

JCD: Would it be accurate to say that a girl and guy are "stealing" some of the excitement and connectedness that should have been reserved for a future husband and wife?

Dr. McIlhaney: Exactly. We have reviewed more than 250 studies, most of which confirmed these changes occurring in the brain and what they mean. Our observation is that human beings are designed by God to have one sexual partner for life. When you share that experience with others repeatedly and casually, the chemistry and the neurological wiring inevitably changes, sometimes irreversibly.

JCD: Do these findings relate only to sexual intercourse, or does the same interference with bonding occur for those who engage in oral sex?

Dr. Bush: Imaging shows that the same areas of the brain are stimulated in both experiences, so it has the same effect.

Dr. McIlhaney: You can actually see brain activity when a person is lusting. When a person is experiencing genuine love for a person of the opposite sex, a different part of the brain is stimulated and shows up on PET scans.

Dr. Bush: To summarize, when a couple has a sexual experience but then does not stay together, it affects both of them emotionally, which then tinkers with the function of pleasure-giving neurotransmitters. That, in turn, rewires the brain. Ultimately, the bond that should occur in marriage is weakened. As you said, something has been "stolen" from their relationship.

JCD: I am reminded of the Scripture in 1 Corinthians 6:18 that says, "All other sins a man commits are outside his body, but he who sins sexually sins against his own body." It is remarkable to see just how accurate that verse is today, in light of the research you are describing. We are doing irreparable damage to our own bodies when we disobey God's moral laws in a sexual relationship.

Dr. McIlhaney: There is another Scripture that relates to what we are saying. It was written by Solomon, the wisest man who ever lived, who was giving advice to a young man. He wrote in Proverbs 7:6–8:5:

At the window of my house
I looked out through the lattice.
I saw among the simple,
I noticed among the young men,
a youth who lacked judgment.
He was going down the street near her corner,
walking along in the direction of her house
at twilight, as the day was fading,
as the dark of night set in.
Then out came a woman to meet him,
dressed like a prostitute and with crafty intent.
(She is loud and defiant,
her feet never stay at home;
now in the street, now in the squares,
at every corner she lurks.)
She took hold of him and kissed him
and with a brazen face she said:
"I have fellowship offerings at home;
today I fulfilled my vows.
So I came out to meet you;
I looked for you and have found you!
I have covered my bed
with colored linens from Egypt.
I have perfumed my bed
with myrrh, aloes and cinnamon.
Come, let's drink deep of love till morning;
let's enjoy ourselves with love!
My husband is not at home;
he has gone on a long journey.
He took his purse filled with money
and will not be home till full moon."
With persuasive words she led him astray;
she seduced him with her smooth talk.
All at once he followed her
like an ox going to the slaughter,
like a deer stepping into a noose
till an arrow pierces his liver,
like a bird darting into a snare,
little knowing it will cost him his life.
Now then, my sons, listen to me;
pay attention to what I say.

Do not let your heart turn to her ways
or stray into her paths.
Many are the victims she has brought down;
her slain are a mighty throng.
Her house is a highway to the grave,
leading down to the chambers of death.
Does not wisdom call out?
Does not understanding raise her voice?
On the heights along the way,
where the paths meet, she takes her stand;
beside the gates leading into the city,
at the entrances, she cries aloud:
"To you, O men, I call out;
I raise my voice to all mankind.
You who are simple, gain prudence;
you who are foolish, gain understanding."

JCD: That is a powerful warning. I'm convinced that it is as relevant to women as it is to men. Sometimes the snare is in the hand of a guy, "calling out" to a gullible girl. Those of us who ignore these inspired words are doing so at our own peril.

Dr. McIlhaney: In keeping with the warning of Scripture, some promiscuous young people are dying today of AIDS or cancer. However, even those who don't die of a disease have often hurt themselves emotionally and may be literally killing their chances of having a happy marriage in the future.

We brought something with us today that will help to illustrate this understanding. It is a CD featuring a young man who has an urgent story to tell. May I share it with your listeners?

JCD: Please do.

[Recording]: What can compare to the joy of holding your newborn baby? For me that joy is overwhelming. My name is Sean. I've been married five years and love my wife more than ever. We have an amazing son and the news we were expecting a baby girl made our future even brighter.

But choices I had made in my past would cloud our bright future and leave our newborn daughter fighting for her life. At first, Linda seemed healthy, but after a few days, my wife said something about Linda didn't seem right. Linda was sluggish and not very responsive to us. Our pediatrician said not to worry. "All babies are different," he said. "She won't act the way your son did."

Then one night while my wife was holding Linda, our baby girl stopped breathing and turned blue. I thought my daughter was dying. Finally, we got a devastating diagnosis. Linda had been born with herpes. The casual sex I'd had in college left me infected with the incurable virus. I told my wife I had herpes before we married, so throughout our marriage, we were careful to have sex only when we thought it was safe.

Yet, as careful as we were, my wife still contracted the virus sometime while she was pregnant with Linda. My wife didn't know she had contracted herpes. She never had a single symptom. The anger and guilt I felt, knowing I had passed the virus to my wife and she had passed it to my daughter, was overwhelming.

As we watched my daughter struggle to stay alive, I thought, *We were so careful; how could this happen?* It happens more easily than you think. You can catch herpes even with condom use. You can catch herpes from a partner even when they don't have an outbreak. You can pass it on to an infant even when you don't have an outbreak.

Herpes attacks an infant's brain like Pac-Man, eating through it. Babies who survive are usually left with severe disabilities. The virus was already eating through Linda's liver. We prayed her brain would not be next. Our prayers were answered. Linda made a miraculous recovery. The virus did not attack her brain. Developmentally, she is a normal fifteen-month-old, but that could change any minute. The virus could attack again.

It's heartbreaking to watch the painful medical procedures Linda must undergo every month. She will never outgrow herpes. It'll be a threat to my little girl's health for the rest of her life, and it all started with the lie of casual sex, the lie that casual sex feels great and hurts no one. It's the lie I was taught in high school sex-ed class. It's the lie that kids are now taught in middle school sex-ed class. Some politicians want it taught to kids in kindergarten.

I'm reminded of that lie every day, reminded by the recent news reports that one out of every four adults in New York City has herpes—adults who think casual sex doesn't hurt anybody, because that's what our culture tells them.

But mostly, I'm reminded of the lie of casual sex by the blisters on my daughter's tiny fingers—painful blisters that never seem to go away. And I'm reminded by her fight for life. Casual sex . . . see for yourself. Then ask, "What can I do to help stop the lie?"

JCD: That is a very sad story.

Dr. Bush: And it is true.

Dr. McIlhaney: Sean told me this story personally and said he wanted to go public with their tragedy so that others might avoid the mistake he made when he was in college. He would do anything to be able to relive those early years. Now he has to deal with guilt and regret every day.

I have seen thousands of women in my medical practice who are suffering because of premarital sex. Like Sean, they didn't know what they were doing until it was too late. It never occurred to them that they might become infected with diseases that would cause such pain later, or in Sean's case, that would disable and stalk a little child yet to be conceived. She is suffering because of her dad's youthful irresponsibility.

Other young people are generally unaware that their hookup behavior is rewiring and changing their brains in ways that will weaken their bond to the person they will someday marry. As you said, it is very sad.

JCD: This is why you left your practice in obstetrics and gynecology, isn't it?

Dr. McIlhaney: Yes, it is also why I founded the Medical Institute. I felt such an obligation to get the truth out to teens and young adults. That has become the passion of my life.

Dr. Bush: This is also why we wrote the book *Hooked*. We were trying not only to warn teens and young adults of the consequences but also to speak to their parents.

JCD: What do you say to the moms and dads who were

promiscuous before they were married—doing things that they now regret—and feel like they can't talk to their kids about it because it would be hypocritical to do so?

Dr. Bush: I think it is appropriate to admit that they made mistakes too but that God has forgiven them and they have forgiven themselves. Then if they speak candidly and honestly to their children, they can still have a powerful influence on them. They can empower them to abstain. The studies show that mothers and fathers have a greater influence on the behavior of teens than anyone else, even when teenagers don't appear to be "getting it."

Dr. McIlhaney: College-aged students are the most vulnerable to the hookup culture. When they leave home, they find themselves in an environment that is so destructive. They think they can get away with everything, but it is untrue. If they violate the moral code that most of them were taught as kids and ignore the medical realities that we have talked about, they *will* suffer the consequences. That is why I hope and pray they will read our book, *Hooked: New Science on How Casual Sex Is Affecting Our Children*. Maybe we can prevent some of the tragic mistakes that have wounded so many members of this generation—and those that are yet to come.

JCD: Thank you so much, Dr. McIlhaney and Dr. Bush. I hope you sell a million copies.

❈   ❈   ❈

One more comment: I would like to hear Dr. Joel Becker and his liberated colleagues try to refute the powerful argument we have just read. He is unlikely to respond, but it doesn't matter. *You*, Mom and Dad, can get the message in the hands of your teens and college students. Doing so could help them weave their way around the land mines I have described.

GOOD NEWS
ABOUT GIRLS

WHEN ONE CONSIDERS adolescent society and its obsession with the dark side of popular culture, we have reason to be discouraged about where it is headed. There is, however, a definite sunny side to be celebrated, and it is time we heralded it. The good news is that there are millions of teens who are *not* sleeping around, are *not* using illegal drugs, are *not* binge drinking, are *not* at war with their parents, and are *not* failing in school. These are wonderful kids who are loved at home. Many of them, like Daphne from Boulder High School, are deeply committed to Jesus Christ and aren't afraid to share their faith. So while it appears at times as though an entire generation of teens and young adults is totally lost, it is definitely not true.

According to data culled from the U.S. Centers for Disease Control and Prevention, 52 percent of high school students are still virgins.[1] What's more, this is a significant improvement from the early 1990s, when less than half of high schoolers (46 percent) reported never having had sex.[2] Though obviously I wish these numbers were higher, it is remarkable that so many of today's teens have not succumbed to the enormous pressures of our hyper-eroticized society. The entertainment industry has thrown everything but the kitchen sink at these kids since they were in kindergarten, but some have chosen to take the high road. When the safe-sex advocates say that it is unrealistic to expect teens to remain chaste and that they are all going to do it anyway, the "experts" are wrong in the majority of cases. And remember this: some of those who experience intercourse once or twice subsequently abstained entirely. We call these individuals "secondary" or "renewed" virgins.

I say this to offer hope and encouragement to today's parents. You have a real shot at keeping your kids moral in a very immoral world. Don't believe those who say, "It can't be done." There is much you can do to help resist the popular culture, if you have the "want to." When I was sixteen, my parents sold our house and moved seven hundred miles away to protect me from the negative influence of some friends. It cost my father professionally, but he never looked back. He and my mother were willing to do whatever was necessary to pull me back from the edge. Are you willing to pay a similar price?

Your strong-willed teens may rebel for a time, but you owe it to them to hang tough and continue to point them in the right direction. Your task is to be *intentional* about teaching chastity and common sense to your children while they are still young. I'll offer some suggestions about how to do that in a moment.

There is more good news on the home front. Sixty-two percent of high school students have never tried marijuana, 93 percent have never used cocaine, 96 percent have never used methamphetamines, and just over 55 percent do not drink alcohol.[3] Many of them are good athletes or disciplined students or hard workers who are determined to do something significant with their lives. In short, there is plenty of good news about this generation that we can applaud.

One of the most encouraging developments is that many girls appear to be realizing that sex without commitment is utterly empty. They are rejecting the lie that the only way to get the love they crave is to throw off all vestiges of modesty and to behave like predatory males. They know this is a popular myth that delivers only tragic consequences. These girls have seen their peers returning from racy prom nights, frat parties, or spring breaks feeling used and rejected. When their passions have cooled the next morning, they look in the mirror with disgust and disdain. Some have hangovers or drug-induced depression. Then they have to deal with apprehension about possible pregnancy, disease, and a return to loneliness. Many girls have watched their friends fall into this trap and have chosen to avoid it, in some cases because of a personal commitment to Jesus Christ.

The observation that attitudes are changing is reported in numerous publications, including a 2008 article that appeared in *Christianity Today* entitled "Zipping It."[4] It features an interview with Donna Freitas, professor of religion at Boston University, and author of *Sex and the Soul*. The interviewer was Katelyn Beaty, assistant editor at *CT*. This is a portion of their important conversation:

Beaty: The cultural myth says that secular schools are the places where faith goes to die. Or, secular colleges are for adults who don't need religious beliefs to prop up their worldview. But what you found is that spirituality, even though it takes various forms and is often private, is thriving. Students are just not being given the tools to know what to do with it.

Freitas: Absolutely. For example, take the sexuality and spirituality class I taught last fall at Boston University, where we studied books by Joshua Harris, Lauren Winner, and Rob Bell, in addition to different sexual-ethics scholars. Almost all the students were as liberal as liberal can get. One of the big hits of the semester was Wendy Shalit's *A Return to Modesty*. The students were floored by her critique of hookup culture, and they spent so much time talking about modesty as a virtue. It allowed them to say, "Wow, we're witness to all this vulgarity on campus. We pretend that we're okay with it, but we're not." I actually had students who for their final project proposed a modesty club. I'm sitting here thinking, *This is Boston University*. It made me think Shalit published her book 10 years too early, because the Left reviled her when she published it [in 1999]. For my class, she could do no wrong. I think that's really telling.

At different points I have received flak from scholars for the in-class resources I use. You're not supposed to teach Harris's *I Kissed Dating Goodbye* or Winner's *Real Sex* because they're not "ivory tower material"—except that it's in these books where robust conversations are happening about the things students care about. I'm a feminist and a liberal, but this is something beyond ideology. It's not a Left or Right issue. It's about responding to young people who are struggling. It's a mistake of many people to tense up about ideology in the middle of this kind of conversation. Part of my job is to figure out what professors do about the issues students are struggling with. They want modesty. And we can give them rich resources on modesty. So why don't we then?[5]

Good question! The answer, as I wrote earlier, is because of the enormous power of political correctness on university and college campuses today. It sometimes turns truth and reason on their ear. As the comment by Dr. Freitas indicates, Wendy Shalit deserves the credit for taking on the hookup culture and explaining why girls and young women are usually its victims. Once again, I highly recommend *Girls Gone Mild* and its predecessor, *A Return to Modesty*, to parents and teens. Here are some direct quotes that present what I consider to be very good news:

> Having grown up in an oversexualized culture, [these young girls] were sick of it and were trying to rally other girls to not present themselves as mere sex objects.[6]

> History has taught us a surprising lesson. Intimacy flourishes where there is also restraint.[7]

> The majority of young people who are participating in the hookup behavior are miserable.[8]

> All of the sexually active girls the reporters talked to wished they had waited until marriage. . . . By the time girls are fourteen to sixteen . . . they don't have any concept of sex as something special. After awhile it makes them feel worthless.[9]

> Young people report that trivializing sex also takes the fun out of it. . . . There is no longer any mystery or power to sex—it is just expected that everything will be sexual, and so nothing is. There is nothing to wait for, or to look forward to. . . . It's as if the concept of innocence were illegal.[10]

> Some young people are seeing the limits of the "let it all hang out" philosophy. . . . Sex may sell, but at our current degree of saturation, mystery and honor will sell even more. . . . We are hungry for examples.[11]

> I'm interested to see that young women are rising to this challenge. At some level they seem to recognize that they are the only ones who can change things.[12]

Shalit's observations are precisely on point. Systematic research has confirmed that girls are often remorseful after early sexual experience, and some have determined not to make the same mistake again. Consider the following corroborating findings from the Heritage Foundation.

> A recent poll by the National Campaign to Prevent Teen Pregnancy asked the question, "If you have had sexual intercourse,

do you wish you had waited longer?" Among those teens who reported that they had engaged in intercourse, nearly two-thirds stated that they wished they had waited longer before becoming sexually active. By contrast, only one-third of sexually active teens asserted that their commencement of sexual activity was appropriate and that they did not wish they had waited until they were older. Thus, among sexually active teens, those who regretted early sexual activity outnumbered those without such concerns by nearly two to one.

Concerns and regrets about sexual activity are strongest among teenage girls. Almost three-quarters of sexually active teen girls admit they wish they had delayed sexual activity until they were older. Among sexually active teenage girls, those with regrets concerning their initial sexual activity outnumbered those without regrets by nearly three to one.

The dissatisfaction and regrets expressed by teenagers concerning their own sexual activity is striking. Overall, a majority of sexually active boys and nearly three-quarters of sexually active girls regard their own initial sexual experience unfavorably—as an event they wish they had avoided.[13]

Michelle Malkin, in her article "Standing Up to the 'Girls Gone Wild' Culture," describes a courageous youngster who has not fallen victim to early sexual experimentation. Instead, she is fighting for decency. Malkin writes:

First, let me tell you about my new hero. Her name is Ella Gunderson and she's a student at Holy Family Parish School in Kirkland, Washington. As reported in the *Seattle Times* a few months ago, Ella recently wrote a remarkable letter to the Nordstrom's department store chain.

"Dear Nordstrom," she began. "I'm an 11-year-old girl who has tried shopping at your store for clothes, in particular jeans, but all of them ride way under my hips, and the next size up is too big and falls down. They're also way too tight, and as I get older, show everything every time I move. I see all of these girls who walk around with pants that show their belly button and underwear. Even at my age I know that that is not modest. With a pair of clothes from your store, I'd walk around showing half of my body and not fully dressed. . . . Your clerk suggested there is only one look. If that is true, then girls are supposed to walk around half naked. I think maybe you should change that."

All it took was one little girl to speak her mind about the excesses of our "Girls Gone Wild" culture. And guess what? The market, in a small way, responded. Nordstrom executives wrote back and pledged to young Ella Gunderson that they would try to broaden the clothes choices for girls. "Your letter really got my attention," wrote Kris Allan, manager of the local Nordstrom's where Ella shopped. "I think you are absolutely right. This look is not particularly a modest one and there should be choices for everyone." . . .

Here's the best part. She and her friends didn't wait around for Nordstrom's to change its inventory. With help from her mom and 37 of her classmates, Ella organized a fashion show to model decent clothes for girls aged 10 to 16. The sold-out show, called "Pure Fashion," drew a crowd of 250; two other clothing stores donated modest clothes; the girls got a standing ovation; and the event raised money for the Catholic Challenge Club network, which encourages young girls to stand up for their faith and their values in an increasingly secular and hostile world.[14]

Congratulations, Ella. We are proud of you. And thank you, Michelle, for bringing Ella to our attention.

Similar efforts are occurring throughout the culture. Have you heard about the Girlcott Girls? They were a group of twenty-four girls who originally banded together in a youth program called "Girls as Grantmakers" run by the Women and Girls Foundation of Southwest Pennsylvania.[15] They were formed with the goal of fighting back against Abercrombie & Fitch, i.e., "girlcotting" or protesting the company's sexist slogans on clothes. (A & F sold T-shirts with such messages as "Who needs brains when you have these?") The teenagers launched what became a cause célèbre and a successful social action.

The Girlcott Girls garnered national attention through radio and television—and more than 23,000 stories about them appeared online.[16] As a result, A & F pulled the demeaning T-shirts from the shelves and agreed to meet with the Girlcott group at A & F headquarters to discuss how the company could incorporate more empowering slogans on T-shirts for women.[17]

Now that the pressure is off, however, A & F has launched a new line of T-shirts targeted at youth with similarly egregious and demeaning images and messages. One such shirt depicts a cartoon-drawn woman opening her blouse and exposing herself to a man with the words "Show the Twins" in large red letters. Two other shirts for sale include such phrases as "Female Streaking Encouraged" and "Female Students Wanted for Sexual Research."[18] Why does it surprise us that Abercrombie & Fitch care more about their profits than the wishes of their customers, including protesting parents? I would never patronize this company!

I hope we have established the fact that teen girls are beginning to understand why morality and modesty are vitally important to them. If given half a chance, they will recognize that they have much to lose by engaging in raunchy behavior. That should not be a difficult case for parents to make, even to starry-eyed adolescents who think they have met the man of their dreams. It is the task of parents to do everything possible to communicate truth to their kids, and the earlier they get started, the better.

You, Mom and Dad, are the centerpiece of that effort. According to Christine Kim, a policy analyst for the Heritage Foundation, "Parental factors that appear to offer strong protection against the onset of early sexual activity include an intact family structure; parents' disapproval of adolescent sex; teens' sense of belonging to and satisfaction with their families; parental monitoring; and to a lesser extent, parent-child communication about teen sex and its consequences."[19]

Dr. Robert Blum, professor and chair of the Department of Population, Family, and Reproductive Health at Johns Hopkins, published a study designed to gauge parental influence on a girl's sexual behavior. His overall conclusion? The quality of the relationship between teens and their mothers was the primary factor in support of virginity.[20] Attachment, anyone? When the girls felt close to their moms and were aware that they disapproved of premarital sex, they were less likely to engage in such activities. Parental closeness was pivotal, but it resulted less from family activities and "lectures" than it did from parents' regular involvement in their children's lives.

Dr. Blum said, "We went out and asked kids in focus groups around the Twin Cities, 'How do you know if you're connected to your parents?' and they gave us fabulous answers. . . . They said things like, 'My mom works two jobs but she always calls when I come home to see how my day was.' Or 'When I go on a date, my dad doesn't say, 'How was what's his name.' To kids, being connected means 'My parents remember me. They think I'm important in their lives and they give me that message all the time.'"[21] It is also helpful to talk to the parents of your daughter's friends.

Blum said talking about sex is important, but it does not mean sitting down in the living room for a serious discussion with diagrams and charts.

The kids tell him, "Spare me that one." Instead, he suggests, "Talking about sex is reading the newspaper and saying, 'Hey, what do you think about that?' It's turning off the television and saying, 'What's happening in your world?' It's also driving in your minivan with your daughters, discussing the latest episode of *Oprah*."[22]

Dr. Blum's findings make sense, but it's important to note that the nature of those conversations is critically important. Sadly, today's kids are regularly given mixed messages by their moms and dads. The so-called safe-sex culture has indoctrinated parents to such a degree that many will say to their kids, "I hope you don't have sex, but if you do, I hope you'll be smart enough to use protection." Is that wise advice to give a hormone-driven teenager who is eager to explore the pleasures of adult sexuality? I certainly think not! In fact, a recent survey asked teens if that qualifying statement left them thinking their parents were basically giving them a green light to have sex with their girlfriend or boyfriend. Nearly half of those kids responded in the affirmative.[23]

Other studies reveal that older teenage girls who have better relationships with their fathers tend to postpone sexual activity longer. The researchers concluded that those who are close to their fathers tend to have fewer boyfriends, feel more guilty about having premarital sex, and tend to eat more meals together as a family.[24]

In short, having a healthy relationship with your daughter (or son) helps to inoculate her against immoral behavior. Clearly, the best birth control for teens is not only Mom, but also Dad! In a world where ten thousand American teenagers contract a venereal disease every day, that is very good news.[25] Unfortunately, mothers and fathers are often *unaware* of their impact, or else they misinterpret it.

In one survey of seven hundred teens, 58 percent reported being sexually active, but only 34 percent of their mothers believed they were.[26] Clearly, there is a major disconnect at this point. Of course, since time began, curious and crafty teenagers have been pushing the envelope, often trying to hide their sexual escapades from Mom and Dad, but never before have the stakes been so high. Now more than ever, parents should invest themselves in their children, building bridges to them stone upon stone and precept upon precept.

How is that accomplished? With generous amounts of that most precious of commodities: time. The National Center on Addiction and Substance Abuse (CASA) at Columbia University conducted a study debunking the catchphrase "It's not the quantity of time spent with children that counts; it is the quality."[27] In fact, that transparent little rationalization is responsible for millions of children being given *neither*. Quality moments don't occur in the absence of time. Unfortunately, time is in short supply in most of today's homes. Mihaly Csikszentmihalyi and Reed Larson found that adolescents spend only 4.8 percent of their time with their parents and only 2 percent with adults who are not their parents.[28]

Chap Clark, Ph.D., professor at Fuller Theological Seminary, laments this lack of intimacy between generations. He writes:

> Adolescents have been cut off for far too long from the adults who have the power and experience to escort them into the greater society. Adolescents have been abandoned. They have, therefore, created their own world, a world that is designed to protect them from the destructive forces and wiles of the adult community.[29]

Pollster Frank Luntz addressed this problem in his book *What Americans Really Want . . . Really*. In addition to his other objectives, he wanted to determine what parents could do to help their teens cultivate a commitment to good, clean living. Specifically, he hoped to ascertain what moms and dads could do to draw their children toward their values and further into the family itself. I think Dr. Luntz's findings are insightful and would be useful to parents trying to create "good news" at home. He kindly gave me permission to quote from his book:

> The American family is broken. Not entirely shattered, but certainly broken. When more than half of marriages end in divorce, we have a problem with broken families. When one in three children lives in a home with only one biological parent, we have a problem with broken families. There are countless households where single parents and even responsible older siblings are stepping up and stepping in to fill the void created by the absence of another parent. Unconventional families are doing what they can to make do, but it's an uphill struggle. The strains on time, resources, and money that result from raising a family are increasingly difficult for two-parent households, let alone for single parents. . . . Good examples are best set and opportunities for children to learn are greatest when they have a mother and a father to teach them. We know we have to do better.
>
> We should find hope in the fact that the American people realize the importance of the family, even if we struggle to protect it. When asked what mattered most to them personally,

Americans agree that having "a loving family" is the single most important priority among a list of many high priorities (combined top three answers):

A loving family	54%
Good health	50%
Financial security	43%
Happiness	33%
Eventually going to heaven	25%
A chance to give something back	24%
Getting as much as I can out of life	17%
A great career	9%
Staying young at heart	9%
Doing something truly memorable	9%
A long life	8%
Opportunities to travel	8%
More time to do what you want	5%
Fewer day-to-day hassles	4%
More choices in life	1%

For a number of years, my research firm did the polling for the Center for Addiction and Substance Abuse (CASA) at Columbia University. Led by Joe Califano—the Secretary of Health, Education and Welfare under Jimmy Carter and a passionate advocate for healthy living—we were encouraged to examine the aspects of parental behavior that might trigger harmful pathological behavior by their teenage children. What we learned should be tacked up on every refrigerator door and on the back of every BlackBerry in America. Wake up, America. Here are the six parental behaviors that are most likely to help—or destroy—your own children:

Healthy Children to Healthy Adults: The Six Steps Parents Really Need to Know

1. Having dinner with your children. Nothing says "I truly care about you" more than spending dinnertime with your children at least five nights a week. More than any other day-to-day behavior, parents who dine with their children produce healthier adults because it sends the clear signal

that their children are a high priority. Parents who miss dinner—no matter what the excuse—are sending the wrong message, and that message is unfortunately being heard loud and clear.

Let me interrupt here and say that Dr. Luntz found that teens who eat dinner at home three to five times per week have a lower risk of using cigarettes, alcohol, and illegal drugs, including marijuana. Only 34 percent of those teens say the television is on during family dinners, and only 12 percent say the family doesn't talk much. Of those who dine infrequently with their parents, 45 percent say the television is usually on as they eat, 29 percent say that the family does not talk very much, and 16 percent say that their dinners are often cut short.[30] The application for parents is crystal clear. Now, back to Dr. Luntz's list.

2. Taking your children to church or synagogue weekly. It is no coincidence that the most successful anti-drug and anti-alcohol programs have a spiritual component. If your children are taught at a young age that there is something out there bigger and more important than themselves, they are more likely to respect and appreciate the wonders of life and less likely to destroy it with drugs and alcohol.

3. Checking your child's homework nightly. There are two components at work here. First, a parent's daily participation in the homework assignments communicates that their children matter, and it also serves as an early warning sign if something is off track. Furthermore, children need to see that their intellectual development is just as important as their physical development. The more engaged a child is in intellectual pursuits, the less likely he or she is to engage in harmful physical behavior.

4. Demanding the truth from your children—and getting it. Parents who insist on knowing exactly where their children are on Friday and Saturday nights are sending a clear message that not every place, every friend, or every behavior is acceptable. Children who tell them the truth are acknowledging those boundaries, but if they would lie about where they are, they are most assuredly lying about what they do. Deceit in the name of "teenagers will be teenagers" should never be tolerated.

5. Taking your children on vacation for at least a week at a time. Long weekends don't qualify because it just isn't long enough to break the daily routine or reconnect the relationship. You need a week without their texting, your e-mailing, and everyone's cell phones. There are no shortcuts here. Switching your portable devices to vibrate is not enough. Turn them completely off so that you can turn your children back on.

6. Encourage them to participate in a team sport. Sorry, but individual sports and other group activities like band and drama don't count. Team members are often even less tolerant of substance abuse than parents—for good reason. When teenagers are forced to depend on each other's physical health and performance, they are less likely to engage in harmful physical behavior. Peer pressure to do the right thing can be a powerful motivating force.

What practical information Dr. Luntz has provided with these findings. I appreciate his allowing me to share his conclusions with you.

I will close with this thought. In the Broadway musical *The Music Man*, a traveling salesman sings a song offering advice to the mothers and fathers of River City. It is called "Ya Got Trouble."[32] He proposes getting the kids involved in a marching band as a way to keep them moral after school. Well, even though the salesman was something of a con man, he was onto something. Parents do need to think hard about protecting their children from harmful influences after school and at all other times. The solution is to be found in building good relationships, in providing close supervision, in keeping your eyes and ears open, in enjoying wholesome recreation with your children, in encouraging team sports, in getting involved in a caring church, in enrolling your kids in a good school, in careful monitoring of their friends, in talking a lot at evening meals, and in praying constantly. These are the contributors to "good news about girls"—and boys.

CHARMING YOUR DAUGHTER

PROVIDED BELOW IS a story you might want to consider sharing with your sixteen-year-old daughter. I found it delightful, and think it might be useful in your family. Enjoy.

The Charm Bracelet
by Sarah Kistler

Sweet sixteen had finally come! I never thought I'd make it. But I did. And it was amazing. My parents threw the birthday party of the century, and I had more people over than I could count. The whole day had been awesome. But as I watched the sun begin to set, I knew the best part was soon to come.

It was late in the evening. Confetti had been swept up, helium balloons had started to sag, and gift wrapping had been folded neatly and tucked away for my mom's later use. As I sat at my window studying the dusky sky, Dad peeked into my room with a smile.

"Ready to go, Sweetie?" he asked.

Was that a trick question? I wondered as I scrambled to my feet. I'd been waiting for this night for five long years, and it was finally here! I was now officially allowed to date!

The plan was for my parents and me to go to my favorite restaurant on the night of my sixteenth birthday and officiate the agreement, go over standards, and discuss rules and such. And now we were finally on the way.

I sat across from my parents in a quiet corner booth. Having just placed our orders, I figured it was time to get on with it. "So. I can go out with any guy I want to, right?" I squealed, hardly able to contain my excitement.

Mom and Dad chuckled. Dad answered, "Well, we agreed to that, didn't we?"

"Sweet!" I exclaimed, doing a little victory dance in my seat. My parents had held me off for years, but now that the time had come, they would let me date any guy I wanted! Of course they knew I had a good relationship with God and wasn't too short on common sense, either.

"Now wait just a second," Mom interrupted with a smile. "You have to agree to a little something yourself."

I was expecting a lecture of some sort, so I was already prepared. "So what do I have to do now?" I asked, leaning forward on my elbows.

"Just open this," Dad answered, producing a small white box. He gave a mysterious smile.

I hesitated a moment before removing the curly pink ribbon. I slowly opened the lid and saw a beautiful silver bracelet. But not just any bracelet. It was a charm bracelet. And they weren't just any charms. They were gemstones, small but gorgeous. A dozen dainty charms dangled gently.

"Wow." I didn't know what else to say. I wasn't expecting this at all.

"Now you have to understand this isn't just any bracelet," Mom informed me.

"I know," I said. "It is so beautiful!" I studied it closer. There were six small charms alternating with six tinier ones. The smaller ones were a deep blue. Sapphires, I guessed. And the other six were each different. One appeared to be just a rock, one was pink, a white one, a red one, green, and . . . was that a diamond?

"This charm bracelet is symbolic," Dad explained, leaning in closer to study it with me. "It represents you and your purity. This is what will guide you through your dating relationships. Your mother and I can only tell you what's right. We can't make you believe it yourself. Hopefully, this will."

I looked up solemnly. "I'm listening."

"This represents the first time you hold a guy's hand," Mom said, pointing to the gray one. "It's just a piece of polished granite. Seemingly cheap, yes, but it's still a part of your bracelet. This is pink quartz."

Then she gently rubbed the next one between her fingers. "It represents your first kiss."

"This green one is an emerald," Dad continued. "This is your first boyfriend. The pearl is the first time you say 'I love you' to a man other than me."

I giggled. This was so amazing.

"The ruby stands for your first engagement. And the diamond represents the first time you say 'I do,'" Mom finished.

After letting it all sink in, I cleared my emotion-clogged throat. "What do the six tiny sapphires stand for?" I asked.

"Those are to remind you how beautiful and valuable you are to us and to God," Dad replied. "Now here's the hitch in all this, the one and only rule you'll ever have to follow when it comes to dating."

Only one rule. Sounded good. But little did I know . . .

"Whenever you give one of these actions of love—a kiss, an 'I love you,' a hand to hold—you also have to give the recipient the gem to match."

I must've misunderstood. "I have to give him the gem?"

"You have to give it to him," Mom restated.

I was silent for a moment. I thought they must be joking. But they weren't even thinking of cracking a smile.

"But Daddy!" I suddenly shrieked. "These are insanely expensive! I can't just give them away!"

He gave a soft, loving chuckle. "Did you hear what you just said?"

I thought about it.

"Baby, your purity, your heart, they're far more valuable than a few little rocks. If you can't find it in your heart to give away your little charms, I don't think you should be giving away the things they represent."

I could feel my insides melting, ready to gush out my tear ducts. On the one hand, it made me feel valuable and precious. But on the other, it made me furious. It made no sense. But it would.

A few weeks after that night, I was hanging out with my

friends at the beach. Chad wouldn't swim because I wouldn't swim. I was more interested in reading than getting caked with sand, and he was more interested in sitting with me than swimming with his buddies. He was sweet. He was cute. And he tried to hold my hand.

I was thrilled for a nanosecond when a certain piece of ugly granite flashed through my mind and made me move out of his reach. I was severely annoyed—annoyed at my parents, annoyed at my bracelet-turned-handcuffs, but most of all, annoyed at myself. I was letting a little rock dominate my romantic life.

I furiously glared at it during the whole embarrassing walk to the bathhouse. But then God hit me upside the head with a shocking epiphany. I couldn't give up my little chunk of granite. It was a part of my bracelet, which in a sense made it a part of me. I wouldn't be whole without it. It wasn't a priceless gem, yet it was still valuable. It made sense after that.

Kevin came along eventually. We had fun. We hung out a lot. I thought I might love him. I thought I might tell him so.

I thought of my pearl.

It turned out that I didn't love him as much as I thought I did.

So my parents had been right. They couldn't make me believe the things they wanted me to believe. So they let God and my bracelet do the work instead. Among the four of them, I figured out how valuable I was. How valuable my purity was. How not valuable guys were who were just wasting my time and emotions. If they weren't in it for the whole bracelet, why should they get one part of it?

Nate. He thought my bracelet was awesome. So he never tried to hold my hand. He never tried to kiss me. But he asked me to marry him.

I never knew that so many years of torture could amount to so much happiness. I'd thought it was silly. I'd thought it was overrated. But now, I have never been more glad of anything in my life.

As I gave my husband the charm bracelet in its entirety, I wondered why I had found it so hard to hang on to those little rocks when it was so amazing to give them all to the man I truly loved.

But it didn't end there. Now our daughter wears it.[1]

PUBERTY AND ADOLESCENCE

LET'S RETURN NOW to chapter 4 ("Why She Is Who She Is") and pick up the story of female development where we left it in early childhood. We talked there about "juvenile puberty," which is a period of estrogen saturation that begins in girls between six and thirty months of age. You'll remember that this hormone and others wire the brain for femininity and prepare it for all that will come thereafter. Then at about three years of age, estrogen levels fall dramatically, and a period of relative quiet occurs hormonally. This is called the "juvenile pause," and it lasts for five to eight years.[1] During that period, girls are typically disinterested in boys and don't even like them very much. The feeling is certainly mutual.

I hope you will stay with me now, because what I will share at this point might get a bit technical. I'll try not to overwhelm you with details, although it is important to understand what is about to happen to your girls. So if you will, please consider these next few paragraphs very carefully as I describe a fascinating but complex developmental journey. The changes that are about to occur will affect the rest of their lives.

Immediately after the juvenile pause, puberty comes on like a house afire. The girl enters a period of intense physical, emotional, and neurological transformation. The timing of this new phase is genetically controlled, although it also appears to be affected by family stability and other factors such as weight gain.[2] Ultimately, however, puberty is set into motion by signals from a remarkable area of the midbrain called the hypothalamus.[3]

This part of the brain closely monitors much of the body's internal environment, including temperature, blood pH, blood sugar levels, and the concentration of many hormones. If a particular chemical is deemed to be out of balance, a signal will be sent to other parts of the brain or body to effect needed changes.

When the time is right, the hypothalamus begins barking orders to the pituitary gland by the secretion of hormones. They are powerful chemical messengers that circulate through the bloodstream and tell the body and cells how to react.[4] The pituitary is an aspirin-sized structure that sits at the base of the brain. In spite of its tiny size, it plays a very important role in regulating numerous body functions. It has been called "the master gland" because it controls a multitude of hormonal functions.[5] Responding to the direction of the hypothalamus, among other glands, it secretes two hormones, LH and FSH, into the bloodstream that flow to the ovaries and cause the production of massive amounts of estrogen. Thus, the girl's brain is marinated for a second time in this female hormone, which begins to spur maturation and sexual development. Three other primary hormones are involved in puberty: progesterone, testosterone, and growth hormones.[6] When they work in concert, it is like fireworks on the Fourth of July.

As LH and FSH stimulate the production of estrogen and progesterone by the ovaries, these hormone levels are monitored by a set of receptors in the hypothalamus and pituitary. In other words, a delicate feedback mechanism comes into play that fine-tunes the constantly fluctuating hormones in a specified fashion, thereby allowing the miracle of ovulation and, as some would say, the curse of menstruation. These elevated levels also influence a multitude of functions and emotions, including anger, sorrow, joy, memory, aggression, thirst, appetite, weight, fat distribution, the development of secondary sex characteristics such as pubic hair, and higher intellectual functioning. In short, they bring about a makeover of the body and the personality. It all begins happening very quickly. So brace yourselves, Mom and Dad. When you see "tiny green buds" appearing on your little girl's tree, you know that childhood is over and she is growing up.

Don't be surprised if your prepubescent kids have heard from older siblings or friends that something exciting and scary is coming, even if they don't yet know what it is. I am reminded of a ten-year-old boy who had a speaking part in a school performance. He was supposed to quote the immortal words of Patrick Henry, but he became confused at the last moment and shouted out, "Give me puberty or give me death!" For some parents, the choice seems to come down to those alternatives.

Once these developmental changes begin to occur, they can be deeply disturbing to a girl who hasn't been told what is happening to her body.

Because it is all so bewildering, she can worry herself sick about sore breast buds ("Do I have cancer?"), menstruation ("Am I bleeding to death?"), and other fears associated with physical changes. That is why it is so very important for you to prepare your daughters for puberty and adolescence. Not only should they come to understand the approaching physical changes, they should also be informed about the wildly fluctuating emotions that will accompany this time of life. Doubts about personal self-worth should also be anticipated and explained. They are inevitable.

By the way, in the addendum at the conclusion of this book is a description of a CD and book series for prepubescent boys and girls titled *Preparing for Adolescence*.[7] I designed it to assist parents in talking with their kids about what is about to happen to them developmentally. Tens of thousands of families have used the recordings and the book to ease the transition from childhood to the teen experience.

Moms and dads should understand that the hormonal barrage that initiates puberty is highly traumatic to the female brain, and it can throw a girl into complete disequilibrium until she begins to adjust to it.[8] This is why parents must take the time to understand what she is going through. From pubescence through adolescence, there will be recurring times of moodiness, anxiety, anger, self-pity, and depression. There will also be periods of giddiness, glee, elation, and happiness. Emotions are on a roller coaster from the peak to the valley, and from one day—or one hour—to the next. The entire family sometimes hangs on for dear life until things start to settle down. For some girls, the return to equilibrium can take five years or longer. In the meantime, surging levels of estrogen and progesterone affect behavior and personality dramatically. They have the female brain (and parents) rocking and reeling.

Dr. Louann Brizendine, a Yale-trained psychiatrist and the author of *The Female Brain*, describes the adolescent experience like this:

> Drama, drama, drama. That's what's happening in a teen girl's life and a teen girl's brain. "Mom, I so totally can't go to school. I just found out Brian likes me and I have a huge zit and no concealer. . . . How can you even think I'll go?" "Homework? I told you I'm not doing any more until you promise to send me away to school. I can't stand living with you for one more minute." "No, I'm not done talking to Eve. It has not been two hours, and I'm *not* getting off the phone." This is what you get if you have the modern version of the teen girl brain in your house.[9]
>
> With this new estrogen-driven reality, aggression also

plays a big role. The teen girl brain will make her feel power-ful, always right, and blind to consequences. Without that drive, she'll never be able to grow up, but getting through it, especially for the teen girl, isn't easy. As she begins to expe-rience her full "girl power," which includes premenstrual syndrome [PMS], sexual competition, and controlling girl groups, her brain states can often make her reality, well, a little hellish.[10]

Hellish, indeed! According to a report issued by the National Institute of Mental Health, approximately 10 to 20 percent of teen girls are in con-tinuing states of crisis.[11] Those upheavals are physical, emotional, and men-tal in nature. They produce large amounts of the stress hormone cortisol. This hormone prepares the body for emergencies, but when cortisol levels are continually high, both the mind and the body are affected adversely. The result is an interference with normal female development.

These findings do not apply to every girl, of course. The NIMH report implies that 80 to 90 percent of girls are *not* in constant states of crisis, and they go through this time of hormonal imbalance without serious conse-quences.[12] Most struggle one way or another, however.

What does a girl need from her parents when everything has gone topsy-turvy? The answer, in a word, is more attachment, not less. (Remem-ber chapter 7?) Even when she is most unlovable, she needs love and con-nectedness from her mother, but also from her father. She needs them to be as calm, mature, and parental as possible. There is no room in their relationship for an out-of-control, screaming, confused, and scared adult. A voice of reason is desperately needed, even with a child who has become entirely unreasonable. I know this is difficult advice to receive or implement because a pubescent girl can be absolutely maddening. But she typically has little self-control and certainly doesn't need a mom with the same problem. The 10 to 20 percent of adolescent girls who are in crisis mode need all the stability they can get from their families. Strange impulses are urging them to do things that make no sense to a rational mind, and many of them can't help responding the way they do.

And let me emphasize this: the divorce of parents during this time is always devastating! Marital breakups are difficult for a child of any age, but they are especially stressful when puberty is in full swing. If moms and dads love their kids, they will do everything possible to avoid this tragedy during the toughest years of their child's life. Divorce can send an unstable kid, and even a mature one, over the edge.

Furthermore, because the onset of puberty is occurring earlier today, and because women are tending to marry later, it is not uncommon for mothers to be going through the stresses of menopause at the same time their daughters are entering the age of sexual awakening. The proximity of those two volatile hormonal experiences within a family can cause a train wreck between generations.

Physician Nancy Snyderman and her teen daughter experienced just such a collision in their relationship. It led the doctor to write an outstanding book titled *Girl in the Mirror*. In it she observed that in previous generations these pivotal journeys had been separated by time. But the simultaneous occurrence of two highly charged hormonal phases adds another dimension to the mother-daughter relationship. It often creates catfights between generations.[13] All I can say is, dads, beware. Maybe you ought to get out of Dodge every now and then.

That last sentence was intended to be tongue in cheek. In reality, fathers are extremely important in the midst of this chaos. If their temperaments allow, they can be the "voice of reason" to which I referred. Fathers can help interpret motives, mitigate harsh words, and soothe hurt feelings across the generational gap. But if Dad also starts to go berserk, it's Katie bar the door. A pubescent girl, a menopausal mother, a couple of adolescent siblings, and an emotionally unstable dad become a volatile cocktail.

Don Imus, the longtime radio shock jock, once told his audience that as the father of four daughters and the husband to an emotionally wired wife, he never experienced a day in a month when someone in his house wasn't either kicking the dog or slamming a door.

The surprising thing is that at the same time puberty is causing girls to pull away from the people they love, other forces inside them are creating an inexplicable longing for connectedness. Just as estrogen drives the need for intimacy in infancy, it has the same effect in puberty and adolescence, only this time it is even more intense. The desire for social bonding, especially with peers, causes great vulnerability. This is why adolescents travel in packs. It is to protect themselves. The most paralyzing fear for a girl in these years is the prospect of being left out, rejected, criticized, or humiliated. Even the most minor criticism from parents can produce a tsunami of tears and retribution. Overreaction becomes an everyday event. Heaven help the mom or dad who tries to convince a sobbing girl that "it's no big deal." They are wrong. *Everything* is a big deal.

To be wounded by a boy can seem like a fate worse than death to a vulnerable girl. That is because during puberty and adolescence, the most urgent biological impulse is to be perceived as sexually desirable. It explains why girls spend hours in front of mirrors, examining, fretting, preening, rearranging, enhancing, wishing, and caking on makeup. Most do not like what they see. Looking back at them are images of braces, acne, misshapen noses, protruding ears, freckles, or "impossible" hair. As parents, your job is to understand these pressures and then to help your daughters cope as much as possible.

Let's talk now about the monthly cycle and how it influences the female mind and body. It is *impossible* to comprehend how a teen girl feels about herself, about her family, about her life, and about her peers without considering the impact of her cycle and the fluctuating hormones that drive it. I refer to that physiological and emotional oscillation as "the seasons of a woman's month."[14]

Note that every woman is different, and some individuals experience and exhibit these characteristics more than others. The description that follows is also more typical of adolescents and younger women than those who are more mature. This, however, is the way the system usually works.

The first week after a menstrual period might be considered the springtime of the month. Estrogen levels are on the rise, producing surging amounts of energy, ambition, and optimism. The world looks bright, and the mood is upbeat. Neurotransmitters in the brain, including serotonin, dopamine, and norepinephrine, are more active, facilitating thought, memory, and intellectual capability. It is a most pleasant time of the month.[15]

I'm reminded of the commercial for a brand of margarine that aired endlessly. It exclaimed, "Everything's better with Blue Bonnet on it." Likewise, everything seems better when estrogen is "moving on up."

Summertime arrives during the second week of the menstrual month. Estrogen reaches its peak and then levels off. A pubescent or adolescent girl in this phase remains energetic, but she paces herself more moderately. She is still confident, creative, and, depending on other circumstances, might be euphoric. It takes a great deal to upset or worry her, and she wishes every day could be like these waning days of summer. Alas, they will soon be a memory. Estrogen is about to take a nosedive.

Then comes the fall. About midcycle, during the start of the third week, a young woman experiences ovulation and her time of fertility. Estrogen levels then rebound for a few days. These developments coincide with her peak of sexual desire. It is also during this week that she feels deep devotion, affection, and closeness for the boy or man she loves. Two hormones are influential in producing those responses. The first is testosterone, the male sex hormone, and the other is progesterone, called "the bonding hormone." Progesterone makes a girl feel close to the one she believes she loves. We can say with a smile that there is a God-designed "conspiracy" at work here to assure the propagation of the human race. You and I would not have existed without it.

Progesterone levels continue to rise at this time. This hormone has two primary functions related to fertility. First, it counteracts the influence of estrogen. Conception cannot occur in the presence of high levels of estrogen. Second, progesterone produces the "fertile soil" of a thickened uterine lining.

Then comes the winter. Estrogen levels continue to plummet in this fourth week. So do progesterone and endorphins. As a result, a girl's mood darkens and she becomes more "within herself." These hormonal changes are very toxic to the brain and can create depression and foreboding, low self-esteem, hypersensitivity, sadness, and anger. Also, she typically feels unloved and insecure. She may sense she is "in a fog" and may walk into a room and not remember why she is there. Even her performance in school can be affected. Alas, she is experiencing the symptoms known around the world as premenstrual syndrome. It is followed in about three days by a period, with its cramping, bloating, and malaise.

And so ends the four-week cycle. It is followed quickly by a surge of estrogen and the return of good times.

I wish I had understood the emotional characteristic of the menstrual cycle when Shirley and I were first married. We had a wonderful relationship following the fun and laughter of college life and three years of courtship. Nevertheless, there was so much about her that I had to learn through "on-the-job training." There was a recurring conversation that we came to call "the talk." It would typically occur late at night when she couldn't sleep. Then my wife, whom I adored, would begin telling me how I wasn't meeting her needs for love and affection, and that I had become too busy for her. Sometimes she would cry, and at other times she would be angry. It bewildered me, because there had been no change in our relationship that I could identify. Those were good days in our lives, and I had no idea what I had done to reject or hurt her. "The talk" was not precipitated, as far as I could tell, by fights or marital disagreements. I was just a young husband who wanted to please his wife. I remember saying repeatedly, "Shirley, for Pete's sake, I want the same thing you want. Why are we having this conversation again?"

I eventually cracked the code. Her irritation had very little to do with me, although a man can always be more caring and considerate. But that was not the problem. Shirley was apparently experiencing the fall and winter of her month. That's when I realized what she needed in those times. My job was not to explain or promise or get angry in response. I needed to simply hold my wife close, tell her how much I loved her, and listen as she talked. That was enough.

Your pubescent daughter has the same need. When she is wailing and complaining and despairing over this or that, she needs attachment. She needs comfort and love. And she needs a few more days to move on past the winter and into the sunlight of the spring. Sounds easy, right? It ain't.

Before we leave the subject of hormones that come into play at this time, there is another secretion that is almost mischievous in its influence. It is oxytocin, which—you guessed it—is stimulated by estrogen. It is nicknamed "the cuddle hormone,"[16] and you can figure out where it leads. When a girl gets to know a guy and feels safe with him, her oxytocin levels rise, giving her a rush of hope, trust, optimism, confidence, and a feeling that all her needs will be met.[17] She may start to fall in love with him, or something that feels like love for a while, but not because he is the perfect human being. He is perceived as the perfect human being because she starts to feel like it. Hugging and snuggling cause oxytocin levels to surge, which leads to more hugging and snuggling. Talk about a tender trap!

Let me say what I implied a moment ago. Our biochemistry is designed to guarantee the continuation of the human race, with hormones, receptor sites, brain wiring, and neurotransmitters effectively carrying impulses from cell to cell. Oxytocin is a powerful component of that apparatus. Dr. Brizendine says, "From an experiment on hugging, we also know that oxytocin is naturally released in the brain after a twenty-second hug from a partner—sealing the bond between huggers and triggering the brain's trust circuits. So don't let a guy hug you unless you plan to trust him."[18] Do you think you can help your daughter understand that hormone? No chance. You just have to hope her boyfriend doesn't know how it works.

On a side note, oxytocin is wonderfully important in the development of maternal attachments. Jeffrey Kluger is the author of an article entitled "The Science of Romance: Why We Love." It was published in *Time* (January 28, 2008) and included this finding about oxytocin:

> New mothers are flooded with the stuff during labor and nursing—one reason they connect so ferociously to their babies before they know them as anything more than a squirmy body and a hungry mouth. Live-in fathers whose partners are pregnant experience elevated oxytocin too—a good thing if they're going to stick around through months of gestation and years of child-rearing. So powerful is oxytocin that a stranger who merely walks into its line of fire can suddenly seem appealing.
>
> "In one study, an aide who was not involved with the birth of a baby would stand in a hospital room while the mother was in labor," says Sue Carter, a professor of psychiatry at

the University of Illinois. "The mothers later reported that they found the person very sympathetic, even though she was doing nothing at all."[19]

There is so much more to say about this complex topic, but we have to get on to "the rest of the story," as the late Paul Harvey was fond of saying. What I have tried to share to this point is an understanding of what your pubescent daughter is experiencing and why. Moms and dads, do you remember those days of exhilaration and despair? Do you recall falling madly in love over and over and over? Perhaps our own memories can help us understand our kids and help them deal with similar highs and lows.

I'll close with another personal recollection. When I was thirteen, my family took a car trip to see relatives in Idaho. Something was definitely going on inside of me, even though I didn't have a clue as to what it was. I just remember fantasizing from the backseat about meeting a cute girl—*any* cute girl—who would be standing on the street corner when we drove into town. I actually looked in vain for that nonexistent girl. Would you believe, she *did* exist. I met her a few afternoons later on a tennis court. She was an older woman of fourteen and was carrying a big tennis racket. I took one look at her and said to myself, *I knew it!* I was drunk on testosterone, and she had to be high on estrogen and oxytocin. It was a match made in heaven.

This little princess and I banged the ball at each other until sundown. I then went home knee-deep in love, even though she beat me soundly. It was one of the most thrilling afternoons of my life, but the affair never went anywhere. In fact, I never saw her again. She did, however, give me much to think about in years to come.

Later that summer, my family flew to Fairbanks, Alaska, where my father was the visiting preacher. That gave me an opportunity to meet a number of teens in the church who invited me to go out for a Coke after the evening service. As we rode in the car, a beautiful native Alaskan girl sitting in the front seat whirled around and said to me with a grin, "I'll bet you a nickel that I can kiss you without touching you."

I said, "How are you gonna do that?"

She just smiled and said, "You'll see." It sounded like a good deal to me, and I took her up on it. This little cutie then gave me my first kiss, dropped the nickel in my hand, and said, "You win!"

Man! Did I love it! I offered to make her the same deal, but she refused. It was all very innocent, but I remember that exhilarating experience with fondness to this day. I had just meandered into adolescence. Eight years later, I met a college homecoming queen named Shirley, and she turned my world upside down. She is the mother of my grown children and is still my sweetheart today. That's the way the system is designed. And guess who the grand Designer is?

I have felt an obligation to tell you the downside of puberty for girls and their parents. This experience need not be the bugaboo that it is held out to be. Wise parents can shepherd their youngsters through these early experiences and make them fun and clean. Adult supervision is absolutely necessary, however, to keep a girl or boy from getting too far ahead of themselves and doing things that will be harmful for decades to come. They also need help in understanding what is happening inside and recognizing that the unstable emotions that come flooding over them at times are temporary. Most of all, stay connected, especially in the dark days when the sky seems to be falling. It usually isn't.

The next chapter will present questions and answers dealing with what we have just discussed. If we were together today, these are some of the things I would want to talk to you about.

BULLIES, BUDDIES, AND BEST FRIENDS

EVERY PARENT HAS reason to be concerned today about the rise in violence among teen girls. The FBI's Uniform Crime Reports indicate that the
number of female arrests for aggravated assault has been increasing for more
than a decade.[1] Some researchers are calling it an epidemic of violence.[2]
They say it reflects emotional pressures resulting from the breakdown of
family, church, community, and school. Others believe girls have become
more masculinized in an effort to imitate and compete with boys, and to
seek their approval. There is validity to all these hypotheses, but the broader
explanation is much more complex.

I want to focus our attention in this chapter on bullying behavior
among girls, which has its own unique purposes and methods. Boys usually
assault one another physically, by kicking, hitting, pulling down pants, and
threatening weaker boys. Girls do it relationally, by backstabbing, harassing,
name-calling, isolating, spreading rumors and lies, and just being nasty.
Taunting behavior of this ilk is pervasive wherever girls are found. Approximately one in three students is either a perpetrator or a target of bullying,
but every student is touched by it in one way or another. That means your
daughter is likely to be impacted emotionally by bullying at some time
during her developmental journey. She might even be the one who is doing
the dirty work.

According to the National Education Association, more than 160,000
children stay home from school every day because of fear of intimidation.[3]

One mother told me that her daughter awakens early each morning and lies in bed wondering, *How can I get through this day without being humiliated?* She worries about not having someone to sit with at lunch and how to do her hair and select clothes in ways that will not bring her ridicule. For this girl and millions of others, school is a minefield through which they walk every day. A bomb could go off underneath them at any moment. Girls whose weight is normal are called "fat," and those who have unusual physical characteristics are mocked unmercifully. They are given nicknames to highlight the features they most want to hide. This insecure world in which children live has a huge effect on them and influences the women they will someday become. And sadly the harassment often begins in early childhood, when they are least able to deal with it.

The implications for naturally fearful and shy girls are highly significant. As they grow older, some will develop ulcers, eating disorders, and depression. In her article "Terrorists in the Schoolyard," journalist Joanne Richard helps explain the scope of the problem and what very young boys and girls often have to endure.

> "Sticks and stones may break my bones but names will never hurt me."
>
> "That's a crock. It's wrong. It hurts," says parenting educator Kathy Lynn. The most common form of bullying is verbal and, according to Lynn and many other experts, school playgrounds are rife with taunts, torment, gossip and exclusion.
>
> The problem of social bullying is widespread and strikes fear in most children and parents: "It should. It's ugly and destructive," says [Barbara] Coloroso. "Bullying is a conscious, willful and deliberate hostile activity intended to harm—pleasure is derived from another person's pain," says Coloroso, an educational consultant and author of *The Bully, the Bullied, and the Bystander*.
>
> Janet Henderson (not her real name) knows: Her 10-year-old daughter, Sara, has been tormented and picked on for the past five years—"ever since kindergarten, when a child told her she was fat."
>
> Henderson, 36, a stay-at-home Mississauga mother of four, quietly sobs as she recounts Sara's painful school years: "It's been hell. Bullying has destroyed her. It's taken her from being a sweet, joyful and easy-going child to being suspicious and afraid—now she'd rather be alone.
>
> "This makes me so angry. It's heartbreaking and has

affected our entire family. How can kids be so mean and their parents not do anything about it? Some parents want their kids to belong so much that they allow them to attack others in order to be part of the group, instead of teaching them to stand up for others. I see so many teachers and parents turn a blind eye."

Experts have seen it all too many times: "Bullying isn't about conflict—it's about hatred and contempt," says Coloroso, and it has deadly effects.

"Bullying is a life-and-death issue. We have enough incidents in our recent past to convince us that it is not only the bully who may terrorize and haunt our community," she says. "Some targets whose cries went unheard, whose pain was ignored, whose oppression went unabated and unrelieved, have struck back with a vengeance and a rage that has racked our communities with incomprehensible horror and sorrow.

"Others, who reached what they felt was an utterly hopeless and irretrievable point, have turned the violence inward and killed themselves. Feeling they had no other way out of the pain and torture heaped on them by their tormentors, no one to turn to, no one to tell, they made the tragic and final exit."

And it's happening in younger and younger kids, says [Ann] Douglas, author of *The Mother of All Parenting Books*. "In fact, it seems to start during the kindergarten years. Girls can be particularly cruel at this age, excluding a particular child in the class because he or she didn't know it was suddenly 'uncool' to still be carrying a Blue's Clues backpack or wearing Teletubby socks.

"It's the loneliest feeling in the world to be the only kid in the class who isn't invited to someone's birthday party," adds Douglas.

Online bullying is now common with older kids: Bullying via e-mail, instant messages, online diaries, and personal websites. Messages that you thought were for your former best friend's eyes only can be quickly shared with an entire school community, along with a blow-by-blow description of all your shortcomings.

According to the experts, you're not born a bully: "It is learned, maybe at home or at daycare or in the classroom or from other kids. Children learn how to relate to others by watching how older people act and mimicking them," says Lynn.

"You have to be taught to have contempt, to hate," adds Coloroso, who adds that bullies harm without feeling empathy, compassion or shame. They feel a sense of entitlement and intolerance towards difference.

The bullied share one thing in common: "They are targeted, plain and simple," says Coloroso. "Each was singled out to be the object of scorn, merely because he or she was different in some way."

The cycle of violence must be broken in our homes, schools and communities: "We as individuals, families and entire communities must create safe harbour for all of our children. We must do what is necessary to take the weapons out of the hearts, minds and hands of our kids," says Coloroso.[4]

"Mrs. Henderson" said the twisting and warping of young minds by other children makes her "so angry." I share her irritation. Bullying is, indeed, a life-and-death issue for an increasing number of teens as well. Perhaps you read the news story about thirteen-year-old Megan Meier, who was an overweight, unhappy middle school girl. She met a boy named Josh online, and he began expressing an interest in her. Once Megan was involved emotionally, he started sending her hurtful e-mails and eventually dumped her viciously. She became so distraught that she hanged herself in her bedroom closet. After Megan's death, it was learned that "Josh" didn't even exist. He had been invented to taunt Megan.

What happened to this sad young woman is unconscionable. Unfortunately, many other middle school students are also subjected regularly to personal assaults of various forms. This harassment doesn't usually result in death, but something does begin to die inside these girls and boys. I have seen it firsthand, having taught science and math earlier in my career to 230 seventh and eighth grade students every day. The challenges these kids faced from their peers were very familiar to me. My students arrived at the beginning of the year hoping and praying for the best. Their adolescent hearts were pounding with excitement and expectation, but mostly they were afraid. Some had been abused for years and were scared half to death. They were thinking, *Will others like me? Will they laugh at me? Will I have any friends?* Their parents were wondering, *Will they make the right friends?*

For girls, the issue of what to wear is pivotal in surviving the dog-eat-dog world of middle school. The clothes a girl wears are the admission ticket to cliques that can protect from ridicule and relational bullying. A mistake at this point can be catastrophic. Cliques are governed by rigid rules and can be most unforgiving. Even the color choices become important. Writer Vanessa O'Connell describes the rules this way:

> Dorothy Espelage, a professor of educational psychology at the University of Illinois, Urbana-Champaign, who has studied teenage behavior for 14 years, says she has seen an increase in "bullying related to clothes." She attributes that to the proliferation of designer brands and the display of labels in ads. In the more than 20 states where she has studied teens, she has been surprised by how kids revere those they perceive to have the best clothes. Having access to designer clothing affords some kids "the opportunity to become popular—and that protects you and gives you social power and leverage over others," she says. . . .
>
> In one study, more than one-third of middle-school students responded "yes" when asked whether they are bullied because of the clothes they wear. Susan M. Swearer, associate professor of school psychology at the University of Nebraska in Lincoln, surveyed a total of more than 1,000 students at five Midwestern middle schools from 1999 to 2004, with about 56% of the sample female. While the prevalence of fashion bullies was greater in wealthy cities and towns, where more designer clothing is available, she found the problem is significant in poorer communities, too.
>
> Teens and adolescents are expected to wear not just any designer brands but the "right" ones. "The better brands you wear, the more popular you are," says Becky Gilker, a 13-year-old eighth-grader from Sherwood Park in the Canadian province of Alberta. "If you don't wear those things you get criticized."[5]

"Friends and enemies" will be the key to everything for your daughter in the middle school years and beyond. Remember that her brain was wired for intimacy with others during infancy, and now in puberty she yearns for close relationships with her peers. Intimacy is the air she breathes and her reason for living. That's why when adolescent friendships go sour and rejection settles in, emotional crises are inevitable.

Friendships change constantly during adolescence. Rosalind Wiseman describes this social pattern in her powerful book *Queen Bees and Wannabes*:

> Especially in sixth and seventh grade, girls change cliques frequently. When this happens, it's common for girls who used to be friends to turn on each other, and the bad teasing can be brutal. . . .
>
> Best friends are two girls who are truly inseparable. . . . They have their own language and codes. They wear each other's clothes. They may have crushes at the same time on the same person. . . . It's almost certain that they'll break up around seventh grade (if not before) when at least one will want to expand her social horizons. And then they'll make up, then break up, then make up. . . . Sometimes your daughter will be the dumper, sometimes the dumpee.[6]

Though breakups and realignments are common, they are terribly painful for the girl who has been thrown overboard. To her, the parting can seem like the end of the world. Two girls may have grown up together and spent countless hours sharing their most intimate feelings and fears. Trust was once the hallmark of their relationship. Then suddenly the rejected girl is treated like the scum of the earth. Her former best buddy won't return text messages or phone calls. They pass in the hall at school without even a "Hi" from the former friend. Barbed humor is used to embarrass and humiliate the rejected girl in front of others. No one wants to sit with her at lunch or at a ball game for fear of alienating the more powerful girl. The rejected girl may have no idea why it has happened, and indeed, there might have been no precipitating event—at least not a visible one. Without warning or explanation, she appears to be hated by the girl who matters to her most.

Our greatest concern must be for the vulnerable girl who lacks a social network to sustain her when her best pal becomes an enemy. Being rejected by a soul mate is a miserable experience, but it is even worse when the victim has no one else to whom she can turn.

Rachel Simmons, author of the book *Odd Girl Out*, says realignments of relationships often flow out of struggles for higher status. She writes:

> For girls on the popularity treadmill, friendship is rarely just friendship; it's a ticket, a tool, an opportunity—or a deadweight. You can own everything Abercrombie ever made, but if you don't have the right friends, you're nobody. . . .
>
> If popularity is a competition for relationships, getting

ahead socially means new relationships must be targeted and formed, old ones dismissed and shed. . . . In friendship, girls share secrets to grow closer. Relational competitions corrupt this process, transforming secrets into social currency and, later, ammunition. These girls spread gossip: they tell other people's secrets. They spread rumors: they invent other people's secrets. They gain calculated access to each other using intimate information.[7]

Being spurned by a particularly popular girl, especially one who is pretty, confident, and well connected socially, has a demoralizing effect on the personhood of a "lesser light." Author Dan Kindlon has described these highly successful and dominant teens in his book entitled *Alpha Girls*:

An "alpha girl" [is] a young woman who is destined to be a leader. She is talented, highly motivated, and self confident. The alpha girl doesn't feel limited by her sex; she is a *person* first and then a woman. . . . Clearly not all girls are alphas. Some lack self-confidence and are anxious, depressed, anorexic, or bulimic.[8]

When an alpha girl resorts to treachery and bullying tactics against a former friend, she does so with the combined power of an entire social network. She commonly recruits her "in" group buddies to engage in seek-and-destroy missions against those she dislikes. Together, the group can devastate an opponent so badly that it will take years for her to recover. Some girls never fully get over such an experience and will not trust other women thereafter. The majority of adult females, I believe, harbor painful memories of such occurrences during their adolescent years when they were ridiculed, ignored, uninvited, taunted, isolated, and lied about. Just ask your female friends if they remember such a time. Some will describe an early experience in vivid detail, perhaps through tears.

Many of the girls who are at the bottom of the social ladder at school are also rejected at home by their siblings, by kids in the neighborhood, and by absentee parents. They are chronically lonely, which makes them try too hard to make friends at school. Hunger for acceptance is like carrying a neon sign saying, "I am desperate." It drives away both male and female peers.

The need for warm and caring friendships has implications for physical and emotional health. Study after study has demonstrated that human beings are social creatures and thrive better when they are loved and appreciated, even by a few people. Dr. DeWitt Williams is director of health ministries of the North American Division of Seventh-Day Adventists. He addresses this understanding of human nature, offering this remarkable illustration:

> A friend sent me pictures of twin babies that were born prematurely. The nurses looked at these tiny babies and didn't think they were going to survive. The larger one might have a slim chance, but the smaller one didn't have much of a chance. So on the night that they thought the smaller baby would die, one of the nurses put her in the incubator with her sister. Almost as soon as the larger twin felt her sister next to her, she reached out and put her arm around her. Lying in bed, she cuddled up to her all night and that arm was wrapped tightly around her. Tubes were in their arms and noses, but they were close to each other. And that's all that mattered. The nurses said that from that moment on the little baby thrived. When they came in the next day, they were surprised to see how alert and responsive the little girl had become. From then on, she grew and gained weight. They both lived and thrived. A big hug and intimate closeness made the difference.
>
> There must be some truth in what someone has said: You need at least four hugs a day for survival, eight hugs for maintenance, and twelve hugs for growth. Have you had your hug today?[9]

Dr. Williams's point is that human beings desperately need the affirmation and support of one another at every stage of their lives, beginning when we are newborns. It is the way we were designed. The Creator could have put within us the temperaments of leopards, great white sharks, European bison, or other animals that remain solitary except when mating or raising young. Instead, He gave us an innate longing for human friendship and affection, and then told us to meet those needs for one another.

When Jesus was asked by a teacher of the law which of the commandments was most important, He replied, "The most important one . . . is this: . . . 'Love the Lord your God with all your heart and with all your soul and with all your mind and with all your strength.' The second is this: 'Love your neighbor as yourself.' There is no commandment greater than these" (Mark 12:29-31).

Given this emphasis, it is easy to understand why teens suffer so terribly when they are rejected and ridiculed. The need for belonging and emotional support during adolescence is greater than at any other time of life.

That is why the experience of being bullied as a teen is always devastating. The natural reaction of the wounded young man or woman is to develop a spirit of bitterness and anger. According to Rachel Simmons, bullying creates a hotbed of resentment and jealousy. Until it is exposed, it exists below the radar of teachers, counselors, and parents. Girls, however, are quite aware of what is going on.

This is what many girls are dealing with today. What can be done to help them? Let's start with what Wendy Shalit writes in *Girls Gone Mild*:

> Public health researchers at Tufts and Harvard tell us that bullying is learned behavior—learning to feel good at someone else's expense—and that this pattern can be unlearned. And Jennifer Connolly, the director of York University's LaMarsh Centre for Research into Violence and Conflict Resolution, has found that 90 percent of the time bullying will stop if adults in authority respond speedily and let the aggressor know that their behavior is completely unacceptable. Can it be "live and let live" attitudes are actually more likely to cause bullying than any belief in girls' niceness?[10]

I agree entirely that the incidence of bullying is increasing because more adults are permitting it to happen, and they may even encourage it by their unwillingness to teach girls to "be nice." Strong, independent, aggressive, and assertive girls appeal more to some modern adults' biases. For whatever reasons, parents, teachers, Scout leaders, and church supervisors often ignore taunting behavior. They become passive bystanders while beleaguered youngsters are desperate for adult intervention.

Let me illustrate: Every classroom has a few boys and girls at the bottom of the social hierarchy who are subjected to frequent harassment. Their ranks include those who are physically unattractive, intellectually challenged, or uncoordinated; boys who are effeminate and girls who are masculine; kids who are larger or smaller than their peers; those who are disabled; and members of racial minorities. Anyone who is different is an easy mark for the "wolf pack."

We've all heard the argument that says, "Kids will be kids—adults should stay out of the conflict and let the children settle things for themselves." Thus, adults become enablers. Let me say it clearly: I consider it child abuse for an adult to stand by passively while a defenseless boy or girl is assaulted by peers, physically or emotionally. The damage inflicted in those moments can reverberate for a lifetime.

Some years ago a woman told me about her experience as a room mother for her daughter's fourth-grade class. She visited the classroom on Valentine's Day to assist the teacher with the traditional party. Valentine's Day can be a painful day for an unpopular child. Every student counts the number of valentines he or she is given, which becomes a direct measure of social status.

This mother said the teacher announced that the class was going to play a game that required the formation of boy-girl teams. That was her first mistake, since fourth graders have not yet experienced the happy hormones that draw the sexes together. The moment the teacher instructed the students to select a partner, all the boys immediately laughed and pointed at the homeliest and least respected girl in the room. She was overweight, had protruding teeth, and was too withdrawn even to look anyone in the eye.

"Don't put us with Nancy," they all said in mock terror. "Anybody but Nancy! She'll give us a disease! Ugh! Spare us from Nasty Nancy." The mother expected the teacher to rush to the aid of the embarrassed girl, but nothing was said to ease her discomfort. Instead, the teacher left Nancy to cope with that painful situation on her own.

Ridicule by one's own sex is distressing, but rejection by the opposite sex is like taking a hatchet to the self-confidence. What could this devastated child say in reply? How does an overweight fourth-grade girl defend herself against nine aggressive boys? What response could she make but to blush in mortification and slide into her chair? This child, whom God loves more than all the possessions of the entire world, will never forget that moment (or the teacher who abandoned her in her time of need).

If I had been the teacher that day, I assure you that I would have come after those boys. Of course, it would have been better if the embarrassment could have been prevented by discussing the feelings of others from the first day of school. But if the conflict occurred as described, with Nancy suddenly being humiliated for everyone to see, I would have thrown the full weight of my authority and respect on her side of the battle.

My spontaneous response would have been something like this: "Wait just a minute! What gives you boys the right to say such mean, unkind things? Which of you is so perfect that the rest of us couldn't make fun of you in some way? I know some of your personal secrets. Would you like me to share them with the class so we can all laugh at you the way you did at Nancy just now? I could do it! I could make you want to crawl into a hole and disappear. But listen to me! You need not fear. I will never embarrass you in that way. Why not? Because it hurts to be laughed at by your friends.

"I want to ask, have any of you ever had boys or girls make fun of you? If you haven't, then get ready for it. Someday it will happen to you too. Eventually you will say something foolish—something that will cause everyone to point at you and laugh in your face. And when it happens, I want you to remember what happened here today."

Then, addressing the entire class: "Let's make sure that we learn a couple of things from what took place this afternoon. First, we will *not* be cruel to each other in this class. We will laugh together when things are funny, but we will not do it by making other people feel bad. Second, I will never intentionally embarrass anyone in this class. That is a promise. Each of you is a child of God. You were made with His loving hands, and we all are equally valuable to Him. This means that Sarah is neither better nor worse than Troy or Megan or Brent. Sometimes I think maybe some of you believe you are more important than others. It isn't true. Every one of you is priceless, and I love each of you too. God wants us to be kind to other people, and we're going to be practicing that kindness through the rest of this year."

I know, I know! Someone would complain about my references to God, but I would have to be ordered not to refer to Him. Children need to know what was written by the Founding Fathers in the Declaration of Independence. It says we humans "are endowed by their Creator with certain unalienable Rights, that among these are Life, Liberty and the pursuit of Happiness." Who is this Creator referred to, if not the God who made heaven and earth and all of us human beings? I wish that historic statement were memorized and discussed in every grade, because it gives worth and dignity to each child.

When a strong, loving teacher comes to the aid of the least respected child in the class, something dramatic occurs in the emotional climate of the room. Every child seems to breathe an audible sigh of relief. The same thought is bouncing around in many little heads: *If Nancy is safe from ridicule—even Nancy—then I must be safe too.* You see, by defending the least popular child in the room, a teacher is demonstrating (1) that she has no "pets," (2) that she respects everyone, and (3) that she will fight for anyone who is being treated unjustly. Those are virtues that children value highly and that contribute to mental health.

Let me suggest to parents that you defend the underdog in your neighborhood. Let it be known that you have the confidence to speak for the outcast. Explain this philosophy to your neighbors, and try to create an emotional harbor for the little children whose ship has been threatened by a storm of rejection. Don't be afraid to exercise leadership on behalf of a youngster who is being mauled. It is a worthy investment of your time and energy.

Many authorities on the prevention of bullying emphasize the importance of talking to children and teens about what they are experiencing. Dr. Cheryl Dellasega says, "Support your daughter: If she comes home talking about a specific incident, help her explore the details and her emotions, [and] look for alternative ways to respond and practice what she will do next time."[11]

Similar advice is given by Drs. Cheryl Dellasega and Charisse Nixon in their book *Girl Wars: 12 Strategies That Will End Female Bullying*. What follows is a summary of twelve suggestions about preventing bullying. Instead of using the word *bullying*, the authors refer to it as "relational aggression," or RA.

1. Inform yourself and others about RA.
2. Build her anti-RA skills at a young age.
3. Give girls the courage to be kind.
4. Begin with the first hurts.
5. When RA is sustained, avoid the blame game.
6. Enlist the help of others.
7. Change the RA way of life.
8. Offer her other outlets and opportunities.
9. Give her a dose of emotion lotion to soothe and support.
10. Give her a tool kit of options.
11. Change the culture.
12. Develop your own action plan to make a difference.[12]

At the core of these strategies is the importance of parents talking with their children and teens. That can be difficult to do. Many kids don't want the involvement of their parents for fear of making matters worse. "Leave me alone" is their typical response. There is nothing more humiliating than for moms and dads to interject themselves into peer relationships. Some of these bullied teens may take out their anger and frustration on Mom and Dad, who have done nothing to deserve the abuse to which they are subjected. At the root of it all is embarrassment at home and at school.

The question, therefore, is how can parents engage in conversation with sons and daughters who don't want to talk? I have found it helpful to gather small groups of teens in a comfortable setting and interact with them together. That is often less stressful than having one-on-one time with Mom and Dad.

I did exactly that some years ago when a group of teens gathered in my family room to talk with me about their experiences and struggles. We taped our discussion, and I included it in my book *Preparing for Adolescence*. The book was written specifically for teens, and is still available in stores and online. I am including a short section of that discussion to illustrate how adults can help kids articulate the problems they face and how to avoid the social mistakes that bring ridicule and bullying. As such, this conversation might be a model for helping your daughter get through a difficult period of life.

JCD: Tell us about those difficult days.

Gaylene: Well, my dad died during the summer following my fifth grade in school. This death happened at a time when I was going through many physical and emotional changes, and I didn't handle it very well. So I entered junior high school without knowing who I was. I wasn't involved in anything and I had nothing to look forward to. It was a very difficult time for me.

JCD: How did you overcome those problems?

Gaylene: My mother encouraged me to reach out, to get involved in as many activities as I could. Also, we got interested in Christianity during those years. Neither my mother nor my brother knew which way to turn, but my grandparents were very religious people. We moved in with them, and that's when I got involved in a Sunday school program, which helped a lot.

JCD: Gaylene, you said this difficult experience occurred during your first year of junior high school. That doesn't surprise me, because the seventh and eighth grades are often the most upsetting period of a person's life. Feelings of inferiority frequently become the strongest during those two years. . . . I know hundreds of thirteen-year-olds who have concluded, "I'm worthless!"

Has anyone else fallen into this same canyon of inferiority?

Darrell: I did, although my situation was different from Gaylene's. . . . I remember one disastrous beach trip in particular. I had looked forward to going, but I came home and I just bawled. I really did. I felt so rotten because I was teased by people throughout the trip. I didn't know why everybody was picking on me. . . . In my group you were supposed to hate school. I was expected to say, "Forget it, teachers are a drag, school is lousy, and anybody who gets interested in schoolwork is a freak." Even now, most of my friends are bored with school, and they work only to get good grades. They say, "I'm not going to study this because it won't be on a test." And that's no good. So when I was in junior high, I was interested in my studies and tried to share my experiences and be open about them, but nobody else wanted to do that. They wouldn't open themselves like I did, and it caused problems for me. From that moment I didn't want to open myself either. It has taken about two years for me to get over these feelings and start talking again in Sunday school and wanting to be free.

JCD: How beautifully you stated it, Darrell. Young people get laughed at . . . teased . . . ridiculed for being open with each other. Their feelings are deeply hurt, and they come home and cry, as you did. Then they begin to "close down." The next day they will be more cautious . . . more reserved . . . more phony in their social contacts.

Have you ever wondered, Darrell, why your friends were not as open as you? It's likely that they had been burned in the same way you were, only earlier. They had already learned the dangers of being free and spontaneous. The result was a very uneasy, tense society where everyone knew he could be laughed out of school if he made one social mistake. What a tough way to live!

Darrell: The pressures are great. For example, everyone is supposed to be "cool" now. I mean, you're not expected to show your feelings or reveal your true self. If you do, someone will laugh at the tenderness, the softness, inside. Well, some people recognize that it is not worth it to be so cautious. I've even seen posters at our school that say, "It's not cool to be cool anymore." That's a quick way to rip yourself apart . . . to do more harm to yourself than others can do to you.

Ceslie: I remember the third week of my first year in junior high—it was a brand-new school for me. I knew a few people there, but I wasn't familiar with everything. I was really little. I was about four feet, nine inches tall, and that's very short. I knew this one girl at our school named "Big Bertha," and she was about five feet eight. Bertha was the meanest girl in school, and everybody would run away when she came around. I thought that was really awful . . . that people shouldn't run away from her. But one day we were going up the stairs and Bertha kicked me. I didn't like that, and I turned around and said something to her, and she kicked me harder. So I went home and didn't say anything to anybody, but I was so upset that I started crying. When I told my parents why I was crying they thought it was very unkind for a person to do something like that. So they called the principal and told him the story. Then they told me to treat Bertha just like I would treat anyone else, because the reason she was kicking me was because she was so embarrassed about being too large. It wasn't because she was really that mean; she just felt bad about herself.

JCD: That was very good advice, Ceslie. . . . Can't you imagine how she felt, first by being called Big Bertha, and then by having everyone run away from her? Those two experiences would probably make *me* want to kick people too. Bertha had been hurt deeply, and that caused her to hurt you. How did you deal with Bertha the next day at school?

Ceslie: Well, she had a little group of friends; there were three of them that stayed together. Every time I saw them in the halls, I just smiled at them. I think it kind of made them mad at me, but I just kept smiling and they never did anything to me after that.

JCD: Did you gradually come to accept yourself?

Ceslie: I think I'm still . . .

JCD: You're still working on that?

Ceslie: Yes.

JCD: You'll probably work on that the rest of your life.

Ceslie: I know.

JCD: Most of us are working on the same project. Page, you started to say something.

Page: You're talking about people who get hurt by their friends. Well, when I was younger, I had an accident that crippled me for a summer. I had to wear these crazy-looking shoes to school. I had broken my leg and I had to wear elevated shoes. I didn't want to. I used to sneak my other shoes from my house and put them on later so people wouldn't laugh at me. This went on for a couple of years. People used to call me "Cripple," you know, and I really wasn't, but it hurt me to be teased. Even now I sometimes feel like, "Oh, I wish I could be like a certain person because he's so great, and boy, you know, all the people would really like me because I'd be such a great athlete." That's what I always wanted to be—somebody that would stand out and not be someone that people laugh at.

JCD: Isn't it interesting that you all have had the *same* feelings? That is precisely my point. If we selected a thousand teenagers and asked each one the question I've asked you, nearly every person would tell us a story like those we've just heard—about being laughed at, about being different, about not being accepted by others. It's something everybody goes through today.

Now tell me why—why is it that we have to endure these difficult moments? Is there any way to avoid them?

Gaylene: I tried to solve my problems in the wrong way—by becoming friends with the popular crowd. There were two different groups in my high school. There was this group that was into partying all night and then coming home late and lying to their parents; then there was the other group that tried to be more responsible. They believed that being wild wasn't going to fulfill their lives. But it wasn't easy for me to choose between these friends. I barged into the tenth grade and met people from the different groups and I didn't know exactly where to turn. There were more people in the rebellious group than in the responsible group, and that's just the way it is, and I didn't want to be laughed at and I didn't want to be rejected, and I didn't want everybody to think I was weird. So I just stood there, at a crossroads in my life, not knowing where to turn.

JCD: Did you feel tremendous pressure to do things that you knew were wrong?

Gaylene: Yes! I was just a sophomore this year, and that's when you get most of the pressure; you get a tremendous amount.

JCD: And that pressure can cause you to behave in ways that you know are harmful. I believe, for example, that most of the drug abuse in our country occurs because of the enormous pressure that Gaylene described. It's not the drugs that attract kids—the problem is that they lack the courage to choose the right group. Did the rest of you have a similar choice to make?

Darrell: I had to decide whether or not I was going to follow the "rules" of my peers at school. I knew that if I didn't go along I would be "out."

JCD: Give us an example of what you mean, Darrell. What kind of rules were you expected to follow?

Darrell: Well, like the "being cool" rule. You must not

show your feelings because people might find something to laugh at. But there were other rules in almost every area.

JCD: What about your clothes—did the group tell you what to wear?

Darrell: Yeah.

JCD: How to talk?

Darrell: Yeah.

JCD: And what slang to use?

Darrell: Yes. You sort of convince yourself after a while that it's what you really wanted anyway. I mean, you like to think that you're not conforming, that you just happen to like the same kind of Levis and shoes and sweaters that everyone else is wearing. But as styles change, you realize there must be some other force that is working on your attitudes. That other force is group pressure.

JCD: How about the matter of drugs? Have any of you ever had anybody offer narcotics to you?

Gaylene: I have, in junior high. We had this bulletin board, and the librarian put up a poster about the dangers of taking drugs. While I was reading it, somebody came up to me and said, "Look nice, don't they?" Right there, they were offering the stuff to me! At the time (this was back in seventh grade), I didn't know much about medicines or anything, and when I told my mom about it, she was completely horrified. She said, "They never did that back in my day." She was always saying things like that. . . .

JCD: Have you ever been offered drugs, Ceslie, or have you ever seen them being used?

Ceslie: No, I've never hung around the wild group. I was always in the group that was quiet and—

Page: Gaylene said her mother couldn't believe drugs were actually available at school. Well, my parents have a hard time believing it too. But, you know, our society has changed. A new trend will come along and everybody wants to be part of the craze. But I worry about what will happen when we're older and we have our kids. How are we going to face this situation with our kids, if we've taken drugs and done wrong things? What answers can we give to our children?

JCD: Those are good questions, Page, because that day will come very quickly. You'll find yourself trying to keep your own children from making the mistakes that worry your folks today.

Ceslie: I think many of our problems occur because we don't talk to our parents enough; we keep everything inside and we never talk to anybody who could help us. We talk to our friends who are having the same problems, but they don't have the answers and they don't know what to tell us. For example, Gaylene talked to her mom. That was probably the best thing she could have done. I would never have said anything to my parents, because they would have just blown up, you know, and gotten mad at the school. But I think that's very important—to have a relationship with your parents where you can talk openly to them, and not have to worry about how they'll respond. Then they can give you the answers that will be helpful to you.

JCD: Two of you have now mentioned this matter of talking to your parents. How about the other two? Darrell, have you been able to talk to your mom and dad?

Darrell: I haven't had that much opportunity to talk to them because drugs have never been a problem with me. But I agree that adults can help us handle our difficulties if they're "tuned in." But sometimes they don't know what's going on. For example, I had one teacher in ninth grade who was out of touch. We were sitting in class one day and here comes this sweet, sickly smell of marijuana down the hall, as clear as could be. It drifted into the classroom and everybody knew what it was except the teacher. (Laughter.) We were sitting there reading and looking at each other and just, you know, trying to hide our laughter, but the teacher was grading papers when all of a sudden she looked up and said, "My! what's that marvelous smell?" (Laughter.) She had no idea why we broke up. It would have blown her away, you know? She was the kind of teacher who would never give a thought to that kind of thing. But they're doing better at our school now. They have big drug-prevention programs, but even that's not going to be enough.

JCD: How about talking to your parents generally about other things that bother you, Darrell? Can you express your feelings to them? Let's go back to that painful night when you went to the beach. (I had a night very similar to that, by the way.) Did you come home and talk to your mom and dad about it?

Darrell: Yeah, I talked to my dad. Both of my parents were brought up in a very strict Christian environment, and my mom is still—well, I'm not saying she's narrow-minded, but because my dad has had more experiences, he's more flexible. He is a minister and so he knows how to counsel people with problems. He told me not to pay too much attention to all this laughter, and helped me understand it. But you know something? I discovered that I brought some of that scorn on myself. I'd worn this real goofy-looking thing—it wasn't funny, but it was goofy. (Laughter.) There's a difference between the two. You can cause people to make fun of you, and that is what I had done. Well, I got rid of that clothing the next day, you know?

JCD: A person gradually learns to keep his peers from laughing at him. After he's been stung a couple of times, he finds out what's "dangerous" and what is not. Page?

Page: Sometimes I feel like I can talk to my father better than I can talk with my mother. Mainly, I guess, because he was a boy himself and he understands some of the situations that I'm going through. He always encourages me to choose the right kind of friends.

JCD: Well, Page, your comment raises an extremely important point. All of us are influenced by people around us. Even adults are swayed by social pressure. For this reason, the most critical decision you must make will involve the friends you choose. If you select the wrong group, they *will* have a bad influence on you. It is a certainty. Very few people have the self-confidence to withstand criticism by their closest friends.

Darrell: I'm in an interesting situation now. Junior high isn't that far behind me, but my little sister is already in junior high, and just last night she was really upset about the possibility that she might have to go to a different school next year. She talked to me about her worries, and I found myself saying the kinds of things we've been saying tonight. As I was talking to her I said to myself, "What am I doing? This is an echo from about three years ago. I am my father and she is me." (Laughter.) You know, it's like my father's words were bouncing off the wall and coming back to her now. I could see that her problems weren't serious at all because I had been through them, and I kept saying, "Why can't she see I'm giving her the clearest answers in the world?" But when I was in that situation I had no idea at first what my father was talking about.

JCD: You have to experience it before it makes sense, don't you? And, in that way, this tape recording may be a mystery to that listener who is between ten and twelve years of age who hasn't gone though the experiences we're describing. You may not fully understand what we're talking about, but when it happens to you, then it will be like turning on a light bulb in your head. You will remember this tape and our conversation about feelings of inadequacy and inferiority. When that happens to you, remember this very moment when I said that you *do* have great worth as a human being.[13]

As you can see from this transcript, adolescents love to talk about themselves if they are in a safe environment and are led by an adult they trust and admire. This kind of group discussion might be a useful vehicle to help you draw out the youngsters who are under siege at school. Regardless of the method you choose, the more you can demonstrate to your sons and daughters that you care and are on their team, the better the outcome.

I will conclude now with the most important suggestion I have to offer to parents of daughters who are in the midst of the storm. There might come a time to get them out of it. You have to be prepared to do whatever is necessary to preserve their tender spirits. When you realize your child has lost the battle against the taunters and harassers, it might make sense to sit down with her and say, "Well, Katelyn, you are really going through a tough time, aren't you? I want you to know that we love you and will do anything we can to help. Would you like to change schools? You can start over with new friends and avoid some of the mistakes that caused others to give you grief. Even if it requires us to move, we will do it if you think it will help."

In some cases, a child can completely recalibrate socially in a new setting with an increased level of confidence. Perhaps there is a Christian school nearby that would be affordable and consistent with your beliefs. Maybe a private school would be appropriate. This is an individual decision for each family to make, of course, but the point is that you can't just sit idly by and watch your child go down for the count. When I was sixteen years old, my parents moved us seven hundred miles away to give me a new start. I corrected some mistakes, learned some new lessons, and made a large number of new friends. Everything changed for me during my last two years of high school. My mom and dad cared enough about me to help me land on my feet.

Another option for you might be homeschooling. It can be a wonderful alternative for the immature child in the early grades who is not able to cope socially. Spending each day in the warm and safe company of a loving parent can circumvent a lifetime of pain inflicted by aggressive peers. I am a firm believer in homeschooling and could write a book on its benefits. It isn't for everyone, but when the circumstances are right and parents are committed, it is an option to be considered carefully.

And so ends our discussion of bullying, buddies, and best friends.

QUESTIONS
AND ANSWERS
ABOUT PUBERTY
AND ADOLESCENCE

Question: I was at the mall the other day where there were hundreds of kids hanging out. They were all flirting with each other and doing what teens do. They couldn't have been more than thirteen or fourteen, but most of the girls were rather developed and many of the guys had acne. Are kids maturing earlier today?

Answer: Yes, although the trend has been going in that direction for at least 175 years. Historical records indicate that the average age of menarche, or first menstruation, for girls in Western nations dropped from 17 years in 1830 to 12.8 in 1962, at the rate of about four months per decade. German medical records from 1860 indicate that the average age of menarche was 16.6 years. Professor Emeritus Norbert Kluge recently predicted that the average age of menarche in German girls would be around ten or eleven in a few years.[1]

American records show it was 14.6 in 1920, 13.1 in 1950, 12.5 in 1980, and 12.2 in 1992. A recent study of 2,510 American girls found that menarche occurred on average at 12.43 years. This age seems to have stabilized in the past fifty years, although secondary sex characteristics such as breast development and pubic hair are continuing to appear earlier.[2]

Obviously, girls are "growing up" very quickly today, especially in industrialized countries around the world.

Question: Do we know why this decline in age has occurred?

Answer: Genetics provide a window during which maturation occurs, of course, but environmental and physical factors appear to influence the timing inside those parameters. For example, as the quality of nutrition and general health improve for children in a population, puberty tends to occur at earlier ages. The most interesting finding to date, however, has revealed a significant link between family cohesion and the onset of sexual development. Specifically, girls who have close, positive relationships with their fathers tend to mature later than those whose dads are cold, distant, and uninvolved.

Investigators at Vanderbilt University studied 173 girls and their families for eight years and drew that striking conclusion. Their findings were reported in the *Journal of Personality and Social Psychology*:[3]

> Researchers found that a father's presence in the home, more time spent by fathers in child care, greater supportiveness in the parental dyad, more father-daughter affection, and more mother-daughter affection, as assessed prior to kindergarten, each predicted later pubertal timing by daughters in 7th grade. In summary, the quality of fathers' investment in the family was the most important feature of the family environment relative to daughters' pubertal timing.[4]

The Vanderbilt study has been replicated numerous times, including an investigation conducted in the United States and New Zealand. Researchers there followed the development of 762 girls ranging in age from five to sexual maturity.[5] They drew similar conclusions:

> [Bruce Ellis, et al,] found that daughters from homes in which the biological father was present tended to experience puberty and their first sexual encounter at a later age than those whose father was absent. The closer and more affectionate the father-daughter relationship, the later the child's sexual development occurred. A supportive relationship between parents delayed puberty still further. In contrast, the biological father's absence, or friction between parents, was associated with earlier puberty, sexual activity and pregnancy. Girls who had lived without their fathers from an early age were almost twice as likely to have

completed puberty by the seventh grade (age 12 or 13) and were seven times more likely to experience pregnancy in adolescence. This effect was magnified by the presence of a stepfather: the more prolonged a girl's exposure to a stepfather or mother's boyfriend, the greater the chance of early puberty. . . .

The study clearly shows that stressful family relationships and the absence of a girl's father are each independently associated with earlier timing of puberty in daughters, both having a similar impact. Ellis suggests that girls "detect and internally encode" information about the quality of their relationship with their fathers, and that this calibrates the timing of their reproductive development and sexual behavior in adolescence.[6]

There are other factors at work in the trend toward earlier maturation. It is believed that obesity and the distribution of fat are implicated. Furthermore, the onset of puberty appears to have declined because of the presence of estrogen in the environment, perhaps from exposure to discarded birth control pills and hormones in meat and dairy products. Other scientists suggest that pesticides and other chemicals that have qualities like estrogen may play a role.[7]

Finally, the onset of puberty is related to race. African American girls develop earlier than white girls, by twelve to eighteen months on average. The beginnings of breast development occur on average at 8.9 years for African American girls and 10.0 for white girls. Forty-eight percent of African American girls and 15 percent of white girls are showing clear signs of puberty by age nine.[8]

Question: What are the implications of early versus late sexual development for girls? Is one more beneficial than the other?

Answer: You've asked a very important question. The early onset of puberty presents children and their parents with predictable challenges. Since girls typically develop earlier than boys, those who mature first among female contemporaries are miles ahead of everyone else. This can produce serious problems, because it isn't socially advantageous for nine- or ten-year-old girls to be boy crazy, have monthly periods, and develop breasts when their friends are still thinking and acting like children. A precocious girl may also lack the emotional maturity to handle the attention she garners from boys. She is at greater risk of being sexually active, contracting a sexually transmitted disease, and experiencing an early pregnancy. We received a letter recently from a writer who said simply, "I am a twelve-year-old girl and I am pregnant." How tragic.

There are additional dangers for early maturing girls: they are more likely to be aggressive, socially withdrawn, and moody, and they experience depression at a higher rate. They also have more problems in school and are more likely to smoke, use alcohol, and do drugs. They are also more prone to breast cancer as adults.[9] So in answer to your question, girls typically do better when they experience menarche at about the same time as their girlfriends, or perhaps even shortly thereafter.

This much is certain: girls who experience menarche when they are younger than their peers need close supervision, careful guidance, constant reassurance, good medical care, good nutrition, and an abundance of love. Don't we all!

Question: What can parents do to prevent early puberty from occurring?

Answer: The answer may be nothing, although endocrinologists and other physicians can give a child hormone injections to slow down very early development. Most doctors are reluctant to do that, however, unless there are concerns about growth.[10] Either way, it is wise to implement a three-part strategy if possible: (1) try to keep the stress level of your family at a minimum while powerful hormones are bombarding your daughter's brain; (2) stave off adolescent attitudes and activities until sexual maturity makes its grand entrance; (3) and most important, develop and maintain a warm and caring relationship between dad and daughter. This is a good time for him to be giving her many hugs, writing affectionate notes, and having bedtime chats as they are welcomed. As writer Mairi Macleod writes: "If you don't want your little princess to grow up too quickly, she had better be daddy's girl."[11]

Question: What is the mechanism that causes a "daddy's girl" to mature later? How does that happen?

Answer: We now know from recent findings that fathers emit chemical signals that inhibit menarche and delay the onset of sexual maturity. These emissions are called pheromones, which are hormones detected through the sense of smell, although neither girls nor their dads are aware of them.[12] When fathers are absent or uninvolved and the pheromones are not emitted, menarche occurs earlier. Interesting, huh? This is just one of the reasons I wrote earlier that girls need their dads as much as boys do. They unwittingly "engineer" the timing of their daughters' maturation!

❀ ❀ ❀

The next two questions were sent by parents who asked for medical information about their girls. I relayed these questions to a colleague, Dr. Roy Stringfellow, a gynecologist in private practice in Colorado Springs, Colorado.

Question: I have a seven-year-old girl who just had her first period. Isn't this too early for her to be developing in that way?

Dr. Stringfellow: It is not normal for a seven-year-old girl to menstruate. The youngest person on record to have a baby was seven years old when she delivered. She proved to have a pituitary tumor that caused her premature puberty. Your little girl needs to be seen by a gynecologist, preferably a gynecologic endocrinologist. If she is markedly overweight or especially large for her age, that may account for the changes, but even then, seven years of age is too early. Have your child examined medically as soon as possible.

Question: My ten-year-old daughter has a noticeable feminine odor a lot of the time. She bathes regularly, but it seems that by midday, or maybe after playing outside, this odor is back. I am concerned that she will become the focus of other children's jokes and put-downs. My wife says she does not know what is causing the odor, other than it might be hormonal. My daughter is developing early. She is not overweight but is one of the largest girls in the children's ministry at church. I wondered if this early development is part of the issue. Can you offer any advice?

Dr. Stringfellow: Your daughter's condition is unusual and suggests several possible causes. She could have a vaginal infection, but that would be rare. Another possibility is a foreign object placed in the vagina. Young girls will sometimes notice there is an opening "down there" and experiment to see how deep it is and what will fit. Then something lodges inside, and the girl is ashamed to tell anyone. Eventually, an odor results. If it is noticeable to the mother and others around, an exam is indicated, especially if there is no vaginal bleeding to indicate early menarche (ten years is not too early for puberty). Even if your daughter has begun to develop, it would be unusual for her to have a persistent odor. There is no such thing as a "hormonal odor" per se, though hormonal changes with bleeding and a change in vaginal discharge can cause an odor. Still, proper hygiene should resolve any noticeable odor. She should be seen by a *female* gynecologist (a vaginal exam is embarrassing enough to a ten-year-old girl, even without it being a man doing the exam), preferably one specializing in adolescent gynecology.

❀ ❀ ❀

Question: I would like for you [Dr. Dobson] to elaborate on your statement that the timing of puberty in girls is related to fat distribution in the body. Does that mean that overweight girls always mature earlier than those who are thin?

Answer: No, but weight does seem to be involved in early and late development. For example, children who participate regularly in gymnastics and are therefore very thin are often late in developing. If you have watched women's Olympic gymnastics competitions, you must have noticed how the female participants usually have smaller breasts, have childish little voices, and are generally immature. Maturation usually occurs when they leave the sport. It is not uncommon for very thin female marathon runners to have amenorrhea, which refers to an absence of menstruation.[13]

Vigorous training was once believed to be very harmful to girls. When I was a boy, I remember that girls were restricted from strenuous exercise. Though it seems silly to us today, girl basketball players were not even allowed to run up and down the court. They could only play offense or defense. The rules required them to stand at the centerline waiting for the ball to be advanced to their end of the court.

How things have changed! Today, some of the best female athletes in the world, such as professional tennis players, are ranked in the top five at seventeen or eighteen years of age. Tracy Austin became the youngest player ever to win a major tournament when she claimed the U.S. Open title at the age of sixteen in 1979; Serena Williams was only a few weeks shy of her eighteenth birthday when she won the title in 1999.[14] The Russian darling Maria Sharapova won the 2004 Wimbledon championship when she was just seventeen.[15]

As for overweight girls, it was believed until recently that obesity was causing the age of sexual maturation to decline.[16] That view is now questioned. Instead, Dr. William Lassek of the University of California, Santa Barbara, says that the key factor is where the fat is located. He writes,

> What our findings suggest is that menarche is likely to occur when girls have stored a certain minimal amount of fat in the hips and thighs, and that girls who tend to

store more fat around the waist—who have abdominal obesity—are more likely to have delayed menarche.

Fat deposited in the hips and thighs is especially rich in omega-3 fatty acids, which are essential for the growth of the infant brain in the womb. This fat is protected from everyday use like money deposited in a bank. You are not allowed to withdraw it until late pregnancy.[17]

Question: I am very concerned about the phenomenon of "cutting." Can you explain to me what would motivate a teenager to slash her arms, legs, and stomach? It has to be painful to do this, and the wounds leave ugly scars. This makes no sense to me, but my daughter and her friends talk about it all the time. One of these girls wears long shirts and skirts to conceal what she has been doing to herself, but she doesn't fool anyone. What is going on here?

Answer: Unfortunately, cutting among teens has become a very common and disturbing disorder. We hear regularly from girls who are engaging in it, and from their parents and friends who are worried about those who are. To illustrate the scope of the problem, let me share some of the recent e-mails, transcripts, and phone calls that have come to Focus on the Family:

I am a cutter. I am miserable, and the problem is getting worse. I really don't know what to do. I don't want to tell my parents because they don't even care. I want to stop hurting myself, but don't know how.

I have a friend who is somewhat of a cutter. She told me to keep it a secret. I don't want to lose her as a friend, but I am worried about her.

I have not yet started cutting myself, but I want to. Can you help me?

My best friend is a cutter and recently started having sex with her boyfriend. I would like to help her, but I am not sure where to start.

I'm only thirteen years old, but one of my close friends is struggling with cutting herself. I've tried to help her in every way I know of, but she is still doing it. Her parents have known about it for months and haven't stopped her or taken her to a counselor. I know they love her and have a plan, but I'm worried about her. I recently found out that she has also made a couple of suicide attempts, and I don't know how to help her. The shocking part is that she is a Christian and goes to church regularly. Her dad is even the minister of music. Before she began to cut herself, she went through anorexia and bulimia. As far as I know, she is over both of these problems—but now she is into cutting. What can I do?

Over the summer I got curious and wanted to know if cutting myself would make me feel better. I didn't feel anything when I cut my arm. I cut myself four other times after that, and I'm afraid that I'm going to continue. I've asked God for the strength to stop, and I just cut myself again and again. My friend knows that I've done it . . . but he thinks that I've stopped and that the cuts on my arms are just me being a klutz. I hate lying to him, but if I don't, he'll tell my mom. What should I do? I just need prayer . . . any prayers would be welcomed with a warm heart.

I am an eighteen-year-old girl who struggles with cutting, and I can't find a Web site to help me out. I am scared.

Note that several of these girls who called or wrote were supposedly asking questions on behalf of "a friend." I suspect that they were actually referring to themselves. That is characteristic of cutters. They are desperate for help but don't want to risk being identified to their parents or friends. Typically, they inflict their wounds when they are alone.

Self-inflicted injuries have become a major public health problem, especially when adolescents and young adults are involved. The instruments used by cutters range from razors to knives, and sometimes even paper clips, scissors, or letter openers. About 4 percent of the general population engages in self-mutilation of various sorts.[18] Among chronic sufferers, 72 percent are cutters, 35 percent burn themselves, 30 percent hit themselves, 22 percent engage in interference with wound healing, 10 percent pull out their hair, and 8 percent actually break their own bones. Fifty-seven percent of self-mutilators have overdosed on drugs at least once.[19]

Question: Why do these poor teenagers mutilate themselves like this, and what can be done to help them?

Answer: As with every other aspect of human behavior, motivation is often complex and varied. This is what is now believed: The profile of a person who deliberately inflicts nonfatal injuries on herself is a female in late childhood or early adulthood. The individual, if untreated, may continue the behavior into her midtwenties or early thirties.[20] She is likely to have experienced physical or sexual abuse and has had at least one alcoholic or clinically depressed parent. As we saw earlier, she is also likely to have had sexual intercourse as a very young girl, perhaps repeatedly. Her greatest pain comes from perceived rejection and circumstances that produce feelings of anger, guilt, and helplessness. The result is utter self-hatred.

In short, these girls have been seriously wounded by people and by life in general. One young woman, described in the *Journal of Mental Health Counseling*, said she cut her thighs where she had been abused "to remind herself that she had not imagined the painful experience."[21]

Harvard University researcher Judith Lewis Herman found that sexual abuse victims were the most likely of all respondents to cut themselves. The earlier the abuse begins, the more severe the injurious behavior is.[22]

Henry L. Shapiro is a developmental-behavioral pediatrician specializing in the evaluation and treatment of learning, developmental, and behavioral problems in school-age children. He reports: "Sexual abuse survivors often blame themselves for the abuse, and as adults, harm themselves physically as punishment for their 'bad' behavior. In perpetuating the cycle of abuse, they may express feelings of intense rage turned inward. Survivors often cannot imagine themselves as lovable human beings. Further, because they cannot physically strike out at the abuser, they often end up striking out . . . at themselves."[23]

Question: I understand that those who hurt themselves are experiencing "rage turned inward." But why do they make things worse by continually damaging their own bodies?

Answer: Here is an oversimplified explanation that is, nonetheless, useful. Girls who cut themselves lack the ability to regulate the anxiety, painful memories, and "bad feelings" that percolate inside. When a girl injures herself, endorphins are released in the brain that produce a sense of pleasure and well-being. The experience is very temporary, but these girls are desperate for even momentary relief. That comes closest to explaining the behavior.

There is one more thing that parents should know. At the risk of being too technical, cutters and other self-mutilators sometimes have a condition called borderline personality disorder.[24] It is characterized by eating disorders, emotional instability, difficulty maintaining friendships, impulsivity, and a high incidence of suicide or attempted suicide, especially among adolescent females and young women. According to one study, 87 percent of the girls in treatment had made at least one suicide attempt.[25] People with borderline personality disorder are also susceptible to addictive behavior, especially to drugs and alcohol.[26]

Finally, adolescents have lower levels of serotonin, which is a neurotransmitter in the brain. In other words, the behavior that "makes no sense" to onlookers is not just an emotional syndrome. It is a chemical and a psychological disorder.

Question: It breaks my heart to tell you that I have a fifteen-year-old daughter whom you have been describing. What can I do to help her? We have had long talks about it, but then she quietly goes into her room and cuts herself again. I don't think she even understands why she does it and is always embarrassed about it later. I must know how to help her.

Answer: I urge you to seek medical and psychological help immediately. Find a program that is staffed by trained professionals who understand the condition and know how to reach teens. Your daughter can be helped, but you are not likely to lead her to wholeness without specialized care.

Now that you know what she is likely to be feeling, you can certainly come alongside her with encouragement and compassion. But as with anorexia and other eating disorders, simply talking and reasoning will not help. Nor will getting angry or saying, "I insist that you stop doing this." There is far more going on inside your teen than meets the eye.

Forgive me for offering such detailed replies to these questions, but girls who are caught in this destructive pattern need our understanding and our intervention.

Question: I am twelve, about to be thirteen. I have a boyfriend, and we want to kiss. I wish I could marry him now. I know marrying a middle school boyfriend is rare, but I feel like he's the one for me. Do you personally think I'm too young for anything I just explained? In love, Jackie

Answer: Hello, Jackie. Thank you for writing to me. I read your letter carefully, and frankly, it made me very sad. I know you will think I don't understand your feelings, but I do. I was once twelve about to be thirteen. Let me just say as strongly as I can that your kissing a middle school aged boy (or a boy of any age) and wanting to marry him at such a young age is a great mistake. He may look like "the one for you," but I promise you, he is not. You are moving toward adult behavior much too quickly, and there is pain and disappointment waiting for you down that road.

You see, life is laid out according to a timetable, and getting ahead of that plan messes up everything. It also leads to doing things that you will regret for as long as you live. Look around you. Do you see anyone else who is planning to marry at twelve years of age? The law will not even permit it, which tells you something.

What you really need is an adult to confide in—hopefully your parents or a youth pastor or a school counselor. Tell that person what you are thinking, and listen carefully to what is said. He or she will know how to guide you.

You should also pray about what God wants you to do, because He does not make mistakes. He loves you, Jackie, and so do I. Give yourself time to grow up. It will happen very quickly. I hope this has been helpful.

Question: My eleven-year-old girl is physically, and otherwise, way too grown up for her age, despite my concentrated efforts to keep her a kid. I don't know how to handle her disrespectful teen attitude. It seems she's always grounded, and I am always yelling and unhappy, which affects everyone in our family. Unfortunately we cannot afford counseling, and I have read many resources to no avail. Help!

Answer: Whatever happened to childhood? I can only imagine what life is like in your household, having a daughter who is still a child but already dealing with all the hormonal influences of puberty.

There are many aspects to your circumstances that I should know in order to help you deal with this situation. For example, where is Dad? If I were consulting with your family, I would look to him as a potential resource. He should be spending more time with your daughter than ever. If you have a grown brother or a pastor or coach who can lend a hand, bring that person in on the problem.

You said you are unable to afford counseling. Let me ask if you would pay for medical care if someone had a serious illness. I suspect that would be a priority even worth going into debt. In a sense, your daughter is ill, and the entire family must get the help it needs to bring greater harmony.

You do know, I'm sure, that everything you described is driven by something akin to perpetual PMS. Her brain is reeling, and so is yours. But responding to her ranting and raving with your own angry outbursts is counterproductive. Let me explain.

There is no quick fix for what is happening, but it seems apparent that you are making some management mistakes that are not helping. Yelling and being unhappy will only make matters worse—much worse. It would appear to me that you have gotten down on your daughter's level and are reacting like one of her age-mates. You must be the parent, and then lead like one.

How is that done? You hold the keys to everything your little girl wants and needs: permission to do things, transportation, allowances (if any), coveted clothing, provision of meals, ironing and laundry, and access to television. It is all under your supervision; or at least, it should be. I suggest that you have a little talk with her and tell her that you know she is going through a tough time but that she has to work harder at controlling her anger. It is not helping her, and it is hurting the rest of the family. This is why you are going to help her be more civil. From now on, everything that she wants will depend on her cooperation.

In the conversation you have with your daughter, say something like this: "I want you to know several things. First, I love you more than you will ever know. I brought you into the world, and I would lay down my life for you if necessary. Everything I am going to tell you today is a product of that love. Second, because I love you so much, I can't allow you to continue to act in a way that is harmful to you and to the rest of the family. It *is* going to stop right now. Third, I have an obligation before God to make you respectful to me first and then to your brothers and sisters. If you don't do it, I have many ways to make you miserable, and believe me when I say I will use every one of them.

"You have chosen to be very difficult, and until you decide to cooperate, this is not going to be a pleasant place for you. When you are tired of having no privileges and being cooped up here at home, we will determine where we go from there. Until then, it would be in your best interest to play by the rules, because they are going to be enforced. If you ever want to talk to me, I would be happy to hear your heart on things that you think are unfair or frustrating. But it will be unacceptable to scream, slam doors, and [fill in the blank]. Get it? Got it. Now, is there anything you want to say?"

Then have the courage to dole out those privileges and consequences with consistency and determination. Do *not* try to control your daughter with anger. It doesn't work. She not only doesn't care if you get mad—she has also won a strategic battle when you do. In short, you need to be far tougher than you have ever been, but not by acting like an out-of-control teenager. When she is ready to negotiate, respond with respect and firmness.

This sounds easy to do, but I know it is not. Nevertheless, you must get control of this kid. She is far too young to be terrorizing the entire family in this way. As you indicated, there are other children at home who are watching this titanic struggle. What they see being modeled in your relationship will haunt you with your other sons and daughters. You could lose them even before they get to the teen years. And as for the eleven-year-old, you have very little time left to turn her around. Otherwise, she will give you fits when she is older and perhaps bigger than you are. I am not suggesting in any way that you do anything abusive, but you have to take charge. Never let this child see you frantic again. And by all means, do not cry in front of her!

This battle you are in is not one you can afford to lose. You can win it! God be with you!

Question: My children are almost grown, and I am seeing now that I have made huge mistakes in the way I raised them. My husband and I had marital problems ending in divorce, and there was far too much alcohol in the home. We were also terribly busy trying to handle two flourishing careers. Many times we were not at home at night and rarely ate together. I had no idea when our kids were born that this parenting thing would be so difficult, and so significant. The teen years were so challenging, and I look at these mixed-up teenagers who are about to become adults, and I weep. What can I do now, since the time to make amends is over? Signed, A regretful mother

Answer: I understand your sense of remorse, which is shared by many members of your generation. Let me offer some thoughts that might be helpful. First, the ball game is not over. Your teens will be very different in the future than they are now. Adolescents have a way of becoming adults, and thankfully, maturity begins to set in. What appears to be great failure on your part now may turn out to look very different in a few years.

Second, I'll guess that you were a much better mother than you think you were. Parenting is a very guilty affair, and no one—*not one of us*—does the job perfectly. We can no more be perfect parents than we can be perfect human beings. The task of raising kids in a fast-paced world is infinitely complex, and life itself takes a toll on our good intentions. But kids are resilient, and they usually manage to turn out rather well.

Remember that the Creator in the Garden of Eden also had "children" who were rebellious. In that instance, Adam and Eve had no television, pornography, bad peers, or other unsavory influences to lead them astray. And yet they were headstrong and went their own way. It is the nature of mankind. What I am saying is that it would be a mistake for you to wallow in guilt for everything your children do wrong.

As I tried to say in chapter 14 ("The River of Culture"), kids are exposed to many harmful influences today. It is impossible to shield them from everything negative. We do the best we can to guide them down the River of Culture and try to keep them from drowning. For you to blame yourself for everything disappointing that you see in your children is not biblical, not reasonable, and not fair. On the other hand, it is inappropriate for parents to take the *credit* for everything good in their children. Each individual is a free moral agent who is able to make independent decisions. Some of those choices turn out to be good and others bad, but you are not to blame for them all.

Ezekiel 18:2-4 says:

> What do you people mean by quoting this proverb about the land of Israel: "The fathers eat sour grapes, and the children's teeth are set on edge"? As surely as I live, declares the Sovereign LORD, you will no longer quote this proverb in Israel. For every living soul belongs to me, the father as well as the son—both alike belong to me. The soul who sins is the one who will die.

What this Scripture is telling us is that there is no such thing as "generational sin." Each person is responsible for his or her own choices and behavior. Parents can try to teach moral principles to their children, but ultimately the accountability passes to the progeny. Does that make sense to you?

You did the best job you could when your kids were small. It was done, I'm sure, in love. Now your record is in the books. I don't doubt that the mistakes you and your husband made were serious and regrettable. But what is done is done. Lay it to rest. Your job now is to pray earnestly for the spiritual welfare of your nearly grown children. Ask the Lord to override your shortcomings and failings, and to work to accomplish His purposes in their hearts and lives. Continue to show love to them, and when your advice is asked for, give it thoughtfully. But do not let the demon of guilt ride heavy on your shoulders. That is a short route to despair.

PROTECTING YOUR
DAUGHTER FROM
INVASIVE TECHNOLOGY

As IF PARENTS don't have enough to worry about, they're also faced with a cyber and media world that is enormously dangerous to their children. I have been searching for a primer that will help them cope, and I think I have found it. What I have to share in this chapter is must-reading for moms and dads trying to help their children navigate today's confusing world of technology and entertainment.

I'm going to turn this chapter over to Bob Waliszewski, the director of Focus on the Family's Plugged In department. Bob and his team's award-winning Web site, http://www.pluggedin.com, provides up-to-date reviews of new movie releases and information on the most popular music, television shows, DVDs, and video games impacting popular youth culture. Bob's understanding and insights regarding the media landscape are second to none, and I am grateful for his willingness to share his expertise with you.

Given space constraints and the amount of ground to be covered, the advice in these pages may not satisfy full-fledged techies, but I believe there is valuable information here for parents who are overwhelmed by the challenge of managing the world of technology and entertainment. Frankly, the enticements available to individuals of all ages today are mind-boggling and scary.

If you have reason to be concerned about pornographic images invading your home, online predators stalking your kids, or curious preteens and teens experimenting with who-knows-what on the Web, do read on. Protecting the innocence of your children is a Herculean task, but I'm confident Bob's perspective and recommendations will help equip you to do just that.

Media and Technology Advice for Parents

Are you aware that the average person between the ages of eight and eighteen spends approximately 44.5 hours each week engaging with some form of media?[1] That's the equivalent of a full-time job and several hours of overtime! With consumption at this level, it's little wonder that media has become a type of "super-peer," influencing behaviors and shaping values.

At the top of the list of challenges is the pervasive problem of Internet pornography. Easy access combined with the relative anonymity of personal computing have made hard-core pornographic images just a keyboard click or two away for anyone so inclined. Internet pornography has long been called a "victimless crime," but the reality is quite the opposite.

Parents trying to protect their children have their work cut out for them. The National Coalition for the Protection of Children and Families estimates that there are over 300,000 pornographic Web sites. The National Center for Missing and Exploited Children reports that one in seven children ages ten to seventeen who use the Internet have been sexually solicited online—and 34 percent of them were unwillingly exposed to images of nudity.[2] Over the past ten years there have been nearly 740,000 reports of child sexual exploitation to the federally managed CyberTipline.[3]

Even for young people who never venture into the seedier side of the Internet, pornographic images are increasingly becoming part of everyday life. And Christian young people are no more exempt from media pressure than their peers. Nearly one in five teens who claim that religious beliefs are "extremely important" in shaping their behavior say most or all of the films they view are R-rated.[4] This fact becomes even more disconcerting when one realizes that adolescents who regularly consume sexualized music, television, and movies are more than *twice as likely* to have sex by age sixteen than their less-exposed peers.[5] Even families who avoid R-rated movies risk exposure to pornographic images and dialogue because many of the films rated PG-13—and occasionally PG—are steeped in extreme sexual content (as are popular songs and video games).[6]

What are moms and dads to do? I suggest that parents in this media-saturated culture become more intentional about raising their daughters (and sons) to honor Christ with their entertainment choices. Not just because today's movies, music, video games, Internet, and television have become increasingly hypersexualized, violent, and profane, and often promote drugs and alcohol, but also because all the forms of entertainment can now be delivered through a variety of new platforms and gadgets—with technological changes occurring faster than at any time in history.

Controlling and limiting the use of these electronic devices by the younger generation is a source of conflict for parents and children. Constant arguments may occur over the amount of time kids spend on social networking (Facebook, MySpace, etc.). Many of their peers are online for hours every day. Maybe a daughter demands unlimited texting on the cell phone or she has a tendency to walk around the house with earbuds, listening to countless hours of music on her MP3 player. Perhaps she wants to compete against video gamers around the globe. There is also the age-old argument over movies and television. What's appropriate and what's not? With wireless Internet and phones that double as computers, your daughter could be exposed to all kinds of harmful influences—right under your nose.

Whatever your exact situation, if you have teen or pre-teen girls, it's important to help them become media savvy so they don't fall prey to the more objectionable elements that are proffered as fun, innocent, and amusing. I'm convinced that what we watch and what we listen to often become profoundly moral issues.

Using Technology as a Family Friend

Before my daughter was married, we took one last vacation as a family. While at dinner one evening, the restaurant's background music featured classic tunes from the 1960s and '70s.

I challenged my family to a game of "Name That Artist." It wasn't a fair competition since the music was mostly unfamiliar to my children, and my wife never did care much for the hits of our generation. One tune stumped me, however. It sounded familiar, but I couldn't come up with the band's name. That's when my son pulled out his cell phone and a few clicks later proudly announced the artist. How? His mobile phone has an application that can discern songs and their artists. Go figure!

Products released to rave reviews just a few years ago now gather dust on the shelves of secondhand stores. Yes, technology is moving at a breakneck pace. And evaluating the implications of new devices and technology is a full-time job. The good news is we don't have to become tech geeks. We just need to know what our own children are into . . . and become familiar with the benefits, the pitfalls, and the safeguards. Because no matter where you are on the gizmo-knowledge curve, I believe strongly that protecting our daughters from the negative aspects of technology requires active parental involvement.

Consider seventeen-year-old Mikaela Espinoza: "Whenever I'd hear my phone ring, I would wake up and answer it. I think a whole bunch of kids text all night long."[7]

Mikaela's doctor determined that her migraines were caused by too little sleep due to excessive texting. "Before technology, we went to sleep when the sun went down," says Dr. Myrza Perez, a specialist in sleep disorders. "Now, with all these distractions, teenagers alone in their rooms stay up to extremely late hours on their cell phones and computers. Their parents have no idea."[8]

Dr. Perez's conclusion that parents can be clueless must serve as a reminder. What would you do if Mikaela were your daughter? That is a good question. I would start by asking questions and becoming familiar with the devices and systems our girls choose to obtain information, to network with friends, and to consume entertainment. Mikaela's parents could have headed off those migraines by simply taking a closer look each month at the family's mobile phone bill. But isn't that being a *snoop*? I don't believe so! In this technological age, that's called wise parenting.

I told my children that e-mails, IMs, and Internet history

were open to all of us in our family. They could read mine. I could read theirs. I could check what sites they visited, and they were welcome to see where I'd been. When my children lived under my roof, I regularly visited their social networking sites. I not only checked to see how my kids expressed themselves, but I also clicked on their friends' sites as well, checking out the photos they posted, the polls they answered, and the questionnaires they filled out. Some parents might be reluctant to monitor these activities, believing it to be an invasion of privacy. But consider this: In 2008, 22 percent of managers checked job applicants' social networking profiles before hiring. A year later, that figure jumped to 45 percent.[9] If potential employers have the need to snoop, how much more do parents need to know what is going on? Never before has there been such a constant invasion of harmful stuff coming at our daughters. To fail to monitor these sites is, I believe, unwise.

According to Maggie Jackson, author of *Distracted: The Erosion of Attention and the Coming Dark Age*, adolescents live in "an institutionalized culture of interruption, where our time and attention is being fragmented by a never-ending stream of phone calls, e-mails, instant messages, text messages and tweets."[10] Teens need to learn how to manage that barrage of information, and to know they will be held accountable for their online choices.

So, do you know what songs your daughter currently listens to on her iPod? Or does she prefer a build-your-own radio station online? Do you know what Internet sites she frequents? The security firm Symantec Corporation, with help from OnlineFamily.Norton, identified the top one hundred Internet searches conducted by children. Number one is YouTube. Fourth on the list is sex. Porn is number six.[11]

Not everything served up to your children is problematic, of course. There are educational videos available, and some of these are very funny. What's more, Christians are increasingly using online video for Kingdom purposes. There's nothing inherently wrong with the technology that allows people to see and hear video offerings. But trust me on this: despite many popular online sites claiming they don't allow pornography or violent content, wretched stuff exists on YouTube and similar sites. Soft-core pornography is routine.

Occasionally, hard-core porn slips through the nearly twenty hours of video that are uploaded to YouTube *every minute*.[12] Without parental guidance, YouTube can quickly move from family friend to major enemy—especially when we realize that even children ages two to eleven spend an average of eleven hours on the Internet every week, a 63 percent increase in the past five years.[13]

While the cell phone can be a wonderful tool, it can also introduce a world of hurt. For instance, one out of every five teens admits to having sent risqué photos of himself or herself via cell phone or e-mail, 11 percent of whom have sent such photos to complete strangers.[14] "Sexting" can also be a means of harassment and bullying, especially when not-so-friendly peers use their cell phone cameras in locker rooms and health clubs. In July 2008, a compromising picture forwarded to others resulted in more than just humiliation. Jessica Logan, eighteen, hung herself after a nude picture she'd sent to her boyfriend was forwarded to other high school girls. According to her mother, Cynthia Logan, Jessica began to experience harassment from peers who labeled her a "slut" and a "whore," and even threw things at her.[15] The bullying was so painful that she lost her desire to live.

Space simply doesn't allow an in-depth analysis of the various ways and systems that are currently delivering information and entertainment. (Articles, news, and quotes on this subject are regularly updated at http://www.pluggedin.com.) Once again, your daughter should not be wandering through potential technology land mines without your regular oversight and involvement.

Use Technology to Help Safeguard

While technology can be a foe, it can also be a great family friend. I'd like to highlight a few of today's technological marvels that I believe are essential for the home. They have made it much easier for parents to safeguard their sons and daughters. Here are some that you should consider:

The DVR. Only 31 percent of American homes currently have this TV-recording device. I think parents should consider purchasing the capability. Most importantly, the DVR can be used to record only *positive* programming that meets a healthy family standard. In addition, the DVR allows families to watch programs at their convenience instead of when they are scheduled. Speaking personally, I like being able to zip through an entire four-hour football game in less than half that time. What a time-saver! And who couldn't use a few more hours in their day?.

ClearPlay machine. This device, available at many Christian bookstores and from http://www.focusonthefamily.com, allows families to rent or buy movies and some television series with offensive content edited out. Editing updates for the latest movie releases are provided online at http://www .clearplay.com.

Internet filters. The Internet can help your daughter study for her final exams. But using it also exposes her to inappropriate sites. So a growing number of families are using Internet-filtering products. These software systems search the Web and restrict access to sites with violent or pornographic content. Several products also notify parents when attempts have been made to access such sites or when unsuitable e-mails have been attempted. (Check out the Parenting tab at http:// www.focusonthefamily.com for more information.)

Some Wise Perspective on Media's Influence

A few years back, game show host Pat Sajak had this to say about television and movies: "Television people have put blinders on and they absolutely refuse—and movie people too—to admit that they can have any influence for ill in our society. You know the argument: 'We only reflect what's going on; we don't perpetuate it.' And yet not a week goes by in this town [Hollywood] where there's not an award ceremony where they're patting each other on the back, saying, 'You raised AIDS awareness,' [or] 'There'll be no more child abuse thanks to the fine show you did.' The argument is you can only influence for good; you can't influence for ill. That makes no sense at all."[16]

Sajak hit the nail on the head. Entertainment can be incredibly influential. The systems currently delivering information and media content are also powerful. Fortunately, it's possible to successfully navigate the culture—as parents implement practical media principles to help guide the way.

What's more, although there are many entertainment products that cross gender lines, our daughters face unique challenges when Hollywood, the music industry, and television executives target them specifically.

As I'm sitting down in front of the computer each day, my eyes often land on a favorite quotation from Bill Cosby that I clipped years ago and tacked up on a board beside my desk: "The networks say they don't influence anybody. If that's true, why do they have commercials? Why am I sitting here with Jell-O pudding?"[17]

Hats off to Mr. Cosby. He gets it. He understands that the media has enormous potential for good or evil. If a mere thirty seconds can get us to buy Jell-O, drive a certain car, use a specific toothpaste, or drink a cola, the network that is sponsoring these products can also influence behaviors with their sitcoms, dramas, and movies.

For instance, when these media outlets portray God's gift of sexual intimacy as a *casual* act, it's no wonder some young people imitate what they've seen and heard. In May 2008, ABC News quoted a young woman, then twenty-two, who explained how the television show *Sex and the City* led her to imitate the leading characters. "When you're [a teenager] you try to emulate people on TV," said the woman, pseudo-named Lisa. "Carrie smoked so I smoked. Samantha looked at hooking up with random people as not a big deal, so that's what I did too."[18] Now realizing that *Sex and the City*'s view of promiscuous sex is a myth, Lisa regrets her choices. But there's no way to unscramble scrambled eggs. She was trapped by a series of lies.

Several recent studies have confirmed that Lisa's experience is all too common. In 2004, the RAND Corporation surveyed 1,792 adolescents and found that those who watched TV programs with a lot of sexual content were twice as likely to initiate sexual intercourse as their peers who watched fewer such programs.[19] Two years later, RAND confirmed a similar trend regarding music. Those who reportedly listened to sexualized music were almost twice as likely to engage in intercourse than their peers who listened to very little.[20] Numerous other studies have confirmed this finding. Young people often are impacted by what they watch and listen to.

Ten Practical Steps Every Parent Should Take

Given the media's tremendous power to teach and influence thoughts and behaviors, how can you train up your daughter to plot a safe course through today's entertainment and technological land mines? Here are some ideas.

1. Make media decisions based on God's view of entertainment. I was talking to some Christian friends recently when the conversation turned to current movies. One of them carried an R rating. I was told to plug my ears so that I wouldn't be offended by one friend's positive perspective on the film. I simply noted, "It doesn't matter what I think; it matters what the Lord thinks." Fortunately, this person interpreted my comment in the spirit in which I intended it—as thought provoking. He later told me that my words helped him make changes to his viewing habits.

Our thoughts about media consumption should be determined by God's standards, not those of the culture. As your daughter embraces this concept, it will help her say no to troublesome media products—even when her friends are saying yes.

2. Teach the WWJD Principle. I think it is appropriate for people of all ages to ask the question popularized more than a decade ago by the WWJD bracelets (What Would Jesus Do?). Though this fashion is now passé, the principle behind it will never be out of date. I actually prefer an expanded version of the question that goes something like this: if Jesus were walking the planet today with His twelve disciples, how would He respond if Peter, John, or Matthew came up and asked, "Should we go see or listen to [fill in the blank]?"

Christ's answer to this question—yes or no—would be based upon His *love* for His disciples, not a desire to squelch their fun!

3. Instill media-related biblical principles. Unlike many of life's potential pitfalls, the Bible seems largely silent about entertainment. After all, Peter, James, John, Abraham, and Moses didn't have to worry about what movies their kids might watch, what songs are played at the high school dance, or what TV shows they might see on their cell phones. However, while the Bible never says such things as, "Thou shalt not listen to gangsta rap," the Scriptures are full of passages to help us navigate the culture.

For instance, Proverbs 4:23 says, "Above all else, guard your heart." Colossians 2:8 expounds on the dangers of being duped by the lies of the world: "See to it that no one takes you captive through hollow and deceptive philosophy, which depends on human tradition and the basic principles of this world rather than on Christ." Psalm 1 warns against hanging out with the wicked, sinner, or mocker. Perhaps we should all place Psalm 101:3 above our TVs: "I will set before my eyes no vile thing. The deeds of faithless men I hate; they will not cling to me."

With today's entertainment, we have ways of associating with these "deeds of faithless men" that David could never have imagined! Check out http://www.pluggedin.com for many more Scriptures that can help teach discernment.

4. Model it. Nothing undermines your teaching about righteousness more than when your daughter observes that you're not applying those same principles to your own entertainment choices.

5. Get your youth pastor and senior pastor on board. Encourage your youth pastor to have a parent/teen night to discuss the subject of honoring Christ with entertainment decisions. Also, you might respectfully suggest to your senior pastor that he consider addressing this subject either from the pulpit or in the appropriate Sunday school classes.

6. Develop a written family media covenant. While it's one thing to talk about media discernment, it's another thing to spell out expectations and boundaries in writing. A written media covenant placed in a prominent location serves as a constant reminder of its importance. (Go to http://www .pluggedin.com and type in "family covenant" for a downloadable example.) Furthermore, plan to explore this issue in your family devotions at least twice a year.

7. Encourage positive alternatives. There are wholesome materials available for young people today. The movies *Facing the Giants, Fireproof, Amazing Grace,* and *The Passion of the Christ* are good examples. (Still, be sure to keep in mind the age and maturity level of your child when selecting any movie.) Also, Focus on the Family's Odyssey audio and video productions are outstanding examples of Christ-centered media. And when it comes to Kingdom work, probably no single product exceeds Campus Crusade for Christ's *JESUS* film (1979), which the organization estimates has resulted in more than 225,000,000 people making decisions for Christ. Further, there are scores of other solid entertainment choices that are not overtly Christian but whose themes and approach are entirely consistent with a scriptural perspective.

Attempts to ban all media and electronic devices at home are rarely successful. Some who go this route just give their kids ammunition with which to rebel—especially when they leave home and head off to college. I'm convinced the workable approach for most of us is to find constructive entertainment alternatives.

8. Consider "movie nights." Focus on the Family has published several *Movie Nights* books featuring quality mainstream films you can watch with your daughter as a fun launching pad for discussion. And now *Movie Nights* curricula are available free at http://www.pluggedin.com.

9. Encourage your daughter to develop a buddy system for media accountability. My own daughter honed her discernment skills by teaching the subject to elementary school age students in our church. But before grabbing the microphone, she developed a best friend in high school who shared her commitment to honor the Lord. They found it much easier to walk this path together than alone. As we read in Proverbs 27:17, "Iron sharpens iron." While such friends are not always easy to find, your daughter should seek "iron" in her life too.

10. Teach divine hatred. Yes, you read that right. Sure, as believers we are called primarily to *love*. But we're also taught in Romans 12:9 to "hate what is evil." Jesus did just that. Hebrews 1:9 tells us that He "hated wickedness." In Proverbs 8:13, we learn that "to fear the Lord is to *hate* evil" (emphasis added). We should follow Christ's example and practice *divine hatred*, despising the very things that He died on the cross to save us from, which will logically help us steer clear of entertainment that glamorizes such things.

Know This Is a Reachable Goal

Teaching discernment, staying on top of technology, and dispersing it both wisely and judiciously can be achieved. Of all the letters and e-mails I've received over the years, my favorite is one from Caroline in Atlanta, Georgia: "I rely on your movie reviews, and I very much appreciate your willingness to endure all kinds of cinematic catastrophes so that I don't have to. For several years now, I have been learning the practice of discernment through reading your reviews. . . . You may be slightly surprised to know that I am not a parent, nor am I even legally an independent adult. I am still in high school, and I know that you are well aware that very few of my peers—or my elders, for that matter—acknowledge or act upon the fact that it really does matter what we watch and that with which we saturate our minds."

So, take heart, parents. Success is possible. As you can see, Caroline is proud of her media convictions. There's no reason your daughter can't be as well.

❀ ❀ ❀

Thank you for this advice, Bob. We must protect our children and teach them what is right and wrong. To let them meander into cyberspace and today's entertainment culture unprotected and unsupervised is tantamount to parental negligence.

THE LAST WORD

WE COME NOW to the end of this exploration of bringing up girls. There is so much more that could be written, but parents today are too busy to read voluminous books. I suspect some are inclined to think, *How would I ever find the time to read a massive publication?* Perhaps someday I will come back to what has been omitted. The subject itself is virtually infinite in scope.

Still, to help us bring this discussion to a close, I will return to the poignant words of John and Stasi Eldredge:

> We have all heard it said that a woman is most beautiful when she is in love. It's true. You've seen it yourself. When a woman knows that she is loved and loved deeply, she glows from the inside. This radiance stems from a heart that has had its deepest questions answered. "Am I lovely? Am I worth fighting for? Have I been and will I continue to be romanced?" When these questions are answered, *Yes*, a restful, quiet spirit settles in a woman's heart.
>
> And every woman can have these questions answered, *Yes*. You have been and you will continue to be romanced all your life. Yes. Our God finds you lovely. Jesus has moved heaven and earth to win you for himself. He will not rest until you

are completely his. The King is enthralled by your beauty. He finds you captivating.[1]

These words are inspiring and entirely accurate. As we saw in chapter 3, there is within the nature of girls a yearning to know that they are precious to someone who loves them wholeheartedly. While boys are fantasizing about conquest and heroic deeds, little girls are already dreaming about the arrival of a Prince Charming who will sweep them off their feet. They hope to marry and live together in a little love nest made just for two. But as we know, life does not always deliver on that promise. The prince sometimes turns out to be fickle or flawed, or he may never show up at all.

Even if their storybook marriage becomes a reality, as it has for Shirley and me and millions of others, women often experience a longing for something more. That *something* is not romantic in nature. It is a hunger for a relationship with the compassionate and caring God, whose love is constant and secure. He never disappoints or forgets. He is there in times of loss and sorrow, and He hears the faintest cry. As King David wrote, "The LORD is a refuge for the oppressed, a stronghold in times of trouble" (Psalm 9:9). David also said, "The LORD is close to the brokenhearted and saves those who are crushed in spirit" (Psalm 34:18). Every child, male and female, should become intimately acquainted with this Friend and Savior during his or her developmental years.

If it is true that children should be trained in the knowledge of the Lord, and Scripture tells us it is, then there is one task in parenting that outranks all others in significance. It is the responsibility of Christian mothers and fathers to introduce their children to Jesus Christ and to cultivate their understanding of Him at every opportunity. The apostle Paul gave us that priority two thousand years ago when he wrote, "Do not exasperate your children; instead, bring them up in the training and instruction of the Lord" (Ephesians 6:4).

How desperately today's young people need this training and instruction. Countless numbers of them around the world are growing up in a world that is warping their beliefs and behavior. You can observe that damning influence by strolling through a local mall on a Friday night. Just look around. You'll see girls and boys who appear to be emotionally lost and spiritually bankrupt. The clothes they wear and the profanity they use and the extreme ways they present themselves expose a poverty of the soul. It is sadness on parade.

Dr. Ken Taylor, the godly patriarch who founded Tyndale House Publishers, was invited to attend a local high school football game after he had retired. He accepted the offer and sat in the bleachers with fans until halftime. Then he quietly slipped away without telling anyone where he was going. He confided to a friend later that he hadn't been bored with the game. Rather, he was so profoundly burdened for the kids around him that he went home to pray for them. What he saw on that day can also be observed by all of us who enter the world of the young.

We see evidence of it among the girls who contact us at Focus on the Family to seek advice. They are very different from those who wrote us twenty years ago. Teens used to inquire about the "right" thing to do, which usually reflected a Christian foundation of some variety. Even those who had no faith seemed to know that some things were simply wrong. That has changed dramatically. A significant number of the kids who ask for our counsel now are not interested in what is moral but rather how they should deal with the messes they are in and whether or not they should act on their impulses and desires. Not all adolescents think this way, of course, nor do the majority of them. But we are hearing from more and more youngsters who are greatly influenced by moral relativism. For them, absolute truth does not exist. There is no reliable standard of right and wrong because they acknowledge no God who can define it.

The classical Russian novelist Fyodor Dostoyevsky considered the consequences of moral relativism in his book *The Brothers Karamazov*. He wrote, "If there is no God, everything is permissible." That is what we are seeing in today's culture. In the absence of a moral compass, immature boys and girls are left to flounder in a bewildering sea of destructive options.

In my book *Bringing Up Boys*, I also discussed this spiritual confusion among those living in a world without God. It bears repeating:

> Human beings tend to struggle with troubling questions they can't answer. Just as nature abhors a vacuum, so the intellect acts to fill the void. Or to state it differently, it seeks to repair a hole in its system of beliefs. That is why so many young people today chase after twisted and alien "theologies," such as New Age nonsense, the pursuit of pleasure, substance abuse, and illicit sex. They are searching vainly for something that will satisfy their "soul hunger." They are unlikely to find it. . . . Meaning in life comes only by answering the eternal questions . . . and they are adequately addressed only in the Christian faith. No other religion can tell us who we are, how we got here, and where we are going after death. And no other belief system teaches that we are known and loved individually by the God of the universe and by His only Son, Jesus Christ. . . .

At the top of the list [of what children and teens need from their moms and dads] is an understanding of who God is and what He expects them to do. . . . Moses takes that responsibility a step further in Deuteronomy 6. He tells parents to talk about spiritual matters continually. . . .

Scripture tells us: "These commandments that I give you today are to be upon your hearts. Impress them on your children. Talk about them when you sit at home and when you walk along the road, when you lie down and when you get up. Tie them as symbols on your hands and bind them on your foreheads. Write them on the doorframes of your houses and on your gates" (Deuteronomy 6:6-9).[2]

Notice that Moses didn't just make a "suggestion" to parents about the spiritual training of their children. He called that assignment a *commandment*. There is urgency in his words. It is not enough to mutter, "Now I lay me down to sleep" with your exhausted child at the end of the day. I have concluded that our primary task as parents comes down to four components that will guide our efforts. They are as follows:

1) Talk to your children about the Lord and His mercies continually. This is what Moses told the children of Israel. It is also what King David and the prophet Joel, among other biblical authors, instructed us to do. These passages are too clear to be misunderstood.

Come, my children, listen to me; I will teach you the fear of the LORD. PSALM 34:11

We will not hide them from their children; we will tell the next generation the praiseworthy deeds of the LORD, his power, and the wonders he has done . . . so the next generation would know them, even the children yet to be born, and they in turn would tell their children. PSALM 78:4, 6

One generation will commend your works to another; they will tell of your mighty acts. PSALM 145:4

Tell it to your children, and let your children tell it to their children, and their children to the next generation. JOEL 1:3

My great-grandmother was a saint who understood that God required her to pass along her faith to her family. She talked about the Lord continually, it seemed.

When I was five years old, I was standing with her in our backyard as a plane flew overhead. She looked up and said, "Oh my, we have to pray for the pilot of that airplane."

"Why, Nanny?" I asked. "Is he going to crash?"

"No," she said, "but there is a man up there God knows and loves. We need to pray for him and his family."

I know now that Nanny was referring to the fact that our country was involved in World War II and that the young man in the plane might soon be engaged in mortal combat, although as a child I didn't understand those implications. What I did understand at the time was her concern about other human beings and our obligation to pray for them.

I hope you will take advantage of every opportunity to tell your children that faith in God is extremely important and that He cares about them too.

Begin this introduction to spiritual truths when your children are very young. Even at three years of age, a child is capable of learning that the flowers, the sky, the birds, and even rainbows are gifts from God's hand. He made these wonderful things, just as He created each one of us. The first Scripture our children should learn is, "God is love" (1 John 4:8). They should be taught to thank Him before eating their food and to ask for His help when they are hurt or scared.

In a 2003 nationwide poll, researcher George Barna observed that children ages five through thirteen have a 32 percent probability of accepting Christ as their Savior. That rate drops dramatically to just 4 percent for kids ages fourteen through eighteen. And those who have not become Christians before age nineteen have only a 6 percent probability of doing so during the rest of their lives.[3]

There is no time to lose!

2) Begin teaching your children to pray as early as possible. My parents and grandparents took that responsibility very seriously. The first word I learned to spell was *Jesus*. And

believe it or not, I began trying to pray even before I learned to talk. I had heard my parents praying during their private devotions, and I began imitating the sounds they made. My mother and father were shocked and wondered how that was possible for a child at thirteen months of age. The moral to the story is that your children are observing you too and are influenced by everything you do.

It is fun watching little children as they begin to grasp the art of talking to God. I received a delightful note from a colleague recently who knew I was writing this book. He wrote, "Every evening we pray together with our four-year-old and end by asking him to thank God for anything he wants to mention. The open-ended prayers are often very sweet. Last week he said, 'Thank you God for *everything*—except germs and mosquitoes.'"

My friend continued, "Riley will often ramble on like a senator engaged in a filibuster, thanking God for the air, the grass, baseball, his dog, his crayons, etc. But last night he was apparently tired, and when I asked him to pray he said, 'No, thank you, Daddy. My mouth has run out of words.'"

Our three-year-old grandson, Lincoln, has an extreme dislike for bedtime, and he thinks up every possible excuse to avoid it. He also wakes up at night and tries to figure out how to get up. A few weeks ago, Lincoln called out to his parents at 3 a.m. He said, "Da-Da, I sick." Ryan came to his bedside and said, "Son, where do you hurt?"

Lincoln pointed to his teeth and said, "Right here."

Ryan told him that he wasn't sick and said he had to stay in bed. The toddler then replied with all seriousness, "Da-Da, let's pray."

Are you praying with your little ones? How about your older children? Don't let the golden opportunities slip away.

3) The third component of spiritual training takes us back to King David's writings. He said in Psalm 119:11, "Thy word have I hid in mine heart, that I might not sin against thee" (KJV). If you want your children to be guided morally when they are beyond your reach and after they are grown, you should begin teaching favorite passages to them when

they are young. It is amazing how often a relevant biblical reference zings to the surface just when a situation comes up that requires wisdom and discernment. If those verses have not been "downloaded" to our brains, we will have to figure out what to do based on our own limited understanding.

Memorize key Scriptures with your children, make a game out of the process, and reward them for learning these passages. Some of the stored passages will stay with them for a lifetime, and even if the exact words are forgotten, the truths they contain remain alive and will be remembered.

Music is a wonderful tool for teaching the Scriptures. Introduce your girls and boys to an array of songs that contain biblical concepts and stories. You can begin with "Jesus loves me, this I know, for the Bible tells me so. Little ones to Him belong. They are weak, but He is strong." Being a traditionalist myself, I prefer songs that have endured for many years. Past generations of children have sung them with their parents. You may prefer more contemporary music, of course, but just be sure that your children grow up with the lyrics and stories of the Christian faith. Then get your girls and boys into a strong church that preaches the Word of God and will help you "bring them up in the training and instruction of the Lord" (Ephesians 6:4).

4) "Pray without ceasing" (1 Thessalonians 5:17, KJV). Prayer is one of God's most mysterious and remarkable gifts to us. It is our lifeline to heaven, our lifeline to the most holy of relationships, our opportunity to directly express our praises and desires to the Creator of the universe. There is power in this simple act that cannot fully be explained, yet can never be denied. And it is our most effective means of contributing to the welfare of our children.

You may be aware that my wife, Shirley, is chairman of the National Day of Prayer Task Force. Prayer has been the passion of her life, beginning at six years of age when she gave her heart to the Lord. This is her message to moms and dads:

When confronted with the awesome responsibilities of parenthood—not to mention the evil in today's world—it's no surprise that many parents feel an urgent need to pray continually for their children. When [our daughter] Danae was about three years old, Jim and I realized that as parents we needed divine help. We began fasting and praying for her, and later for [our son] Ryan almost every week (a practice that I continue to this day).

Our prayer went something like this: "Lord, give us the wisdom to raise the precious children You have loaned to us, and above all else, help us bring them to the feet of Jesus. This is more important to us than our health or our work or our finances. What we ask most fervently is that the circle be unbroken when we meet in heaven."

God has not only heard this prayer but blessed it in ways we never anticipated. Our prayer time has become a project that Jim and I enjoy *together*, drawing us closer to each other as we draw closer to God. In addition, the act of fasting each week serves as an important reminder of our priorities: It's difficult to forget your highest values when one day out of seven is spent focusing entirely on them. Finally, our children were influenced by these acts of discipline. When they observed us fasting or praying, it gave us the opportunity to explain why we did these things, how much we loved them, and how much we loved and trusted the Lord.

God hears and honors—in His perfect timing—our petitions on behalf of our children. If you want the very best for your sons and daughters, I urge you to call on the greatest power in the universe in frequent prayer.[4]

Shirley's words go to the heart of what I believe most passionately. It is why throughout my professional life, I have encouraged Christian parents to introduce their boys and girls to Jesus Christ and to continually hold their names before the Lord in prayer. After all, the only way you can be with your sons and daughters in the next life is if you, and they, know Him as Lord and Savior.

Let me conclude by telling you about a little needlepoint plaque that hangs on the wall of our home. It contains the words of 3 John 1:4 (KJV): "I have no greater joy than to hear that my children walk in truth." Thank God, they do!

In this context of eternity, I'll leave you with a story about a little girl whom I never was privileged to meet. Her name is Delaney, and she lived on this earth for only sixteen months before slipping away to be with Jesus. Who can explain why this precious child was given so little time to live and love and grow? Only God knows. But my heart is tender toward her parents, Mark and Becky Waters, with whom I served for many years at Focus on the Family. Mark sent me an unforgettable photograph that he titled, "The Empty Chair." It and his accompanying letter are reproduced below.

"The Empty Chair," photographed by Mark Waters

> *Dear Dr. Dobson:*
> *Today is the sixth anniversary of the day my precious little girl, Delaney, went home to live with Almighty God. As my family and I remember with tears, smiles, and confident thoughts of seeing her again one day, I can't help but think of you as you are writing* Bringing Up Girls.
> *Although we had only sixteen short months with her, Delaney is a*

special gift. As the father of one boy already at that time (now two), I can tell you that she was a completely different being. From the time my boys were old enough to reach out and hug me, I always got the sense that they were practicing their headlocks, which they now use on me every chance they get. To receive a hug from Delaney, however, was an altogether different experience. She never tired of melting into my arms and burying her tiny face deep into my neck. She was pure love. She was my "Sweet Delaney Pie."

When sharing our story with others, especially parents, I am always careful to convey the most important perspective that God has blessed us (yes, blessed us) with through our tragic loss. I always say to them, "I can live my life here on earth without my precious Delaney, but I cannot possibly conceive of spending eternity without any one of my children." God has made the significance of this perspective so very clear to my wife, Becky, and me, and we are eternally (literally) grateful. I wish this truth could become as clear to every parent without having to go through such a tragic experience as ours.

Even through all we've learned, we are still not perfect parents, but we don't have to be perfect in order to pass along God's eternal perspective. Our sons speak often and with confidence of "our sister, Delaney, who lives in heaven." They also smile as they talk about what they will do together when they finally get to see her. The faith of children is so pure. I love that.

I don't know what Delaney will look like when I see her again. Will she still be a little girl, or will she have grown to be a beautiful woman? No matter. We will embrace, and I will weep flowing tears of joy for a long, long time. I will weep because the pain of her death will be gone forever. What will be left will be the only thing that matters: we will share eternity together.

May God bless you, Dr. Dobson, as you write this book, that your readers will take seriously the responsibility of raising, protecting, and loving these special gifts—these tender, loving, precious little girls God has entrusted them with.

Your brother in Christ,
Mark

Thank you, Mark. You have spoken on behalf of many other parents among my readers who live today with "an empty chair." I met many of them during their times of anguish when I served on the Attending Staff at Childrens Hospital of Los Angeles. Some of their children have gone on to heaven now, where they run and play with "Sweet Delaney Pie." But their days on this earth will never be forgotten.

Perhaps those moms and dads, along with Mark and Becky, will find solace and inspiration in the following poem written by Edgar Guest.

Child Loaned

"I'll lend you for a little time
A child of Mine," He said.
"For you to love the while she lives,
And mourn for when she's dead.
It may be six or seven years
Or twenty-two or three,
But will you, till I call her back
Take care of her for Me?
She'll bring her charms to gladden you,
And should her stay be brief,
You'll have her lovely memories
As solace for your grief.
I cannot promise she will stay,
Since all from Earth return,
But there are lessons taught down there
I want this child to learn.
I've looked this wide world over
In My search for teachers true,
And from the throngs that crowd life's lanes,
I have selected you;
Now will you give her all your love,
Nor think the labour vain,
Nor hate Me when I come to call
And take her back again?
I fancied that I heard them say,
"Dear Lord, Thy will be done,
For all the joy Thy child shall bring,
For the risk of grief we'll run.
We'll shelter her with tenderness,
We'll love her while we may,
And for the happiness we've known,
Forever grateful stay.
But should the angels call for her
Much sooner then we planned,
We'll brave the bitter grief that comes
And try to understand.

❀ ❀ ❀

Well, those are my thoughts and suggestions about bringing up girls. It has been a pleasure writing this book for you. I have been working on it for more than three years, poring over a huge volume of research and professional literature. Some of the girls I had in mind in the beginning are now grown, and some of their young mothers had begun to think their daughters would be grandmothers by the time I finished. Now that the book is complete and you have read it, I hope you have found my advice helpful. The girls you are raising deserve your very best.

HELPFUL RESOURCES
FOR PARENTS

LET ME SHARE with you now some resources that might assist you in bringing up girls. My daughter, Danae, has written two books, *Let's Talk!* and *Let's Walk the Talk!* that provide teen girls with "big sister" advice about all the important issues and challenges they face on a daily basis.

Danae remembers what it's like to be a teenager and how hard it can be to live as a Christian in an increasingly secularized world. Her first book, *Let's Talk!* offers advice to girls about six categories: God, family, friends, guys, self, and eternity. The comments about each topic are firmly grounded in Scripture and communicated in a way that teens can relate to. *Let's Walk the Talk!* features wise counsel on subjects such as spiritual maturity, financial responsibility, true beauty, modesty, and God's ultimate plan for our lives. I highly recommend these resources for your teenage daughters (and those preparing for the teen years).

❀ ❀ ❀

Another great tool you might find useful is called *Secret Keeper Girl Kit: Eight Great Dates for You and Your Daughter.* The subtitle reads, *The Power of True Beauty and Modesty.* It is intended for girls between eight and twelve years of age, and was written by Dannah Gresh, with special insights from Rebecca St. James.[1]

I wish this recorded and written program had been available when our daughter was moving through the era immediately prior to puberty. She and her mother would have loved sharing these "great dates" together.

On the CD, Dannah Gresh and others talk to your girls about what they call eight "dates." Each one addresses a different topic in a highly personal and warm manner. There is also a Secret Keeper Girl book that supplements the CD.

❀ ❀ ❀

The third suggestion should also be helpful. Some years ago I recorded a series called *Preparing for Adolescence* that parents and daughters or sons could listen to together. Now available on CD, these recordings are designed to help moms and dads introduce the physical and emotional upheaval that will soon occur. They also give parents the ability to stop their CD player and answer questions as they arise.

I actually prepared these recordings for my daughter when she was heading into puberty. I had no notion of selling them commercially. However, the junior high department at our church heard about the recordings and asked if they could use them with parents. Then a publisher got wind of the series and quickly made them available to the public. A book bearing the same name was then published. The CDs and book can still be found in bookstores and libraries, and many thousands of parents have used them.

Ideally, these recordings should be listened to by girls and boys separately (usually fathers with their boys and mothers with their girls) during the period immediately prior to puberty. If parents wait too long to introduce the relevant subjects to their children, they will be embarrassed to listen. I can just hear a fourteen- or fifteen-year-old saying, "Oh, Mom! You've got to be kidding!" But if you talk about these topics prior to the arrival of the happy hormones, it is much more comfortable for both generations and proves to be more effective. Your obligation, one way or the other, is to get the job done. You owe it to your kids to prepare them for what lies in the path immediately ahead.

❀ ❀ ❀

Finally, I would like to offer an alternative to Girl Scouts of the USA, which I can no longer recommend to parents. That organization has changed radically since 1993, when it began making references to God "optional" and marking the word with an asterisk. Then came mandates against Christmas caroling, praying at meetings, and singing hymns. Now we are seeing a surge toward the left that is deeply disturbing to many Christian parents.

For example, as part of GSUSA's aMAZE program for middle school Scouts, the girls read a quote from Buddha and are encouraged to explore mazes and stone or dirt labyrinths—symbols rooted in pagan mythology and the New Age movement. They are used as meditation tools, along with "transformation circles." Eastern mysticism through Zen gardens and Buddhist writings are part of the curriculum. Moral relativism is evident throughout, which teaches that ethical issues are up to the individual. GSUSA's definition of right and wrong includes this statement: "Whatever is consistent with your character."[2]

The curriculum has a strong anti-boy tone (boys are mentioned only in negative situations). There is minimal emphasis on mother, father, or family. Girls are not taught pride of country. The United States is depicted as antiquated and incompatible with globalism. One program involves girls in the United Nations Population Fund. Translated, that amounts to a massive effort to limit human procreation by means of abortion.

Many of the female role models lauded by GSUSA are radical feminists, lesbians, existentialists, or communists, including the former chairwoman of the American Communist Party. There is much more to disturb parents, including a consistent infusion of lesbian and homosexual propaganda. In short, the organization has been "captured" by advocates of an extreme leftist ideology that is being force-fed to millions of vulnerable girls. Its board of directors and many troop leaders are intent on converting every girl from the youngest Daisy to a mature Ambassador into an "agent of change," programmed to implement an extreme international agenda. The media has kept this transformation a secret for more than a decade.

There is a far better program available for girls, in my opinion. It is a nonprofit organization called American Heritage Girls, founded in 1995 in West Chester, Ohio, by a group of parents wanting a more wholesome alternative for their daughters. These parents were disillusioned with the increasing secular focus of existing organizations for girls. They wanted a Judeo-Christian focused entity and assumed that they were not alone.[3]

American Heritage Girls is dedicated to the mission of building women of integrity through service to God, family, community, and country. It offers badge programs, service projects, leadership opportunities, and outdoor experiences to its members. This program of character building has successfully served thousands of girls since its inception and will continue to do so long into the twenty-first century.

AHG troops are composed of groups of girls ages five to eighteen who meet weekly or biweekly to learn new skills, give service, grow in their faith, practice leadership, experience teamwork, build friendships, and strengthen character. The girls mentor one another in a large group setting and then break into age-appropriate units to achieve the unit's goals for each meeting. According to the president of AHG, "This Christ-centered organization is led by dedicated adult volunteers who facilitate the program while recognizing girls' valuable input."

There are more than ten thousand American Heritage Girls who meet across the United States. Each troop reflects the "personality" of its Charter Partner as it utilizes the AHG program to achieve its ministry goals for youth.

This is the oath taken by American Heritage Girls:

> *I promise to love God,*
> *Cherish my family,*
> *Honor my country,*
> *And serve in my community.*

I recommend American Heritage Girls enthusiastically to parents who want their daughters involved in a traditional Christian-based program that will reinforce what they are trying to teach at home. That certainly will *not* occur at Girl Scouts USA!

You can get more information about American Heritage Girls by contacting their headquarters at http://www.ahgonline.org or at (513) 771-2025.

NOTES

Chapter 1

1. James C. Dobson, *Bringing Up Boys* (Carol Stream, IL: Tyndale House Publishers, 2001).

Chapter 2

1. See http://www.ed.gov/about/reports/annual/osep/2003/25th-vol-1.pdf, figure 1-20, page 26.
2. Michael Gurian, *The Wonder of Boys* (New York: Jeremy P. Tarcher/Putnam, 1996), xvii–xviii.
3. Gennaro F. Vito, Jeffrey R. Maah, and Ronald M. Holmes, *Criminology: Theory, Research, and Policy* (Sudbury, MA: Jones and Bartlett Publishers, 2006), 38.
4. See http://www.sciencenews.org/articles/20060415/mathtrek.asp.
5. See http://ojjdp.ncjrs.org/ojstatbb/nr2006/downloads/chapter6.ppt#264,10,Juvenile%20 court%20caseload%20trends%20are%20different%20for%20males%20and%20females.
6. Peg Tyre, *The Trouble with Boys: A Surprising Report Card on Our Sons, Their Problems at School, and What Parents and Educators Must Do* (New York: Crown Publishers, 2008); "Trends in Educational Equity of Girls and Women: 2004," National Center for Education Statistics, U.S. Department of Education; see http://nces.ed.gov/pubs2005/equity/Section4.asp; "Education at a Glance 2003," Organisation for Economic Co-Operation and Development; see http://www.oecdwash.org.
7. Alaina Sue Potrikus, "Women Making Strides in Education, Grades, Attendance, Graduation Rate Higher than Men," *St. Paul Pioneer Press* (September 28, 2003): A5.
8. "Trends in Educational Equity of Girls and Women: 2004," National Center for Education Statistics, U.S. Department of Education; see http://nces.ed.gov/pubs2005/equity/Section4.asp; Kathleen Deveny, "Girls Gone Bad," *Newsweek* (February 12, 2007), 40.
9. "Trends in Educational Equity of Girls and Women: 2004," National Center for Education Statistics, U.S. Department of Education; see http://nces.ed.gov/programs/projections/ projections2015/sec4b.asp.
10. "Media's Effects on Girls: Body Image and Gender Identity," National Institute of Media and the Family fact sheet (last revised April 3, 2009).
11. Stacy Weiner, "Goodbye to Girlhood," *Washington Post* (February 20, 2007); see http://www .washingtonpost.com/wp-dyn/content/article/2007/02/16/AR2007021602263.html.
12. Ellen A. Schur, Mary Sanders, and Hans Steiner, "Body Dissatisfaction and Dieting in Young Children," *The International Journal of Eating Disorders*, vol. 27 (December 1999): 74–82; Judith Duffy, "Revealed: The Children as Young as Five Years Old Suffering from Eating Disorders," *Sunday Herald* (November 12, 2006): 7.

13. "Cutting Girls Down to Size: The Influence of the Media on Teenage Body Image," *Media & Values* (November 3, 2005): 2–3.
14. National Institute of Mental Health Statistics, 2004; see http://www.nimh.nih.gov/Publicat/eatingdisorders.cfm#sup1>.
15. Ibid.
16. Urmee Khan, "Angelina Jolie Says Fidelity Not Essential for Relationships to Work," *Telegraph* (December 23, 2009); see http://www.telegraph.co.uk/news/newstopics/celebritynews/6870917/Angelina-Jolie-says-fidelity-not-essential-for-relationships-to-work.html.
17. The Center on Alcohol Marketing and Youth, *Out of Control: Alcohol Advertising Taking Aim at America's Youth—A Report on Alcohol Advertising in Magazines* (Washington, DC: The Center on Alcohol Marketing and Youth, 2002).
18. "Teenage Girls Targeted for Sweet-Flavored Alcoholic Beverages: Polls Show More Teen Girls See 'Alcopop' Ads than Women Age 21–44," AlcoholPolicyMd.com (December 16, 2004); see http://www.alcoholpolicymd.com/press_room/Press_releases/girlie_drinks_release.htm.
19. Page Hurwitz and Alison Pollet, "Strip Till You Drop: Teen Girls Are the Target Market for a New Wave of Stripper-Inspired Merchandise," *The Nation* (January 12, 2004): 20.
20. Ibid.
21. Steve Lopez, "A Scary Time to Raise a Daughter," *The Los Angeles Times* (October 26, 2003): B1.
22. Project Safe Childhood: A National Media Campaign; see http://knowwheretheygo.org/DigitalFootprint/pornography.
23. See http://www.amazon.com/Barbie-Scene-Bling-Chelsea-Doll/dp/B000A7S5AU/ref=pd_sim_t_title_2.
24. Weiner, "Goodbye to Girlhood."
25. Bruce Kluger, "Dolls Lose Their Innocence," *USA Today* (December 11, 2006): A23.
26. See http://www.apa.org/pi/women/programs/girls/report-summary.pdf.
27. NPD Fashionworld Data, 2003, quoted by Claudia Wallis, "The Thing about Thongs," *Time* magazine (September 28, 2003); see http://www.time.com/time/magazine/article/0,9171,490711,00.html.
28. Michelle Malkin, "Standing Up to the 'Girls Gone Wild' Culture" (July 27, 2004); see www.michellemalkin.com/ 2004/07/27/standing-up-to-the-girls-gone-wild-culture.
29. Ibid.

Chapter 3

1. *Good Housekeeping* (October 1990): 87–88.
2. Lynn Hirschberg, "The Misfit," *Vanity Fair* (April 1991): 160–169, 196–202.
3. Alan Ebert, "Oprah Winfrey Talks Openly about Oprah," *Good Housekeeping* (September 1991): 63.
4. Deborah Starr Seibei, "Melissa Gilbert's Bittersweet Justice," *TV Guide* (October 15, 1994): 12.
5. Marcia Chellis, *Living with the Kennedys: The Joan Kennedy Story* (New York: Simon and Schuster, 1985), 39.
6. Ibid., 45.
7. John and Stasi Eldredge, *Captivating: Unveiling the Mystery of a Woman's Soul* (Nashville: Thomas Nelson, 2005), 46, 59.
8. Meg Meeker, *Strong Fathers, Strong Daughters: 10 Secrets Every Father Should Know* (New York: Ballantine Books, 2006), 8–9, 18, 28.
9. Angela Kaset, "The Hopechest Song," Purple Sun Music, LLC (1996). Performed by Stephanie Bentley on the album *Hopechest*.

Chapter 4

1. Adapted from Robert Southey's (1774–1843) poem entitled "What Folks Are Made Of," circa 1820.
2. "Brainstorm: Neuroscientist Sandra Witelson Says Men's and Women's Brains Are Different," *Chatelaine* (December 1995): 72–74.

3. Louann Brizendine, *The Female Brain* (New York: Morgan Road Books, 2006), 12.
4. Michael Gurian, Ph.D., *The Wonder of Girls* (New York: Simon and Schuster, 2002), 29.
5. Ibid.
6. Michael Gurian and Kathy Stevens, *The Minds of Boys* (San Francisco: Jossey-Bass, 2005), 140.
7. Michael Gurian and Kathy Stevens, "With Boys and Girls in Mind," *Educational Leadership* (November 2004): 21–26.
8. Brizendine, *The Female Brain*, 13.
9. Ibid.
10. Ibid.
11. E. B. McClure, "A Meta-Analytic Review of Sex Differences in Facial Expression Processing and Their Development in Infants, Children, and Adolescents," *Psychological Bulletin* 126, no. 3 (2000): 424–453.
12. Ibid.
13. Brizendine, *The Female Brain*, 14–15.
14. M. J. Meaney and M. Szyf (2005). "Environmental Programming of Stress Responses through DNA Methylation: Life at the Interface between a Dynamic Environment and a Fixed Genome," *Dialogues in Clinical Neuroscience* 7, no. 2 (2005): 103–123.
15. Brizendine, *The Female Brain*, 21–22.
16. Gurian, *The Wonder of Girls*, 23.
17. Ibid., 53.
18. Ibid.
19. Ibid.
20. Ibid., 55.
21. Ibid.
22. Allan Pease and Allan Garner, *Talk Language: How to Use Conversation for Profit and Pleasure* (London: Simon and Schuster, 1985).
23. Ron G. Rosenfeld and Barbara C. Nicodemus, "The Transition from Adolescence to Adult Life: Physiology of the 'Transition' Phase and Its Evolutionary Basis," *Hormone Research* 60 (2003): 74–77.
24. Ibid.

Chapter 5

1. John Adams and Charles Francis Adams, *The Works of John Adams, Second President of the United States* (Boston: Little, Brown & Company, 1865), 171.
2. John Adams, quoted in his address to U.S. military forces, October 11, 1798; see http://oll.libertyfund.org/?option=com_staticxt&staticfile=show.php%3Ftitle=2107&chapter=161247&layout=html&Itemid=27%3chttps://fofmail.fotf.org/exchweb/bin/redir.asp?URL=http://oll.libertyfund.org/?option=com_staticxt%26staticfile=show.php%253Ftitle=2107%26chapter=161247%26layout=html%26Itemid=27.
3. Abraham Lincoln, the Gettysburg Address (November 19, 1863).
4. Horace Mann, *The Common School Journal: For the Year 1847*, vol. IX (Boston: William B. Fowle, 1847): 181.
5. Quoted in E. D. Hill, *I'm Not Your Friend, I'm Your Parent: Helping Your Children Set the Boundaries They Need . . . and Really Want* (Nashville: Thomas Nelson Publishers, 2008), 16.
6. Venice Buhain, "Young Students Learn How, Why to Use Good Manners," *Olympian*; see http://www.finaltouchschool.com/article_yslearn.htm.
7. Virginia De Leon, "You Could Call Her Our Very Own Ms. Manners," *Spokesman-Review* (April 7, 2008).
8. Sheryl Eberly, *365 Manners Kids Should Know: Games, Activities, and Other Fun Ways to Help Children Learn Etiquette* (New York: Three Rivers Press, 2001).
9. Zehra Mamdani, "Charm Schools Making a Comeback," *Chicago Tribune* (June 29, 2008): 6.
10. Karen Santorum, *Everyday Graces: A Child's Book of Good Manners* (Wilmington, DE: ISI Books, 2003).

11. Caroline Mansfield, Suellen Hopfer, and Theresa M. Marteau, "Termination Rates after Prenatal Diagnosis of Down Syndrome, Spina Bifida, Anencephaly, and Turner and Klinefelter Syndromes: A Systematic Literature Review," *Prenatal Diagnosis* 19, no. 9 (1999): 808–812; see http://www3. interscience.wiley.com/cgi-bin/abstract/65500197/ABSTRACT. This is similar to 90 percent results found by David W. Britt, Samantha T. Risinger, Virginia Miller, Mary K. Mans, Eric L. Krivchenia, and Mark I. Evans, "Determinants of Parental Decisions after the Prenatal Diagnosis of Down Syndrome: Bringing in Context." *American Journal of Medical Genetics* 93, no. 5 (1999): 410–416.
12. "Meet Pro-Life Governor Sarah Palin," *National Right to Life News*, September 1, 2008.
13. "Building Moral Character in Kids," *Focus on the Family* daily radio program (November 7, 2005).
14. Wendy Shalit, *Girls Gone Mild: Young Women Reclaim Self-Respect and Find It's Not Bad to Be Good* (New York: Random House, 2007).
15. Adams, *The Works of John Adams*, 171.
16. This discussion took place on the Focus on the Family campus in October 2008.

Chapter 6

1. Peggy Noonan, "Embarrassing the Angels: Or, That's No Way to Treat a Lady," *Wall Street Journal*, March 2, 2006; see: http://www.opinionjournal.com/columnists/ pnoonan/?id=110008034.

Chapter 7

1. John Bowlby, *Attachment and Loss 1: Attachment* (New York: Basic Books, 1969/1982); Jeffry A. Simpson and William Steven Rholes, *Attachment Theory and Close Relationships* (New York: Guilford Press, 1998), 167; Inge Bretherton, "The Origins of Attachment Theory: John Bowlby and Mary Ainsworth," *Developmental Psychology* 28, no. 5 (September 1992): 759–775.
2. See http://www.zerotothree.org/site/PageServer?pagename=key_brain.
3. Lucy M. Osborn et al, *Pediatrics* (Philadelphia: Elsevier Mosby, 2005), 494.
4. Bowlby, *Attachment and Loss 1*; Simpson and Rholes, *Attachment Theory and Close Relationships*, 167; Bretherton, "The Origins of Attachment Theory," 759–775.
5. C. F. Weems and V. G. Carrion, "The Association between PTSD Symptoms and Salivary Cortisol in Youth: The Role of Time since the Trauma," *Journal of Traumatic Stress* 20, no. 5 (2007): 903–907; A. N. Schore, "The Effects of Early Relational Trauma on Right Brain Development, Affect Regulation, and Infant Mental Health," *Infant Mental Health Journal* 22, no. 1–2 (2001): 201–269; A. N. Schore, *Affect Regulation and the Origin of the Self: The Neurobiology of Emotional Development* (Mahwah, NJ: Lawrence Erlbaum, 1994).
6. Terry M. Levy, Ph.D., "Understanding Attachment Disorder"; see http://www.4therapy.com/ consumer/conditions/article/6578/507/Understanding+Attachment+Disorder.
7. M. Mäntymaa, K. Puura, I. Luoma, R. Salmelin, H. Davis, J. Tsiantis, V. Ispanovic-Radojkovic, A. Paradisiotou, T. Tamminen, "Infant-Mother Interaction as a Predictor of Child's Chronic Health Problems," *Child Care Health Development* 29, no. 3 (May 2003): 181–191.
8. Ruth Feldman et al, "Relations between Cyclicity and Regulation in Mother-Infant Interaction at 3 and 9 Months and Cognition at 2 Years," *Journal of Applied Developmental Psychology* 17 (1996): 347–365.
9. Psalm 139:13-18.
10. Lauren Lindsey Porter, "The Science of Attachment: The Biological Roots of Love," *Mothering* (July/August 2003).
11. National Women's Law Center calculations based on data from Employment Characteristics of Families in 2006, Tables 5 and 6.
12. U.S. Census Data, 2002; see http://74.125.155.132/search?q=cache:JYsjKWy9tEQJ:www.census. gov/prod/2008pubs/p70-113.pdf+Census+and+%22mothers%22+and+2002+and+maternity&c d=1&hl=en&ct=clnk&gl=us.

13. Daphne de Marneffe, *Maternal Desire: On Children, Love, and the Inner Life* (New York: Little, Brown and Company, 2004), ix.

14. Ibid., 22.

15. Ellyn Spragins, "Love & Money: Is My Mom Better than Yours?" *New York Times* (July 1, 2001).

16. Ibid.

17. Ibid.

18. "Fewer Mothers Prefer Full-Time Work: From 1997 to 2007," Pew Research Center (July 12, 2007); see http://pewresearch.org/pubs/536/working-women.

19. Ibid.

20. Ibid.

21. Ibid.

22. Carol Platt Liebau, *Prude: How the Sex-Obsessed Culture Damages Girls (and America, Too!)* (New York: Center Street, 2007), 208–211.

23. Quoted by Mary Ann Fergus, "Author Looks at Mom-Daughter Tensions," *Houston Chronicle* (March 25, 2002): 1.

Chapter 8

1. See http://www.focusleadership.org.

2. Proverbs 18:24.

3. Psalm 34:18.

4. William J. Gaither and Gloria Gaither, "Something Beautiful" (copyright 1980).

Chapter 9

1. John Lennon, "Beautiful Boy" (1980). Versions of this same quote have been attributed to several individuals over the years, including Betty Talmadge, Thomas La Mance, Margaret Millar, Lily Tomlin, William Gaddis, and Allen Saunders.

2. Tanya S. Scheffler and Peter J. Naus, "The Relationship between Fatherly Affirmation and a Woman's Self-Esteem, Fear of Intimacy, Comfort with Womanhood and Comfort with Sexuality," *Canadian Journal of Human Sexuality* 8, no. 1 (Spring 1999): 39–45; Margaret J. Meeker, *Strong Fathers, Strong Daughters: 10 Secrets Every Father Should Know* (Washington D.C.: Regnery Publishing, 2008).

3. National Vital Statistics, Volume 52, No. 10, 2002. See http://www.cdc.gov/nchs/data/nvsr/nvsr52/nvsr52_10.pdf.

4. H. Norman Wright, *Always Daddy's Girl* (Ventura, CA: Regal, 2001), 35–36.

5. Meeker, *Strong Fathers, Strong Daughters*, 96; Debra Haffner, *Beyond the Big Talk: A Parent's Guide to Raising Sexually Healthy Teens—from Middle School to High School and Beyond* (New York: Newmarket Press, 2001).

6. Rebekah Coley, "Children's Socialization Experiences and Functioning in Single-Mother Households: The Importance of Fathers and Other Men," *Child Development* 69 (February 1998): 219–230.

7. A. Morcoen and K. Verschuren, "Representation of Self and Socioemotional Competence in Kindergartners: Differential and Combined Effects of Attachment to Mothers and Fathers," *Child Development* 70 (1999): 183–201.

8. Michael D. Resnick et al, *Journal of the American Medical Association* 10 (September 10, 1997): 823–832.

9. Diann Ackard et al, *American Journal of Preventive Medicine* 1 (January 30, 2006): 59–66.

10. U.S. Department of Health and Human Services, National Center for Health Statistics, "Survey on Child Health" (Washington, D.C.: GPO, 1993).

11. Greg J. Duncan, Martha Hill, and W. Jean Yeung, "Fathers' Activities and Children's Attainments" (paper presented at a conference on father involvement, Washington, D.C.).

12. Joseph E. Schwartz et al, "Sociodemographic and Psychosocial Factors in Child as Predictors of Adult Mortality," *American Journal of Public Health* 85 (1995): 1237–1245.

13. Claudette Wassil-Grimm, *Where's Daddy? How Divorced, Single and Widowed Mothers Can Provide What's Missing When Dad's Missing* (New York: Overlook Press, 1994).
14. N. Zill and Carol Schoenborn, "Child Development, Learning and Emotional Problems: Health of Our Nation's Children," U.S. Department of Health and Human Services, National Center for Health Statistics, Advance Data 1990 (Washington, D.C.: GPO, 1990).
15. E. M. Hetherington and Barbara Martin, "Family Interaction," *Psychopathological Disorders of Childhood* (New York: Wiley, 1979).
16. F. Horn and Tom Sylvester, *Father Facts* (Gaithersburg, MD: National Fatherhood Initiative, 2002).
17. Agnieszka Wiszewska et al, "Father-Daughter Relationship as a Moderator of Sexual Imprinting: A Facialmetric Study," *Evolution and Human Behavior*, published online by Elsevier (2007).
18. James J. Rue and Louise Shanahan, *Daddy's Girl, Mama's Boy* (Indianapolis: Bobbs-Merrill, 1978).

Chapter 10

1. Harry H. Harrison, *Father to Daughter: Life Lessons on Raising a Girl* (New York: Workman Publishing Co., 2003). Used by permission.

Chapter 11

1. See http://generationsoflight.myicontrol.com.
2. Neela Banerjee, "Dancing the Night Away, with a Higher Purpose," *New York Times* (May 19, 2008): A13.
3. Steven Curtis Chapman, "Cinderella," released May 28, 2008. Used by permission.

Chapter 12

1. "The Princess Effect: Fascination with Princesses Could Be Unhealthy," *Good Morning America*, ABC News (April 22, 2007).
2. Peggy Orenstein, "What's Wrong with Cinderella," *New York Times* (December 24, 2006): 34.
3. Beth Thames, "Pretty in Pink but Powerful, Too," *Huntsville Times* (January 2, 2005): F2.
4. Jennifer Dowd, "The Princess Debate: Are Fairy Tale Princesses Really Bad for Our Girls?" see http://parenting.kaboose.com/behavior/emotional-social-development/the-princess-debate.html (accessed September 2, 2009).
5. Orenstein, "What's Wrong with Cinderella," 34.
6. Ibid.
7. Thames, "Pretty in Pink," F2.
8. "Princess Image for Girls Debated," United Press International, (April 23, 2007).
9. James C. Dobson, *The New Hide or Seek: Building Confidence in Your Child* (Grand Rapids, MI: F. H. Revell, 2008), 34–35.
10. Skip Hollandsworth, "Vanity Farrah," *Texas Monthly* (January 1997): 71.
11. Donna Freydkin, "TV Angel's Story Comes to a Sad Ending," *USA Today* (June 26, 2009): D10.
12. "Remembering Farrah: Her Life in Pictures," *People* (July 13, 2009).
13. Freydkin, "TV Angel's Story," D10.
14. Sue Anne Pressley, "From Courting to Court: A Love Story," *Los Angeles Times* (September 7, 1995): E1.
15. Abby Goodnough and Margalit Fox, "Anna Nicole Smith Is Found Dead in Florida," *New York Times* (February 9, 2007): A12.
16. Marc Gellman, "Women as Meat: Reflections on the Death of Anna Nicole Smith," *Newsweek* Web Exclusive (February 14, 2007); see http://www.newsweek.com/id/61487?tid=relatedcl.
17. Nancy Etcoff, Susie Orbach, Jennifer Scott, and Heidi D'Agostino, "The Real Truth about Beauty: A Global Report," Findings of the Global Study on Women, Beauty and Well-Being, Unilever Beauty Brand (September 2004).
18. Ibid.
19. Ibid.
20. "Real Women Bare Their Curves as Part of Dove's Global Campaign to Widen the Definition of

Beauty," Unilever Press Release (June 23, 2005); see http://www.unileverusa.com/mediacenter/pressreleases/2005_PressReleases/Real_Women.aspx.

21. Ibid.

Chapter 13

1. George F. Gilder, *Men and Marriage* (New York: Gretna, Pelican Pub. Co., 1986), 120–121.
2. NICHD Study of Early Child Care and Youth Development: "Does Amount of Time Spent in Child Care Predict Socioemotional Adjustment during the Transition to Kindergarten?"; see http://www.researchforum.org/project_printable_185.html; Brian Robertson, *Day Care Deception: What the Child Care Establishment Isn't Telling Us* (San Francisco: Encounter Books, 2003), 85–86.
3. Jay Belsky, "The Dangers of Day Care," *Wall Street Journal* (July 16, 2003).
4. Karl Zinsmeister, "Longstanding Warnings from Experts," *The American Enterprise* (May/June 1998): 34–35.
5. Robertson, *Day Care Deception*, 85–86.
6. See http://www.pollyklaas.org/about/pollys-story.html.
7. Colorado State Assembly SB200; see http://www.leg.state.co.us/clics/clics2008a/csl.nsf/fsbillcont3/BD7A295EB6F4460E872573F5005D0148?open&file=200_enr.pdf.
8. United States Attorney General's Commission on Pornography, Final Report (July 1986); see http://www.porn-report.com; G. Able, et al, "Self-Reported Sex Crimes of Nonincarcerated Paraphiliacs," *Journal of Interpersonal Violence* 2 (1987): 3–25; see http://www.mayoclinicproceedings.com/content/82/4/457.full#sec-3; Patrick Goodenough, "Online Porn Driving Sexually Aggressive Children," CNSNews.com (November 26, 2003).
9. *New York v. Ferber*, 458 U.S. 747; see http://straylight.law.cornell.edu/supct/html/historics/USSC_CR_0458_0747_ZS.html.
10. See http://www.charleyproject.org/cases/c/culver_lynette.html; http://www.time.com/time/2007/crimes/14.html.
11. *Funny Girl*, directed by William Wyler (Columbia Pictures Corporation, 1968). Lyrics by Bob Merrill.
12. James C. Dobson, *The New Strong-Willed Child* (Carol Stream, IL: Tyndale House Publishers, 2004), chapter 4.

Chapter 14

1. "Is God Dead?" *Time* (April 8, 1966); see http://www.time.com/time/covers/0,16641,19660408,00.html.
2. Laura Mansnerus, "Timothy Leary, Pied Piper of Psychedelic 60's, Dies at 75," *New York Times* (June 1, 1996).
3. Based on numbers reported by the Alan Guttmacher Institute.
4. "Court Tosses FCC 'Wardrobe Malfunction' Fine," *Associated Press* (July 21, 2008).
5. Michael Burleigh, *The Third Reich: A New History* (New York: Hill & Wang, 2001), 235.
6. William Lawrence Shirer, *The Rise and Fall of the Third Reich: A History of Nazi Germany* (New York: Simon and Schuster, 1960), 249.
7. Wendy Shalit, "A Ladies' Room of One's Own," *Commentary* (August 1995).
8. Liebau, *Prude*, 17.
9. Ibid., 31.
10. Ibid.; 2002 National Survey of Family Growth, Advance Data No. 362 (September 15, 2005).
11. B. E. Wells and J. M. Twenge, "Changes in Sexual Behavior and Attitudes, 1943–1999: A Cross-Temporal Meta-Analysis," *Review of General Psychology* 9 (2005): 249–261.
12. Lydia Saad, "Americans Have Complex Relationship with Marriage: Many Supportive of Unwed Families, but Most Still Seek Marriage," Gallup Poll News Service (May 30, 2006).
13. "Most Americans Believe in Sin, but Differ Widely on Just What It Is," Ellison Research (March 11, 2008); see http://ellisonresearch.com/releases/20080311.htm.

14. Family Research Council, *Washington Update* (March 2008).
15. Florence King, "In All, Modesty," *National Review* (January 25, 1999).
16. Liebau, *Prude*, 186, 88.
17. Christopher Kelly, ed., *Rousseau on Women, Love, and Family* (Sudbury, MA: Dartmouth Publishing, 2009), xxx.
18. "Sex and Tech: Results from a Survey of Teens and Young Adults," National Campaign to Prevent Teen and Unplanned Pregnancy (December 2008).
19. Jim Jacobs and Warren Casey, "Look at Me, I'm Sandra Dee" (1978).
20. Randal Kleiser, *Grease* (Paramount Pictures, 1978).
21. Conference on World Affairs panel held at Boulder High School (April 10, 2007), transcript.
22. "School Employees Reprimanded for Sex, Teens, Drugs Assembly," *Denver News* (May 23, 2007).
23. Conference on World Affairs panel (April 10, 2007).
24. Shalit, *Girls Gone Mild*, 38.
25. Ibid., 36, 33.
26. Ibid., 6.
27. Ibid., 7.
28. Leibau, *Prude*, 191–192.

Chapter 15

1. "Girls' Suicide Rates Rise Dramatically: CDC Advises Prevention Programs to Focus on Gender and Age Groups Most at Risk," Associated Press (September 6, 2007).
2. Martha W. Waller, Denise Dion Hallfors, Carolyn Tucker Halpern, Bonita Iritani, Carol A. Ford, and Guang Guo, "Gender Differences in Associations between Depressive Symptoms and Patterns of Substance Use and Risky Sexual Behavior among a Nationally Representative Sample of U.S. Adolescents," *Archives of Women's Mental Health* 9, no. 3 (May 2006): 139–150.
3. Ibid.
4. Ibid.
5. Denise D. Hallfors, Martha W. Waller, Daniel Bauer, Carol A. Ford, and Carolyn T. Halpern, "Which Comes First in Adolescence—Sex and Drugs or Depression?" *American Journal of Preventative Medicine* 29, no. 3 (October 2005): 163–170.
6. Robert E. Rector, Kirk A. Johnson, Ph.D., and Lauren R. Noyes, "Sexually Active Teenagers Are More Likely to Be Depressed and to Attempt Suicide," Center for Data Analysis Report #03–04, Heritage Foundation (June 3, 2003).
7. Ibid.
8. Ibid.
9. Ibid.
10. Ibid.
11. Ibid.
12. Stephanie Dunnewind, "Teens, Drugs and Gender Roles: Markers for Cutting," *Seattle Times* (September 24, 2003).
13. Sexually Transmitted Disease Surveillance, 2007, Centers for Disease Control and Prevention. The full report is available at http://www.cdc.gov/std/stats07.
14. E. Johannisson, "STDs, AIDS and Reproductive Health," *Advances in Contraception* (June 2005).
15. Ibid.
16. Lawrence K. Altman, "Sex Infections Found in Quarter of Teenage Girls," *New York Times* (March 12, 2008); "Teens Unaware of Sexually Transmitted Diseases until They Catch One, Carnegie Mellon Study Finds," *Medical News Today* (January 3, 2006).
17. Genital HPV Infection: CDC Fact Sheet, 2009; see http://www.cdc.gov/STD/HPV/STDFact-HPV.htm.
18. Ibid.
19. Ibid.
20. Ibid.
21. Christine Markham, Ph.D, "Middle School Youth as Young as 12 Engaging in Risky Sexual

Activity," *Journal of School Health* (April 2009); see http://www.uthouston.edu/media/newsreleases/nr2009/index.htm?id=1214820.

22. Duberstein Lindberg, Rachel Jones, and John S. Santelli, "Non-Coital Sexual Activities among Adolescents," *Journal of Adolescent Health* (July 2008): 231–238.

23. National Center for Health Statistics, 2005; Laura Sessions Stepps, "Study: Half of All Teens Have Had Oral Sex," *Washington Post* (September 16, 2005).

24. Teen Sex Survey conducted by Princeton Survey Research Associates International, 2004; see http://www.msnbc.msn.com/id/6839072.

25. Ibid.; *Contraceptive Technology Update* 22, no. 5 (May 2001).

26. Joel A. Ernster, Cosimo G. Sciotto, Maureen M. O'Brien, Jack L. Finch, BS, Linda J. Robinson, Thomas Willson, and Michael Mathews, "Rising Incidence of Oropharyngeal Cancer and the Role of Oncogenic Human Papilloma Virus," *Laryngoscope* 117, no. 12 (January 2009): 2115–2128.

27. "Studies Tie Oral Sex to Throat Cancer in Some Men," *Colorado Springs Gazette* (October 22, 2007).

28. Sexually Transmitted Disease Surveillance, 2007.

29. Conference on World Affairs panel (April 10, 2007).

30. Steve Jordahl, "House Subcommittee Cuts Funds for Abstinence Education," *Citizenlink* (July 14, 2009); see http://www.citizenlink.org/content/A000010497.cfm.

31. Miriam Grossman, M.D., *Unprotected: A Campus Psychiatrist Reveals How Political Correctness in Her Profession Endangers Every Student* (New York: Penguin Group, 2007), 3–4.

32. Ibid.

33. Ibid.

34. Joe S. McIlhaney Jr. and Freda McKissic Bush, *Hooked: New Science on How Casual Sex Is Affecting Our Children* (Chicago: Northfield Publishing, 2008).

Chapter 16

1. Danice K. Eaton et al, "Youth Risk Behavior Surveillance: United States, 2007," Surveillance Summaries, Morbidity and Mortality Weekly Report 57, no. SS-4; see http://www.cdc.gov/mmwr/preview/mmwrhtml/ss5704a1.htm.

2. Centers for Disease Control and Prevention, Surveillance Summaries, data for 1991, YRBSS, "Youth Online: Comprehensive Results."

3. "Youth Online: Comprehensive Results, Alcohol and Other Drug Use," Centers for Disease Control and Prevention (2007); see http://apps.nccd.cdc.gov/yrbss/CategoryQuestions.asp?Cat=3&desc=Alcohol and Other Drug Use.

4. Interview by Katelyn Beaty, "Zipping It," *Christianity Today* (August 26, 2008).

5. Ibid.

6. Wendy Shalit, *Good Girl Revolution: Young Rebels with Self-Esteem and High Standards* (New York: Ballantine, 2008), 233.

7. Wendy Shalit, "Modest Extremes: Why an Observant Jew Understands Sexuality Better than Hugh Hefner," *In Character*; see http://www.incharacter.org/article.php?article=55.

8. Shalit, *Girls Gone Mild*, 11.

9. Ibid., 9.

10. Ibid., xxi.

11. Ibid., 75.

12. Ibid., 149.

13. Rector, Johnson, and Noyes, "Sexually Active Teenagers."

14. Malkin, "Standing Up to the 'Girls Gone Wild' Culture."

15. "Abercrombie & Fitch Target of 'Girlcott'" *Pittsburgh Tribune Review* (October 26, 2005).

16. "The Girlcott Story," Regional Change Agents: A Program of Women and Girls Foundation; see http://www.wgfswpa.org/girl2girlgrants/section_girlsOurVoices/girlcott.htm.

17. "'Girlcott' Leaders Meet A & F Execs," *Pittsburgh Business Times* (December 6, 2005).

18. "Abercrombie & Fitch Pitches New Trashy T-Shirts to America's Youth," American Family Association Press Release (September 1, 2009).

19. Christine C. Kim, "Teen Sex: The Parent Factor," *Backgrounder*, Heritage Foundation, no. 2194 (October 7, 2008).
20. Ibid.
21. Laura Billings, "Best Birth Control for Teens Is Mom," *Saint Paul Pioneer Press* (September 8, 2002), C1.
22. Ibid.
23. Bill Albert, "With One Voice 2007: America's Adults and Teens Sound Off about Teen Pregnancy," National Campaign to Prevent Teen Pregnancy (February 2007); see http://www .thenationalcampaign.org/resources/pdf/pubs/WOV2007_fulltext.pdf.
24. Mark D. Regnerus and Laura B. Luchies, "The Parent-Child Relationship and Opportunities for Adolescents' First Sex," *Journal of Family Issues* 27, no. 2 (February 2006): 159–183.
25. The Centers for Disease Control and Prevention (CDC) estimate that 19 million new cases of sexually transmitted diseases occur each year in the United States, and almost half are among 15- to 24-year-olds. In the United States, 10,000 teens are infected by sexually transmitted diseases (STDs) per day; one out of every four sexually active teens has an STD.
26. James Jaccard, Patricia J. Dittus, and Vivian V. Gordon, "Parent-Adolescent Congruency in Reports of Adolescent Sexual Behavior and in Communications about Sexual Behavior," *Child Development* 69, no. 1 (February 1998): 247–261.
27. Mihaly Csikszentmihalyi and Reed Larson, *Being Adolescent: Conflict and Growth in the Teenage Years* (New York: Basic Books, 1984).
28. Ibid.
29. Chap Clark, *Hurt: Inside the World of Today's Teenagers* (Grand Rapids, MI: Baker Academic, 2004), 21.
30. Frank Luntz, *What Americans Really Want . . . Really: The Truth about Our Hopes, Dreams, and Fears* (New York: Hyperion, 2009).
31. Ibid.
32. Morton DaCosta, *The Music Man* (Warner Bros., 1962).

Chapter 17
1. Sarah Kistler, "The Charm Bracelet." Used by permission.

Chapter 18
1. Ron G. Rosenfeld and Barbara C. Nicodemus, "The Transition from Adolescence to Adult Life: Physiology of the 'Transition' Phase and Its Evolutionary Basis," GHD during Critical Phases of Life, 6th KIGS/KIMS Expert Meeting on Growth Hormone and Growth Disorders, Florence, Italy (November 8–9, 2002).
2. Ibid.
3. Alecia D. Schweinsburg, Bonnie J. Nagel, et al, "fMRI Reveals Alteration of Spatial Working Memory Networks across Adolescence," *Journal of International Neuropsychological Society* 11, no. 5 (2005): 631–644; B. Luna, K. E. Garver, et al, "Maturation of Cognitive Processes from Late Childhood to Adulthood," *Child Development* 75, no. 5 (2004): 1357.
4. Gurian, *The Wonder of Girls*, 70.
5. "What Is the Pituitary Gland?" University of Pittsburgh, Department of Neurological Surgery; see http://www.neurosurgery.pitt.edu/minc/skullbase/pituitary/index.html.
6. Gurian, *The Wonder of Girls*, 75.
7. James C. Dobson, *Preparing for Adolescence* (Ventura, CA: Gospel Light, 2005).
8. Brizendine, *The Female Brain*.
9. Ibid., 21.
10. Ibid., 30.
11. D. Rubinow, C. Roca, et al, "Gonadal Hormones and Behavior in Women: Concentrations versus Context," *Hormones, Brain and Behavior* 5 (2002): 37–74.
12. Ibid.

13. Nancy Snyderman, *Girl in the Mirror* (New York: By the Bay Productions, 2002), 20.
14. Michael Gurian discusses an idea similar to this in his book *The Wonder of Girls*, 83–84.
15. Ibid., 83.
16. I. F. Bielsky and L. J. Young, "Oxytocin, Vasopressin, and Social Recognition and Reduction in Anxiety-Like Behavior in Vasopressin V1a Receptor Knockout Mice," *Neuropsychopharmacology* 29, no. 3 (2004): 483–493; C. S. Carter, "Developmental Consequences of Oxytocin," *Physiology and Behavior* 79, no. 3 (2003): 383–397.
17. Ibid.
18. Brizendine, *The Female Brain*, 58.
19. Jeffrey Kluger, "The Science of Romance: Why We Love," *Time* (January 28, 2008): 54.

Chapter 19

1. Curt Anderson, "Women's Crime Rate on Increase," Associated Press (October 28, 2003).
2. James Garbarino, *See Jane Hit: Why Girls Are Growing More Violent and What We Can Do about It* (New York: Penguin Books, 2006); Deborah Prothrow-Stith and Howard R. Spivak, *Sugar and Spice and No Longer Nice: How We Can Stop Girls' Violence* (San Francisco: Jossey-Bass, 2005).
3. "As I See It: Strategic Ways to Stop Bullying," *Kansas City Star* (February 14, 2008).
4. Joanne Richard, "Terrorists in the Schoolyard," *Ottawa Sun* (October 14, 2004): 56.
5. Vanessa O'Connell, "Fashion Bullies Attack—in Middle School," *Wall Street Journal* (October 25, 2007); D1.
6. Rosalind Wiseman, *Queen Bees and Wannabes: Helping Your Daughter Survive Cliques, Gossip, Boyfriends, and Other Realities of Adolescence* (New York: Three Rivers Press, 2002), 119, 162–163.
7. Rachel Simmons, *Odd Girl Out: The Hidden Culture of Aggression in Girls* (Orlando: Harcourt Books, 2002), 159, 172.
8. Dan Kindlon, *Alpha Girls: Understanding the New American Girl and How She Is Changing the World* (New York: Rodale, 2006).
9. DeWitt Williams, "The Friendship Factor," *College and University Dialogue*, http://dialogue .adventist.org/articles/15_2_williams_e.htm.
10. Shalit, *Girls Gone Mild*, 254.
11. Helena Oliviero, "Bully Girls: Intimidating Practices Grow among Female Teens, *Atlanta Journal-Constitution* (August 26, 2004): B1.
12. Cheryl Dellasega and Charisse Nixon, *Girl Wars: 12 Strategies That Will End Female Bullying* (New York: Fireside, 2003).
13. James C. Dobson, *Preparing for Adolescence* (Carol Stream: Tyndale House Publishers, 1992), 146–159.

Chapter 20

1. Professor Emeritus Norbert Kluge of the Universität Koblenz-Landau wrote in the Internet publication *Beiträge zur Sexualwissenschaft und Sexualpädagogik* that in 1992 girls had their first period on average at 12.2 years old and in 2010 will have it around 10 or 11 years of age.
2. William Cameron Chumlea, Ph.D., Christine M. Schubert, M.S., Alex F. Roche, M.D., Ph.D., D.Sc., Howard E. Kulin, M.D., Peter A. Lee, M.D., Ph.D., John H. Himes, Ph.D., M.P.H., and Shumei S. Sun, Ph.D., "Age at Menarche and Racial Comparisons in US Girls," *Pediatrics* 111, no. 1 (January 2003): 110–113; J. L. H. Evers and M. J. Heineman, *Gynecology: A Clinical Atlas* (St. Louis: Mosby, 1990), 80.
3. B. J. Ellis, S. McFadyen-Ketchum, K. A. Dodge, G. S. Pettit, and J. E. Bates, "Quality of Early Family Relationships and Individual Differences in the Timing of Pubertal Maturation in Girls: A Longitudinal Test of an Evolutionary Model," *Journal of Personality and Social Psychology* 77 (1999): 387–401.

4. "Father-Daughter Relationship Crucial to When Girls Enter Puberty, Researchers Say," *Science Daily* (September 27, 1999); see http://www.sciencedaily.com/releases/1999/09/990927064822.htm.

5. B. Ellis, J. Bates, K. Dodge, D. Fergusson, J. Horwood, G. Pettit, and L. Woodward, "Does Father Absence Place Daughters at Special Risk for Early Sexual Activity and Teenage Pregnancy?" *Child Development* 74 (2003): 801–821.

6. Mairi Macleod, "Her Father's Daughter," *New Scientist* (February 10, 2007): 38–41.

7. Diana Zuckerman, "When Little Girls Become Women: Early Onset of Puberty in Girls," National Research Center for Women and Families; article first appeared in *The Ribbon*, a newsletter of the Cornell University Program on Breast Cancer and Environmental Risk Factors (BCERF) 6, no. 1 (Winter 2001).

8. Ibid.

9. Ibid.; V. G. Phinney et al, "The Relationship Between Early Development and Psychosexual Behaviors in Adolescent Females," *Adolescence* 25 (Summer 1990): 321–332.

10. Zuckerman, "When Little Girls Become Women."

11. Macleod, "Her Father's Daughter."

12. R. L. Matchock and E. J. Susman, "Family Composition and Menarcheal Age: Anti-Inbreeding Strategies," *American Journal of Human Biology* 18, no. 4 (2006): 481–491.

13. A. R. Glass, P. A. Deuster, S. B. Kyle, J. A. Yahiro, R. A. Vigersky, and E. B. Schoomaker, "Amenorrhea in Olympic Marathon Runners," *Fertility and Sterility* 48, no. 5 (November 1987): 740–745.

14. U.S. Open list of past champions; see http://www.usopen.org/en_US/about/history/wschamps .html.

15. Ladies' Singles Finals 1884–2008, Wimbledon Rolls of Honour; see http://www.wimbledon.org/en_GB/about/history/rolls/ladiesroll.html.

16. Aviva Must, Ph.D., "Back to School: Child and Adolescent Health," *Pediatrics* (September 2005); E. J. Mundell, "Puberty Comes Sooner for Overweight Girls," *Health Day* (August 11, 2005).

17. Macleod, "Her Father's Daughter."

18. J. Briere and E. Gil, "Self-Mutilation in Clinical and General Population Samples: Prevalence, Correlates, and Functions," *American Journal of Orthopsychiatry* 68, no. 4 (October 1998): 609–620.

19. Mel Whalen, "Self-Mutilation," Self-Injury Information and Support; see http://www.psyke.org/articles/en/selfmutilation; A. R. Favazza and K. Conterio, "Female Habitual Self-Mutilators," *Acta Psychiatrica Scandinavica* 79 (1989): 283–289.

20. Ibid.

21. Judy A. Stone and Shari M. Sias, "Self-Injurious Behavior: A Bi-Modal Treatment Approach to Working with Adolescent Females," *Journal of Mental Health Counseling* 25, no. 2 (April 2003): 112.

22. B. A. van der Kolk, J. C. Perry, and J. L. Herman, "Childhood Origins of Self-Destructive Behavior," *American Journal of Psychiatry* 148 (1991): 1665–1672.

23. Quoted by Stone and Sias, "Self-Injurious Behavior," 112.

24. "Borderline Personality Disorder: A Brief Overview That Focuses on the Symptoms, Treatments, and Research Findings"; see http://www.nimh.nih.gov/health/publications/borderline-personality-disorder-fact-sheet/index.shtml.

25. Anthony Bateman, F.R.C. Psych., and Peter Fonagy, Ph.D., F.B.A., "8-Year Follow-Up of Patients Treated for Borderline Personality Disorder: Mentalization-Based Treatment versus Treatment as Usual," *American Journal of Psychiatry* 165 (2008): 631–638.

26. "Borderline Personality Disorder."

Chapter 21

1. "Generation M: Media in the Lives of 8–18 Year-Olds," Kaiser Family Foundation (March 2005); see http://www.kff.org/entmedia/7250.cfm.

2. Janis Wolak, Kimberly Mitchell, and David Finkelhor, "Online Victimization of Youth: Five Years Later," National Center for Missing and Exploited Children (2006).

3. Ibid.
4. Christian Smith with Melinda Lundquist Denton, *Soul Searching: The Religious and Spiritual Lives of American Teenagers* (New York: Oxford University Press, 2005), 222.
5. Christine E. Kaestle, Carolyn T. Halpern, William C. Miller, and Carol A. Ford, "Young Age at First Sexual Intercourse and Sexually Transmitted Infections in Adolescents and Young Adults," *American Journal of Epidemiology* 161, no. 8 (2005): 774–780.
6. Ibid.
7. Marissa Lang, "Night Texting Putting Teen Health at Risk," *Miami Herald* (July 21, 2009).
8. Ibid.
9. Jenna Wortham, "More Employers Use Social Networks to Check Out Applicants," *New York Times* (August 20, 2009); see http://bits.blogs.nytimes.com/2009/08/20/more-employers-use-social-networks-to-check-out-applicants.
10. Patrick Welsh, "Txting Away Ur Education," *USA Today* (June 23, 2009); see http://blogs.usatoday.com/oped/2009/06/txting-away-ur-education.html.
11. "School's Out and Your Kids Are Online: Do You Know What They've Been Searching for This Summer?"; see http://www.symantec.com/about/news/release/article.jsp?prid=20090810_01.
12. See http://www.youtube.com/t/fact_sheet.
13. "Growing Up, and Growing Fast: Kids 2–11 Spending More Time Online," Nielsenwire (July 6, 2009); see http://blog.nielsen.com/nielsenwire/online_mobile/growing-up-and-growing-fast-kids-2-11-spending-more-time-online.
14. Brenda Rindge, "Teen 'Sexting' Risky Behavior," *Post and Courier* (January 6, 2009): D1.
15. Mike Celizic, "Her Teen Committed Suicide Over 'Sexting,'" MSNBC (March 6, 2009); see http://www.msnbc.msn.com/id/29546030.
16. John Smyntek, "Names and Faces," *Detroit Free Press* (April 9, 2001): C1.
17. See http://www.goodfight.org/a_v_hollywoodsmission.html.
18. Sheila Marikar, "Sex and the City Fiend: Show Turned Me into Samantha," ABC News (May 21, 2008); see http://abcnews.go.com/Entertainment/story?id=4895398&page=1.
19. Rebecca L. Collins, Marc N. Elliott, Sandra H. Berry, David E. Kanouse, Dale Kunkel, Sarah B. Hunter, and Angela Miu, "Watching Sex on Television Predicts Adolescent Initiation of Sexual Behavior," *Pediatrics* 114, no. 3 (September 2004): E280–E289.
20. Steven C. Martino, Rebecca L. Collins, Marc N. Elliott, Amy Strachman, David E. Kanouse, and Sandra H. Berry, "Exposure to Degrading versus Nondegrading Music Lyrics and Sexual Behavior among Youth," *Pediatrics* 118, no. 2 (August 2006): E430–E441.

Chapter 22

1. Eldredge, *Captivating*, 146.
2. Dobson, *Bringing Up Boys*, 248–249.
3. John W. Kennedy, "The 4–14 Window," *Christianity Today* (July 2004), http://www.christianitytoday.com/ct/2004/july/37.53.html.
4. James and Shirley Dobson, *Night Light for Parents* (Carol Stream, IL: Tyndale House Publishers, 2002), 22.

Addendum

1. Dannah Gresh, *Secret Keeper Girl Kit: The Power of True Beauty and Modesty* (Chicago: Moody Publishers, 2004).
2. Chelsea Schilling, "Girl Scouts Exposed," WorldNetDaily (May 17, 2009); see http://www.wnd.com/index.php?fa=PAGE.view&pageId=97977.
3. See http://www.ahgonline.org.

MORE PARENTING RESOURCES FROM TYNDALE HOUSE PUBLISHERS BY DR. JAMES DOBSON

Bringing Up Boys
978-0-8423-5266-6 (hardcover)
978-1-4143-0450-2 (softcover)
978-0-8423-2297-3 (audio)
978-1-58997-040-3 (home DVD series)

The New Strong-Willed Child
978-0-8423-3622-2 (hardcover)
978-1-4143-1363-4 (softcover)
978-0-8423-8799-6 (audio)
978-1-4143-0382-6 (workbook)

Parenting Isn't for Cowards
978-1-4143-1746-5 (softcover)

Parents' Answer Book
978-0-8423-8716-3 (softcover)

The Complete Marriage and Family Home Reference Guide
978-0-8423-5267-3 (softcover)

The New Dare to Discipline
978-0-8423-0506-8 (softcover)

Visit **www.tyndale.com/drjamesdobson**
for more information.

Tune in to
Dr. James Dobson's Family Talk.

To learn more about
Dr. James Dobson's Family Talk
or to find a station in your area,
visit www.drjamesdobson.org
or call (877) 732-6825.

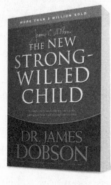

LOVE MUST BE TOUGH
978-1-4143-1745-8 (softcover)

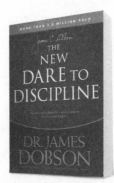

THE NEW DARE TO DISCIPLINE
978-0-8423-0506-8 (softcover)

LIFE ON THE EDGE
978-1-4143-1744-1 (softcover)

DR. JAMES DOBSON'S
Online
DISCUSSION GUIDES

Take your reading experience to the next level!

Visit www.bookclubhub.net for free discussion guides for many of Dr. Dobson's books, including the bestsellers *Bringing Up Girls*, *Bringing Up Boys*, *The New Strong-Willed Child*, *The New Dare to Discipline*, and *When God Doesn't Make Sense*. These bonus resources are perfect for sparking conversations in your church or book group, or for digging deeper into the text on your own.

CP0559